ISSUED TO STUDENT

# Languages of Dress
# in the Middle East

# Languages of Dress in the Middle East

edited by
## Nancy Lindisfarne-Tapper
and
## Bruce Ingham

CURZON
in association with
The Centre of Near and Middle Eastern Studies
SOAS

First published in 1997
by Curzon Press
15 The Quadrant, Richmond
Surrey, TW9 1BP

© 1997 Nancy Lindisfarne-Tapper and Bruce Ingham

Typeset in Sabon by LaserScript, Mitcham, Surrey

Printed in Great Britain by
Biddles Limited, Guildford and King's Lynn

*British Library Cataloguing in Publication Data*
A catalogue record for this book is available from the British Library

*Library of Congress in Publication Data*
A catalogue record for this book has been requested

ISBN 0–7007–0670–4 (Cloth)
ISBN 0–7007–0671–2 (Paper)

# Contents

# Preface

*Languages of Dress in the Middle East* examines the complex relation between clothing practices and natural languages in the Middle East. Treating cases as diverse as the practices of veiling in Oman to the dress reform laws of Turkey and Iran, each of the nine ethnographic papers stands as a separate study. Each is also a contribution to the comparative enterprise which is elaborated in the theoretical and methodological introduction to the volume.

The ethnographic studies are wide-ranging. All of them present new materials based on first-hand field experience in the Arab Middle East, Iran and Turkey and also countries of the Caucasus and the Mediterranean. Thematically, the studies are equally innovative in bridging disciplinary boundaries; they draw on approaches derived from social anthropology, history, ethnology and linguistics. The dress types covered are also varied in style and design from the extremely simple, as in the case of men's dress in rural southern Arabia, to those which are very elaborate, as in the case of the courtly robes of the Ottomans and Persians, and from the ancient, as are preserved stylistically in the masks and cloaks of the Caucasus, to the contemporary, as with fashions which owe their origins to late twentieth Europe.

Ingham, Yamani and Chatty (see below) all offer papers on the Arabian peninsula. Ingham's study of men's dress is historical and distributional, linking dress with Arabian identities over time, while isolating local differences which reveal cultural ties to peoples living outside the peninsula. Yamani, by contrast, offers a single detailed case study of the relation between dress styles and changing identity. She writes of adaptation of dress styles to the new social order, giving a unique insider viewpoint on clothing fashions among the present Hijazi elite.

Like Yamani, Lindisfarne-Tapper too presents an anthropological case study of dress in a particular local setting, in this case among the Shahsevan tribespeople of north-western Iran. She stresses the political significance of dress as a mark of tribal identity in the region, while describing the ways in which, within the tribal community, dress is used to mark other kinds of difference relating to gender, age and wealth and religious status.

Hewitt and Khiba and Chenciner offer papers on dress in the Caucasus. Hewitt and Khiba concentrate on the dress of Abkhazia and Georgia, documenting the terms used for various items of clothing in the many different languages of the region. In this way they illustrate the variety of intimate associations there may be between natural languages and dress. A particularly telling example concerns the *chokha* or tunic which is found throughout the region and was also an important element of the Cossack uniform. Chenciner, by contrast, concentrates in his discussion on the felt capes and masks, clothing items which, as is evident from legends and accounts of the ancient Greeks, have changed little since antiquity. The felt cape, like the Bedouin *farwah* or sheepskin cloak, has been of the utmost importance to Caucasus shepherds over millennia, serving as a coat, sleeping blanket and even a temporary shelter in bad weather. Both the capes and the masks which Chenciner describes are associated with particular styles of warfare, associations which are today preserved in local performances and seasonal celebrations,

In the next section, both Agius, writing of Malta, and Chatty, writing on Oman, deal with the topical subject of veiling. Agius' study is etymological. He concludes that, though the Maltese veil has its origins in the Romance tradition, the elaborate terminology which people have used over centuries has been drawn mainly from dialects of North African Arabic. Chatty is concern with local variation in another sense. Her focus is on the *burqa* (sometimes *burgu'*) face mask which is common to parts of central and eastern Arabia as well as Iran and Baluchistan. Though widely known regionally, Chatty documents the significant variations in the meaning and use of the *burqa* between rural and urban settings.

In the concluding section of the volume, Norton and Baker approach the politics of dress in another frame. Norton's study 'Faith and Fashion in Turkey' chronicles changes in dress conventions of earlier Ottoman times, through the simplicity of dress styles associated with the 1830 reforms to the European fashions which were adopted as part of the changes introduced by Ataturk. Norton also describes an insistent modernity in clothing styles which was later elaborated in another politics of dress whereby Turks distinguished themselves and others as 'of the left or right' or religious or as 'Maoists' or 'Marxists' by the clothing they wore. Baker, in the final paper of the *Languages of Dress in the Middle East*, offers an exemplary analysis of the dress reform laws in Iran in the 1920s and 1930s. She examines contemporary social and historical trends inside the country and internationally and traces their effect on dress legislation.

# Acknowledgements

The idea for this book grew out of a session on Dress at the BRISMES (British Society for Middle Eastern Studies) conference held at the School of Oriental and African Studies in 1991, and also a one-day conference on the Language of Dress in the Middle East held at SOAS in 1993, organized by Jennifer Scarce of the National Museums of Scotland and Bruce Ingham of SOAS. However the articles in this volume do not all originate in those sessions and neither are all the papers read at them included here. The editors acknowledge the support of the Centre of Middle Eastern Studies at SOAS, and particularly its Publications Officer, Richard Tapper, who went to considerable length to see the manuscript to publication, and his Editorial Assistant, Diana Gur. The lively illustrations in the volume were prepared from photographs provided by the authors or the editors by Ruard Absaroka, Sean Bowen, Imshi Burell, Edward Lindisfarne and Howard Tangye; we thank them particularly for their work.

# Notes on Transliteration and Transcription

The articles in this volume include terminology from a number of different languages, namely Arabic (including classical and colloquial varieties), Persian, Turkish, Maltese and Caucasian languages. Certain of the articles such as those of Hewitt on the Caucasus and Agius on Malta deal with comparative dress lexicons. In these the linguistic symbols used are quite elaborate. In others we have followed more generally used transcription systems.

For Arabic the only symbols that require comment for those unfamiliar with the language are -ḥ- 'voiceless pharyngeal fricative', -ʿ- 'voiced pharyngeal continuant', -ṭ- 'voiceless pharyngealized alveolar plosive', -ṣ- 'voiceless pharyngealized alveolar fricative', -ḍ- 'voiced pharyngealized dental fricative or plosive' depending on dialect and -'- glottalstop.

For Persian (Farsi) no particularly unfamiliar symbols are used, while for Standard Turkish -c- equals English -j-, -ç- equals English -ch-, ş equals English sh-, ğ is similar to a Parisian French -r-, but softer and in the environment of -i- or -e- can be pronounced like English -y-. Also in Standard Turkish, an undotted -ı- represents a high back spread vowel, dotted -ö- and -ü- are as in German.

For Azerbaijani Turkish, as in Tapper-Lindisfarne's paper, the same conventions apply, but also there is a distinction between -a- (back -a-) and dotted -ä- (front -a-) and that ğ can be palatalized to -j- and -k- can often be palatalized towards -ç-, -ç- is as English -ch- but often becomes fronted to -ts-, -x- is a velar voiceless fricative as in Scottish 'loch', while -ğ- also becomes like -ch- in 'loch' in final position. Finally -q-, as in Arabic and Persian, is a uvular plosive which however can also become as in Scottish 'loch' finally. For further details see R. Tapper *Pasture and Politics: Economics, Conflict and Ritual among the Shahsevan Nomads of North-western Iran*. London: Academic Press, 1979.

For the Caucasian languages, as in Hewitt and Khiba's paper, a cedilla marks retroflexion; an acute over a consonant shows palatalisation; ejectivity is marked by an apostrophe; labialization by a raised little circle; stress by bold type; /y/ is the palatal glide; ǰ = palato-alveolar affricate; c =

affricate ts; the hachek turns alveolars/dentals into corresponding palato-alveolars; gamma is the voiced back fricative, whose voiceless counterpart is x; a dot under an h makes it pharyngal; G is the voiced uvular plosive; L is a lateral affricate. In Chenciners contribution, also on the Caucasus, a generalized notation system is used.

For Maltese, as in Agius, the Maltese orthography is used with phonetic transcriptions using the same symbols as Arabic.

# Notes on Contributors

**Dionisius Agius** teaches Arabic at Leeds University. His publications include *Arabic Literary Works as a Source of Documentation for Technical Terms of the Material Culture* (Berlin: Klaus Schwarz, 1984), *The Study of Maltese Arabic: 1632–1916* (Louvain: Peters, 1990) and *Siculo Arabic* (London: KPI, 1996). He presently holds a Leverhulme Research Fellowship to study traditional seafaring in the Arabian Gulf. He is a member of the Hakluyt Society and the Society for the Promotion of Byzantine Studies.

**Patricia Baker** is an independent researcher who travels extensively in the Middle East and Asia. She read Islamic History and then Islamic Art and Archaeology at SOAS. She has lectured as the Historian in Ceramics and also in Glass at the West Surrey College of Art (now The Surrey Institute). Her publications include *Islamic Textiles* (London: British Museum Press, 1995) and a number of conference papers on Islamic culture.

**Dawn Chatty** is an anthropologist with long research experience in the Middle East, initially among the Bedouin of Syria and Jordan and for the last fifteen years in the Sultanate of Oman among the Harasiis tribe. Her research interests include development and social change, development planning, gender and development and nutrition and public health. Her publications include *From Camel to Truck: The Bedouin in the Modern World* (New York: Vantage Press, 1986) and *Mobile Pastoralists: Development Planning and Change in the Sultanate of Oman* (New York: Columbia University Press, 1996). She is currently Senior Research Officer at the Oxford Refugee Studies Programme.

**Robert Chenciner** is a senior associate member of St Antony's College, Oxford and an honorary member of the Daghestan branch of the Russian Academy of Sciences. His publications include *Kaitag Textile Art of Daghestan* (London: Textile Art Publications, 1993) and *Daghestan: Survival and Tradition* (London: Curzon Press, forthcoming). Exhibitions include 'Architecture of Baku' at the Heinz Gallery, London (1985),

'Daghestan Today' at the Zamana Gallery, London (1989) and 'Kaitag Embroideries' shown at many international venues including the Institut du Monde Arabe in Paris.

**George Hewitt** is Professor of Caucasian languages at SOAS. His publications include *A Grammar of Abkhaz* (Amsterdam: North Holland, 1979), *A Learner's Grammar of Georgian* (London: Routledge, 1995) and a *Reference Grammar of Georgian* (Amsterdam, Philadelphia: John Benjamins, 1995) and a number of articles on the recent politics of the Caucasus. He has also recently been elected an honorary member of the International Adyghe Association.

**Zaira Khiba** was born in Ochamchira (Abkhazia), where she grew up speaking Abkhaz, Mingrelian and, from the start of school, Russian. She studied Abkhaz and German at the Abkhazian Pedagogical Institute (now the Abkhazian State University) and was engaged on postgraduate work for her Candidate's thesis at Tbilisi University (Georgia) when she met and married George Hewitt in 1976. Since coming to England in 1977, she has collaborated as native-speaker informant for Hewitt's grammar of Abkhaz in the Lingua/Croon Helm/Routledge Descriptive Studies' series, has published an article on the secret language of Abkhazian hunters, and has co-produced with Hewitt the forthcoming 'Abkhaz Newspaper Reader' (Dunwoody Press, Maryland). The couple have two daughters.

**Bruce Ingham** teaches linguistics and Arabic at SOAS. His research interests are in the Arabic dialects and oral literature of the Arabian Peninsula and also in American Indian languages. His publications include *North East Arabian Dialects* (London: KPI, 1982), *Bedouin of Northern Arabia: Traditions of the Al Dhafir* (London: KPI, 1986), *Najdi Arabic: Central Arabian* (Amsterdam, Philadelphia: John Benjamins, 1994) and *Arabian Diversions: Studies in the Dialects of Arabia*, (Reading: Ithaca Press, 1996). He is a founder member of the Association International de Dialectologists Arabes.

**Nancy Lindisfarne-Tapper** is a social anthropologist at SOAS. She has done ethnographic fieldwork in Iran, Afghanistan, Turkey and most recently Syria. She is the author of *Bartered Brides: Politics and Gender in an Afghan Tribal Society* (Cambridge: Cambridge University Press, 1991) and *Dancing in Damascus* (Damascus: Dar al Mada, 1997); she is also co-editor (with Andrea Cornwall) of *Dislocating Masculinity: Comparative Ethnographies* (London: Routledge, 1994).

**John Norton** is Director of the Centre for Turkish Studies at the University of Durham. He has taught modern Turkish Studies at Durham since 1972.

In addition to Turkish language and literature he has conducted research into various aspects of Turkish culture and politics, especially current Islamic religious movements and dervish orders, on which he has published a number of articles.

**Mai Yamani** is an independent researcher and Associate of the Centre of Islamic and Middle East Law, SOAS. She lectures on the culture and life of the Middle East and has edited *Feminism and Islam: Legal and Literary Perspectives* (Reading: Ithaca, 1996).

# List of Illustrations

# Chapter One

# Approaches to the Study of Dress in the Middle East

*Nancy Lindisfarne-Tapper and Bruce Ingham*

In the Euro-American literature on the Middle East, as in art and photography, descriptions of clothing styles and depictions of the clothed (or sometimes lasciviously unclothed female) body, created exotic and sometimes erotic images of people who live in the region. Indeed, Middle Easterners were often characterized by their dress alone, as if their clothing confirmed them as subspecies of racial types: *the* Bedouin warrior, *the* peasant woman, *the* Berber tribesman. Or they were described in terms of their 'costumes', with all the superficial, arbitrary and theatrical overtones such a word suggests.

These images continue to resonate today, appearing in television advertising, women's magazines and in the 'colourful' folkloric images of the travel brochures and national tourist boards. Some are clearly meant to suggest uniqueness and the specificity of a particular setting as a tourist destination. In others – here several of the United Colours of Benetton advertisements come to mind – a simplistic notion of social and cultural diversity is suggested by mixing skin colours and 'ethnic' dress.

Such images are not politically neutral. Rather they constitute new ways of marking difference and inequality. Yet other images partake more directly of older forms of orientalist discourse (cf. Said 1978) which link explicit and repressed sexuality and the putative danger and violence of Islam. Thus consider the opulescence and sexuality suggested by a recent advertisement for an expensive perfume in which a blond model stands in front of the Great Pyramid bathed in a sunset glow, wearing a flowing 'Arab' gown. Such an image of a 'Middle Eastern' woman may be compared with others, especially cliched images of veiled women which represent all that critics see as alien, repressive and threatening in so-called 'fundamentalist' Muslims.

However, such stereotypes are not the only way to approach the topic of clothing in the Middle East. In this volume our ambition is to off-set voyeuristic and politically interested accounts of Middle Eastern dress by focusing on the particular. Each of the studies here describes a specific repertoire of clothing styles in their wider historical, linguistic and ethnographic context. And each poses important questions whose answers lead us to an alternative perspective on dress in the Middle East, one which can embrace a range of materials from the meticulous detail of Edward Lane's *The Manners and Customs of the Modern Egyptians* (1923, orig. 1836), to Shelagh Weir's lively study of Palestinian dress (1989) and Jennifer Scarce's documentary history of women's clothing in the Ottoman Empire (1987).

The deliberate play in our title suggests the scope of our ambitions. For us, *Languages of Dress in the Middle East* refers both to the metaphorical languages of clothing and adornment and to the natural languages from which these metaphors are fashioned. In criticizing the French semiotician Roland Barthes' writing on clothes and fashion (1983), Alison Lurie explores the richness of the metaphor 'the language of clothes',

> Besides containing 'words' that are taboo, the language of clothes, like speech, also includes modern and ancient words, words of native and foreign origin, dialect words, colloquialisms, slang and vulgaries' (1981: 6).

Lurie found, when she wrote about the language of dress in Europe and America, that this metaphor stimulated her to ask about clothing vocabularies and the sartorial repertoire available to any individual. As we have found, the metaphor also insists we make sense of the mixing and matching of local garments with what are often known explicitly as 'foreign' styles. In this way we are obliged to explore phenomena such as Islamist veiling or a global fashion for blue jeans which have excited much wider polemic and ethnographic interest.

As we shall see, some new items of clothing or styles may be borrowed, copied, and integrated into a particular dress tradition with little remark (see, for example, the plastic shoes worn by the Shahsevan, Lindisfarne-Tapper, this volume). Elsewhere, so-called 'foreign' clothes may be used to emphasize differences between people, as when they reflect the personal style, sophistication and wealth of members of the Saudi Arabian elite (Yamani, this volume). New clothing styles elsewhere have been introduced by fiat, as was the case in Iran under both Reza Shah and the Islamic Republic (Baker, this volume) and with the dress reforms initiated in Turkey under Atatürk (Norton, this volume). Indeed, the Turkish case also raises comparative questions about the relation between the reform of the Turkish language and those which concerned clothing. Both were seen as capable of automatically transforming identities from those which were 'eastern' to those associated with the 'west'. In short, the language metaphor also invites us to consider the politics of lingua francas, pidgins and creoles.

More broadly, each of our contributors raises questions about the relation between clothing arts and power: that is, about the political economy of dress. To understand how clothing construes social identity, we must know how clothed bodies are evaluated in a particular setting. As snapshots of local experiences and sentiments, the studies in this volume suggest, in Rugh's words,

> dress styles may occupy a place along the continuum between the extremes according to momentary definitions of what is modest or immodest, form-concealing or form-revealing, appropriate or inappropriate, garish or in good taste (1986: 3).

Such a perspective raises many questions of linguistic, anthropological and social historical interest. How do people alter their appearance? How do they and others understand and describe such changes? Does the impetus for change derive from the movement of peoples and/or ideas and material items both geographically and through time? Do the dialectics of style and notions of 'good taste' or 'high fashion' evince a relationship between those who dominate and others in any particular social setting? How are a vocabulary of clothing items and a dress aesthetic associated with moral evaluations concerning etiquette and good manners, competitive displays of honour and sexuality, piety and spiritual conviction?

## The Breadth of the Study

Following Eicher and Roach-Higgins (1992, and see Eicher 1995; also Yamani, and Norton, this volume), our focus is deliberately on appearance in the widest sense. Eicher and Roach-Higgins write,

> the dressed person is a *gestalt* that includes the body, all direct modifications of the body itself, and all three-dimentional supplements added to it. ... [and] that only through mental manipulation can we separate body modifications and supplements from the body itself – and from each other – and extract that which we call dress (1992: 13).

They continue,

> We also take the position that the direct modifications of the body as well as the supplements added to it must be considered types of dress because they are equally effective means of human communication, and because similiar meanings can be conveyed by some property, or combination of properties, of either modifications or supplements (*ibid.*)

Such a definition is a deliberate attempt to put an end to the dichotomy between ornament and dress which characterized ethnographic descriptions in the past (1992: 12–3; see also Barnes and Eicher 1992). It is also a definition which avoids constructionist arguments which treat the body as 'natural' and a foil against which all that is done to the body may be seen as 'cultural' and socially contrived. Rather, as feminists and others have been arguing for some time, the so-called 'biological body' is also cultural; bodily form and substance are socially construed from a period before conception until death and after (cf. Gaines & Herzog 1990, Mascia-Lees & Sharpe 1992; Bordo 1993).

The papers in this volume tend to focus on clothing per se,[1] touching only briefly on other topics such as gesture, silhouette, masking, the use of jewellery and make-up, grooming head and body hair, tattooing and other body decoration and perfume. In this the papers reflect an older archival desire to document hitherto undescribed Middle Eastern clothing styles. This is a first step to analyses of other processes of body modification, such as the use of henna or perfume, as in Kanafani's account of dress and adornment in the Arabian Gulf (1983), or discussions of ways soft tissue can be altered, including through head-shaping (cf. N. Tapper 1991) and male and female circumcision (cf. Kennedy 1978; Boddy 1989 among many others). We would argue that analytically there is no necessary or intrinsic difference between clothing and any or all of these other means of altering personal appearance. Each set of styles and techniques has its own aesthetic, and each, either separately or in combination, may be used to create and confirm or contest personal and collective identities. Each is an embodiment of pleasure and of social discipline and control.

The papers of this collection also make it clear that there is almost nothing that can be regarded as specifically Middle Eastern in terms of dress. When looked at in contrast to Europe, at first glance it seems that local Middle Eastern dress styles tend towards the elaborate and flowing. However, everyday clothing worn until recently in parts of Russia and eastern Europe is similarly loose and suggests a continuity with dress styles in the Caucasus. Other periods have seen the influence of Central Asian styles from Yemen to the Horn of Africa and, via the Hadhramaut and Oman, to India and Southeast Asia (see Ingham, this volume). Regionally then, our area of focus forms links in a series of fashion chains which stretch from Nairobi to Alma Ata and from China to Europe.

It it important to note how items of clothing seem to have spread across the region. An item known variously as the *chokha, jukha* or *chogan*, a kind of jacket or morning coat associated widely in the Arab Middle East with the word *jukh* meaning 'broadcloth', appears in India as *chogan*, in Iran as *jukheh*, in the Causasus, Turkey and Iraq as *chokha* and in Arabia as *jukha*. In Arabia the jacket described in this way was particularly prestigious and among Bedouin it was associated with horsemen known as 'knights' (*fāris*) and had military-like markings of horizontal bands which distinguished the rider in battle. By contrast, in the Caucasus, *chokha* jackets were regarded as distinctive markers of particular regional identites and were, in the past, an obligatory part of men's formal dress (Hewitt and Khiba, this volume).

Fashions in dress weaponry have also spread through the region, probably along the Middle Eastern trade routes. The sword as the dress weapon par excellence is a good illustration of this process where three main fashions in swords can be distinguished: the Turkish, Persian and Arab. These three are known in their respective languages purely by the word for 'sword', i.e. *kilij* in Turkish, *shamshīr* in Persian and *sayf* in Arabic. The Turkish has a broader blade and a curling hilt of wood or bone, the Persian is finer in shape and shows a narrow hilt with a pommel bending off from the hilt at about 45 degrees, while the Arab has a hilt like the Persian but often with the pommel curving back at about 120 degrees to the hilt and often with a chain from pommel to cross piece, possibly a vestige of a hand guard. Many of the Arab blades are less curved and some are completely straight. These styles are by no means confined to the area of their origin. Among the Bedouin and others of the Emirates and Kingdoms of the 19th and early 20th century Arabia all three were used, as can be seen in 19th century illustrations and later photographs. And as we said above, the swords of the Hadhramaut show definite east Indian affinities reflecting trade links with that area.

## Beginning with the Particular

The most compelling entry point for any critical discussion of the clothing of the Middle East is through particular, fine-grained ethnographic and socio-linguistic studies. Such local perspectives encourage an interest in how clothing styles and other forms of adornment or body-marking construe difference, and how people become aware of such differences. Clothing is not some added extra, some *post facto* 'symbol' of difference; rather, the medium is the message and, in this very basic sense, clothing indeed maketh the woman or man.

It is also the case that all meaning is relational. Thus women's dress may effectively mark gendered differences in a particular setting because it differs from the dress of men of the same age, rank or marital status. Or, as is the case among the Shahsevan tribespeople of Iran, there may be little distinction between the dress of children and adults, suggesting a continuity of attitudes and expectations between them, as well as a sense that, for example, even young children may be engaged to be married (see Fig. 2 and Lindisfarne-Tapper, this volume).

Or, for example, a man's identity as a religious specialist may be created or confirmed sartorially, distinguishing the *mullah* or *imam* from those men who make no such claim to religious expertise. This relational meaning of dress is parallel to the relational social meaning of dialect in language. A particular form such as the pronunciation of [ts] for [k] in words such as ki:s 'bag, pouch' may be a sign of Bedouin identity in

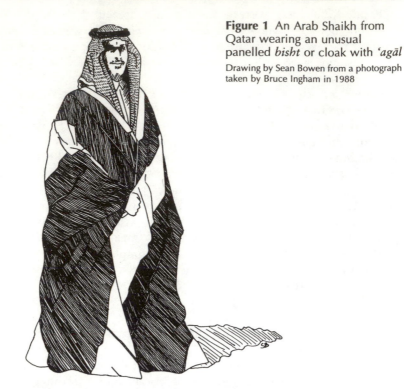

**Figure 1** An Arab Shaikh from Qatar wearing an unusual panelled *bisht* or cloak with *'agāl*

Drawing by Sean Bowen from a photograph taken by Bruce Ingham in 1988

northern parts of Arabia, ie Syria, Iraq and Jordan. In central Saudi Arabia, however, where these dialects originate, the [ts] pronunciation is universal and only signifies a local origin. This is also true of men's dress styles. In parts of Southern Iraq, the wearing of the *'agāl* or 'head rope' over the *ghutrah* 'head scarf' indicates tribal identity in the larger tribal confederations of the Mintifij and Bani Huchaim. Or, in Iraq, people not wearing the head rope *'agal* (see below, p.8), and wearing the head scarf folded back over the head in a semi turban style would be thought to be coastal or palm-cultivating Arabs of the area of the Shatt al-'Arab. Within Saudi Arabia however the absence of the *'agāl* does not have this meaning, and there is a tendency for people from the smaller towns not to wear it. The main signal given by not wearing the *'agāl* in Saudi Arabia and the Gulf States, or by wearing it plainly falling down from either side of the head to the chest, is that one may be a *muṭawwa'* or person committed to the *da'wah* or propagation of Islam. This can be further emphasized by wearing a plain white, twisted cloth in place of the *'agāl*. These signals are therefore relative to the area in which one lives and can easily change their meaning with the passing of time.

**Figure 2** A young Shahsevan girl (left) with her older sisters, one engaged (centre), and one already married

Drawing by Sean Bowen from a photograph taken by Nancy Lindisfarne-Tapper in 1965

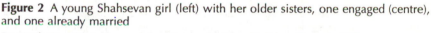

To explore relational meanings it is necessary to focus on specific contexts and the range of local options and strategies of dress. Ideally, a study embraces all members of any particular community whose vocabularies of clothing and dress behaviour change as they act and respond to the opinion of others. We may ask, for instance, how personal clothing choices are constrained and dress conventions established and maintained in any particular setting. Or what are the connections between ideas of the body, local styles and innovation: what, in any one setting is the politics of fashion?

Sciama (1992), writing about Venetian needle-lace (cf. Turkish *oyalar*), which was probably introduced into Europe by Muslims in the 9th century A.D., suggests a range of interesting comparative questions about the sexual politics of dress. One set of questions she raises concerns the extent to which luxury and power were displayed in the dress of both men and women. In some periods a man presented himself as a symbol of his own power, while at others the responsibility was delegated to a wife or mistress in what Veblen, in his *The Theory of the Leisure Class* (1898), called 'vicarious ostentation'. Such questions of conspicuous display are of course relevant to the elite dress styles described by Yamani and Norton (this volume), but they are no less important when we consider how people throughout the region evaluate differences in dress fabrics and ornaments, and dress manufacture and styles.

As Sciama also makes clear, clothing need not be just a repository of monetary value, but may also be given moral value. To borrow Bourdieu's term (1977), items of clothing, and the demeanor with which they are worn, may be a store of 'symbolic capital', or social worth. Such is the case in Sciama's own examples of how a young woman's industry and purity are evinced by her lace-making skills. Elsewhere in the Middle East the same virtues may be represented by the size and quality of a woman's trousseau (cf. Tapper 1985; 1991).

That persons are judged and valued by their appearance and clothing is, of course basic to discussions of social difference. There is, however, wide variation in the specific idioms of such evaluations, the lattitude they allow for change and their complexity. Thus Sciama discusses how the 'purity' of lace was associated with the sexuality of both its makers and wearers, and how it is now also associated with the purity of a pre-industrial past. Once conceived in this far-ranging way, the moral values conveyed through an aesthetics of clothing is a subject ripe for careful study in the Middle East.

Another set of questions Sciama raises concern attitudes to the gendered body and the extent to which sexual dimorphism is emphasized by clothing styles. She compares French and Spanish fashions for lace, showing that there were important regional and national differences in attitudes to parts of the body such as the head and neck. Her study also considers the contrasting degrees of physicality displayed by men and women. At a time when Spanish men's dress revealed muscles and genitalia, women's dress flattened breasts and otherwise hid the shape of the female body; in other periods styles of dress created an androgynous or unisex body.

Of course meanings may change in other ways, particularly over time. A good example of such a possibility is offered by the headrope (*'agāl*) worn in the central Arabian region of Najd and its hinterlands. Apparently the head rope was originally a camel hobble (from the root *'agal*, meaning 'to hobble') which was carried on the head when not in use. Gradually however, this rope came to distinguish the Bedouin of north and central Arabia, and the ruling families descended from them, from other Bedouin. The usage, of course, has persisted long after the camel ceased to be an important part of a way of life. A second example of a continuous dress tradition whose meaning has undoubtedly changed considerably over time is provided by the woven pattern of the Arab *shmāgh* or headscarf. This clothing design is said to have originated in Mesopotamia as a pattern known as either 'ears of corn' or, in some instances, 'fishing nets'; suggesting the two main sources of natural wealth in the Fertile Crescent. Though the motif is now purely decorative, it is notable that it continues to appear on headscarves throughout the region. Equally, the hilt of a type of sword worn in the Hadhramaut now looks like a purely abstract design. However when compared with the Kris, a type of broad sword or dagger of the East Indies, it can be seen to have clear links with the dragons' head designs common there, whence this type of sword would seem originally to have come (see Fig. 3).

As Kroeber's early study of clothing styles and social change suggested (1919), questions concerning how differences created and made salient through clothing are perennial. Why do particular styles become prominent at a particular time? When are fashions associated with one sex appropriated by the other, as is the case with the Saudi Arabian men's *thōb* (see Yamani, this volume), and the hood described by Agius (this volume). In short, how and why do clothing styles change? And to what extent do such changes auger changes or modifications in manners (cf. Harmon 1995:8)?

## Going beyond the Function of Clothing

By framing questions in unexpected ways, as Sciama does, we take the study of clothing in the Middle East beyond conventional wisdoms and tired functionalist arguments, whether these are presented in terms of 'adaptation', 'need' or 'survivals' from an earlier period. As Fiske writes briskly of blue jeans, functionality may be a 'precondition of their popularity, but it does not explain it' (1989: 1). The same may be said of clothing styles and vocabularies everywhere.

Yet the habit of treating clothing and other items of material culture in functionalist terms is widespread in Middle Eastern accounts. Thus, Rugh confronts one functionalist argument in *Reveal and Conceal*, her book on Egyptian dress, when she writes,

> Observers often comment on how dysfunctional Egyptian women's folk dress appears to be with its voluminous layers of material that seem to interfere with mobility, and its extensive use of the colour black that absorbs the hot rays of the Egyptian sun (1986: 12).

But her reply, unfortunately, does not alter the terms of the debate. Rather she too relies on utilitarian premises by citing a recent study in the science journal *Nature* about the character and degree of radiation absorbed by black garments. At the very least such an argument is ethnocentric: it assumes that the debate can be won with an argument from Western science which both patronizes and vindicates folk practice.

More tellingly however, such functionalist arguments cannot account for variation. This may be a variation between individuals, between categories of people or variations between categories of dress: for example, between

**Figure 3** Three Hadhramauti Arabs with dress swords

Drawing by Sean Bowen from a photograph taken in the late 19th century and published in F.M. Hunter, 1877, *Accounts of the British Settlement in Aden*. London: Frank Cass

everyday dress and other garments, such as a wedding dress, which have special and contrastive associations for the people concerned. In short, such arguments cannot explain the great range of Egyptian clothing styles and dress colours Rugh herself describes. Neither can they explain the variety of clothing styles and colours other people living in hot, sunny climates chose to wear or not wear; nor do they cater for the different ways people themselves think it expedient or desirable to dress with respect to heat and sun.

Within functionalist frameworks, contradictory evidence is typically countered with detailed secondary elaborations. Thus Rugh's later account of colour differences between women's and men's dress among the Bedouin poses a further set of problems. Black garments are no longer at issue, rather,

The bright-colored embroideries of the bedouin women's dress may ... have adaptive qualities [being an immediate signal for distinguishing the bedouin female from townspeople or peasants] as well as being aesthetically pleasing to a people who live in a mostly beige and grey world. ... Men's clothing is more subdued and blends more successfully into the scenery. As protectors and potential competitors they are better served by avoiding the high profile of a conspicuous costume (1986: 82).

Clearly, this passsage begs a myriad of questions about Bedouin aesthetics, processes of gendering and display, and even whether or not Bedouin women and men experience heat and colour differently from each other. Yet sadly, such social evolutionary/socio-biological arguments have a continuing popularity, in part at least because of the comfortable way they situate their advocates at the pinnacle of social development and progress. They are arguments which depend on premises which stem from an outsider's point of view, meaning they are most effectively unsettled by viewing clothing through a local lens. This becomes particularly clear when we look at the question of veiling among Middle Eastern Muslim women, a theme which has excited much, often prurient, interest, and then at broader questions about social change.

## Generalizations and Gender

Edward Said has argued that an assocation between the Orient and sex is one of the most persistent themes of Orientalist discourses. It is an association which discredits Oriental 'fecundity, yet titillates, suggesting sexual promise (and threat), untiring sensuality, unlimited desire, [and] deep generative energies' (1978: 188). In its crudest forms, the categorical association of the Orient and sexuality gains its power through generalization. Thus, all women and men – as Arabs, Turks, Middle Easterners or Muslims – are sexualized and treated as members of a single homogeneous category (cf. Moors 1991 for a careful account of the wider implications of this process).

Another such argument is 'philological' (cf. Said 1978: 309 ff., 320–1). It is an argument which focuses on Arabic as *the* language of the Middle East, then reifies the language, rendering it static and timeless. Arabic is also characterized in crude psychological or sociological terms, as, for example, encouraging 'exaggeration' and 'general vagueness'. By separating this mythical entity, *the* language, from its use and interpretation, speakers of Arabic are themselves made to seem childlike, irrational and locked in simple, archaic patterns of thought (cf. Gilsenan 1991). One way of quickly disposing of such a fixed and falsely abstract notion of a language is by exploring actual language usage with respect to material objects. In this volume, Hewitt and Khiba, and Ingham, explore the relation between the articles of clothing worn in a particular setting and the vocabularies used to describe them. To the same end, Agius and Chenciner have used drawings and paintings in tandem with linguistic data. Among a range of other insights, it is also clear from these studies that there has been a considerable degree of borrowing and fluidity between the spoken and written dialects and languages of the Middle East and adjacent regions.

The same process of reification, whereby people, like languages, are reduced to their classification in pseudo-scientific terms, is also evident in many discussions of clothing in the Middle East. Labels such as 'traditional', 'ethnic' and 'folkloric' often construe the people who wear such clothing as variously quaint, simple-minded, partisan or parochial. The immediate consequences of such generalizations are threefold. First, there is again the problem of variation. Perceptions of difference among a particular category or group of women, or men, are ignored. And, of course, the same generalizing tendencies may preempt discussion of other kinds of differences, such as those among people designated as members of a particular ethnic or national group. Secondly, both Western and Middle Eastern rhetorics concerning gendered identities are made to seem natural or god-given, as are the rhetorics which fix ethnic, national or religious identities. Finally, and most tellingly, notions of gender, or other aspects of personhood, are not problematized, nor is there an investigation of the ways clothing and bodily adornment are felt to alter identity.

## Differences among Women

Images of women in the Middle East are frequently reduced to a very limited range of highly emotive themes concerning sexuality, veiling and seclusion, the oppression of women by men and the position of women 'in Islam'. Not only are non-Muslim women often simply ignored, but the fact of being female and Muslim, may be stressed to the exclusion of other attributes of identity, such as age, class or regional origin. Clearly, such a focus suggests a direct, and automatic, link between 'Islam', 'Islamic law' and the 'status of women'; it is a link which is often represented by 'the veil' (see Chatty, and Agius, this volume).

Scarce, in her book on elite women's clothing styles within the period and domain of Ottoman rule, writes scathingly of such generalizations about women's dress,

> about women's role in a predominantly Muslim society, it would be inappropriate and inaccurate to assume it was uniformly and rigidly circumscribed because private and public behaviours were carefully distinguished; there is at present simply not enough evidence to make general statements (1987: 14).

She adds,

'Women's costume presents an evolution equally as complex and varied as that of their masculine contemporaries – a fact which has been overlooked because of the lack of officially defined and recognized feminine public roles ...

Such evidence neatly disposes of the tiresomely persistent myth that 'oriental' costume is essentially timeless and can, therefore, be simply dismissed as a few basic items of clothing assembled together to produce a generalised and pleasingly colourful stereotype' (*ibid.*, 14–15).

Women and women's dress, as Scarce makes clear, are made to seem uniform through accounts which effectively hide their own broad Orientalist origins. In this respect it is worth noting how academic and more popular works on the Middle East employ the image of the veiled woman to create apparent similarities among the people studied; to create, in short, an apparently coherent subject. The numbers of books, papers and popular accounts of the Middle East which have included the word 'veil' in their titles, particularly since the Islamic Revolution in Iran in 1978, is telling. Moreover, the image of the veiled woman is not in any way neutral; it is redolent with Orientalist import. To take only one recent example: the geographically and thematically diverse papers collected in Fawzi El Solh and Mabro's edited volume, *Muslim Women's Choices* (1994; cf. Lindisfarne 1995; Hale 1996) are, for comparative purposes, given an illusory unity by implying that the Muslim women of the title automatically share a common outlook and interests. Further, the cover photographs – two clichés: Iranian women in black chadors on the front and Afghan women in mesh-fronted chaderis on the back – suggest that all the women described in the volume are identically 'Muslim' and identically subject to Islamic strictures because of their veils.

## Naturalizing Political Interests: the Rhetorics of 'Women's Dress'

Generalization also conceals political interests in other ways. For instance, Graham-Brown's chapter 'Dressing the Part' in her *Images of Women*, is admirably clear about Orientalist characterizations. Yet even she begins in a way which barely distinguishes between women's clothing *per se* and particular rhetorics of difference. Thus,

the imagery of women's dress played an important role within Middle Eastern societies. It could be used as a form of social control; or as a symbol of national identity. Equally, it could be used to signify the changing status of women' (Graham-Brown 1988: 118).

Left undeveloped (which Graham-Brown does not), such a statement (and there are many in the literature that are not explored further) deflects attention from the very political positions it posits. Whose 'social control'? 'National' as opposed to what other sort of identity? 'The changing status of women' as measured by whom, according to what standards? The apparent absence of politics comes from the generality of the statement itself.

In this respect, the rhetorics of veiling have proved a versatile political tool. They have been used by Islamists and other Muslims to signal loyalties and interests which may not be particularly 'religious' or sectarian in any sense. Yet others in both Euro-America and the Middle East have focused on the veil to identify and castigate the 'fundamentalist' threat by contrasting the 'repression of women' with their own (whether Western or Middle Eastern) 'emancipation'. The rhetorical power of the imagery of the veil lies in its vacuity: everything depends on who is descibing the phenomena of veiling, for whom and to what end (see Fig. 4).

Such arguments typically leave little space for individual attributions of meaning or individual choice. Rather, they assume that the impetus for sartorial change comes from above (from higher political or religious authorities), or even as some emergent property of 'tradition', 'modernity' or 'post-modernity'; that is, as an expression of late 20th century social forms (see Thomas 1992). This encourages an unreflecting focus on the dictates of good taste and the power of fashion mafias without considering how change actually takes place. Rather, such arguments assume that

**Figure 4** Cartoon in the Islamic radical periodical, *Mektup*, April, 1989. Consider the irony of the caption which reads, 'That's what I'm afraid of. It will destroy our civilization . . .'

Redrawn here by Howard Tangye

sartorial rules change naturally and inevitability transform social identities automatically (see also below), an assumption which has been shared by Middle Eastern rulers among others. Indeed, it is the kind of assumption which lay behind the dress codes and dress reforms introduced by Atatürk and Reza Shah.

One reason why generalizing arguments appear so compelling is that they often suggest that the 'veil', or 'veiling', is a unitary phenomenon deserving of a single explanation or 'solution'. Such arguments work through a sleight of mind. Thus, *the* veil (*sic*) has often been treated as an indicator of class identity, social mobility and/or opposition to the West without ever making clear who, besides the speaker or the author, thinks so, or even what exactly an 'indicator' of social status is.

Confusing and contradictory statements about what veiling 'does' abound. In some contexts, veiling may be associated with the sexual position of the wearer, but elsewhere it is described as a means of distancing women from sexuality. It may be said to prevent a woman from becoming an object of a man's desire. But equally it may by its very presence create a covered body and thus a monolitihic sexualized identity for a woman. Or veiling may denote other stereotypical attributes of gendered difference and inequality. For instance, Hewitt and Khiba quote the 17th century missionary, Lamberti, who compares Italian and Caucasian women's dress in ways which mark them both inferior to men:

> Although the women are far from our country, they still do not fall short of our women in comeliness, especially in the combing of the hair and in covering the head, which plainly bears witness to the emptiness of their heads (this volume, p.104).

Veiling practices may be said to cover the shame of women's dependency on men, act as a measure of the control of men or as mark of the complementarity of women and men (see, for instance, Abu Lughod 1986). The construal of gendered responsibility, respectability and desire are complex, sometimes internalized, sometimes located in the covered body and knowing gaze. In terms of local understandings, 'the veil' often serves to explain both the causes and consequences of many aspects of social life: it is seen as an all-purpose symptom of a social condition *and* as the most effective way of managing that condition. As Makhlouf, writing of the women of San'a, Yemen, put it,

> the modesty code rests on two contradictory assumptions: that woman is weak and needs to be protected from threats to her honour, and that she has strong sexual impulses which threaten the honour of males and the integration of the group ... The veil is a double shield, protecting the woman against external offences of society and protecting society against the inherent evil of woman (1979: 38).

Such ambiguity is indeed likely to be characteristic of local rhetoric. But describing local rhetoric as a *fixed* modesty code is an unfortunate artifact of Makhlouf's own analysis. As Makhlouf herself notes, actual veiling practices are contingent upon other factors (cf. Watson 1994). What is so often missing is some broader perspective which allows the investigator to ask what then is *gender* and how it does figure in people's understanding of the world?

In short, 'veiling' may be held to indicate virtually anything informants *and* the analyst want. The problem is that there is no single garment, nor any single woman or man (remembering the example of veiled Tuareg men, as well as men's use of headscarfs elsewhere), who dresses as she or he does for any single reason: generalizations about *the* veil and *a* category of women or men partake of the absurd. Rather, wearing a head-covering must be understood as a complex act which may generate a myriad of nuanced interpretations (see Fig. 5). As Eickelman succinctly notes, singling out a single attribute of local custom, such as the practice of veiling (in any case not a specifically Islamic practice despite popular assumptions to the contrary, cf. Agius, this volume), often turns out to be relatively unimportant in comparison to overall patterns of sexual ideology and practice (1989: 194). To reintroduce a political perspective, we need to know how, in each particular setting, images of women's dress are understood to have originated, how they are used, in what contexts, to persuade which audiences of what political advantages, and why?

## Islamist Categories and Consumerist Debates

Discussions of consumerism also concern relations of exchange and changing meanings. They offer parallel examples of the kinds of argument often used to talk about veiling and Middle Eastern women. It is instructive to treat the two together.

Initially consumerist debates centred on international labour markets and markets for mass-produced goods, with the suggestion that consumers everywhere were becoming increasingly homogenized, or Americanized, because of their exposure to and desire for identical products: whether Coke, Levis or brand name sports shoes. One such argument occupied a central place in the revolutionary discourse of Iran in 1978. In a process of 'west-toxification' or 'west-struckness' (*gharbzadegi*) (Al-e Ahmad 1982 (orig. 1962)), Iranians and other Middle Easterners were said to have became mesmerized by, and adulatory of, western lifestyles and goods. Their salvation depended on a complete rejection of such material and spiritual dependency.

However, as many have subsequently described, the very protests against Western hegemony and consumerist homogenization reinforced orientalist

**Figure 5** Different headcoverings mark age and generational differences between three women living in the same Turkish household: an elderly woman, her daughter and granddaughter.

Drawing by Edward Lindisfarne from a photograph taken by Nancy Lindisfarne-Tapper in 1983

conceptions of the Middle East among many Euro-Americans. Equally, among Middle Easterners, there was a tendency to essentialize 'The West' in a reverse process often described as occidentalism. In other words, part of the meaning of Islamist veiling styles lies in their contrastive relation with 'Western' or 'non-Islamist, but Middle Eastern' identities. Meanwhile, from either a 'Western' or 'non-Islamist but Middle Eastern' point of view, the television images of the veiled women on the streets of Tehran in the early days of the Islamic Revolution were immensely powerful, making all Iranian women seem the same and creating an essentialized gendered dichotomy between women and men (see below, p.19).

Category creation is an act of power. For some, such as Kandiyoti (1995) or Nader (1989, quoted in Carrier 1992: 207, n. 6), the categorical distinctions between East and West has encouraged quiescence among women throughout the Muslim world. Yet for others, the new veiling practices associated with Islamist groups, whether particular Sufi orders, such as the Naqshibandiyya (see e.g. Atay 1994), or women's groups (see Hegland 1995) are much more complex, as Torab's study of women in Tehran suggests (Torab 1996). Further, new styles of veiling are sometimes, and in some places, understood as an explicit, if somewhat oblique, form of political protest against a national government. Yet elsewhere new veiling styles may be best considered as a kind of transnationalism which originates in contact with, and not simply opposition to, the West (see Carrier 1992, for an account of the various forms 'occidentalism' can take, and cf. Thomas 1992).

Elizabeth Wilson, writing about Euro-American fashion systems, introduces a socio-psychological argument which may also be relevant to understanding aspects of Islamist practices of veiling.

> In fashion we often express our longing for the 'authentic' and the 'postmodern' simultaneously, attemptng to have our cake and eat it, to be both simple and complex. We long for a leftie equivalent of the little black dress (maybe for a long time blue jeans *were* the little black dress of the counter culture). We want a garment that is totally different, and yet that will fix us forever and thereby negate the fluidity of personality. We long for a sartorial nirvana in which fashion – which expresses the change that is life – would be no more (1990: 38).

In rather the same vein, Fiske, writing about the paradoxes of blue jean conformity, argues that presently in Euro-America, individualism is one of the most widely held communal value, yet with jeans,

> the desire to be oneself leads one to wear the same garment as everyone else. ... [this] does not mean the desire to be fundamentally different from everyone else, but rather to situate individual differences within communal allegiance (1989: 3).

The methodological and theoretical problems posed by such insights are easy to see when it is blue jeans which are under discussion, yet the issues are virtually identical with those which so readily ensnare commentators on veiling in the Middle East. Thus, from the point of view of any particular woman, the choice to wear, or not wear, a particular kind of head-covering, and the meaning which she attaches to that choice, must be treated with the utmost respect and as separable from the apparent conformity and communal allegiances such a choice may also convey.

As is the case with the arguments about globalization and the effects of consumerism, what is often lost sight of in debates about contemporary Islamist movements are the political processes which reify apparently monolithic groups of people as 'Westerners', 'fundamentalists' and 'veiled women'. Yet, the counter arguments about consumerism insist that mass-produced items do not have the same meanings or implications everywhere, but are context-related and dependent on individual interpretation. For these reasons it is said that consumerism actually produces greater complexity worldwide (see Appadurai 1990; Featherstone 1990).[2] The same case can be made about Islamist veiling. It is logical that there should also be arguments which deny the reality of political or religious homogenization and insist on the impossibility of describing women's veiling in generalizing terms.

In its crudest form, the consumerist debate, and much of what is written about veiling in the Middle East, depend on constructing two extreme and apparently exclusive points of view: that of the outsider who claims the moral high ground by categorizing others as identical 'Westerners' or 'Middle Easterners/Muslims', and that of the insider who knows intimately that dress styles depend on choices which relate to each individual and their unique material and social circumstances. The lesson, of course, is not that one of these perspectives is more correct than the other, but that they are comparable: both are interested and both must be contextualized in terms of the political dispositions of the particular audiences.

## Gendered Identities

Generalizations about veiling or 'women's dress in the Middle East' raise a third set of questions which may seem remote from the persistent assocation between sex and the Orient, but are central to its continuing force. Such generalizations almost invariably assume that differences between women and men are categorical, comprehensive and completely understood. However, a moment's reflection shows that this is not so.

First, there are considerable differences within each apparently natural gender category. That is, different individuals who are ascribed membership of one gender category are by no means anatomically identical, and some individuals, such as the 'hermaphrodites' described by Sanders (1991), confound local gendered dichotomies.

Or, to take another recent example, Weir makes much of the sexuality and sexual dimorphism 'symbolised' in Palestinian dresses worn early in the 20th century (1989; cf. Gerholm 1980). Yet her account raises questions about what actually is meant by 'sexuality'/'gender' and reveals how unproductive are earlier and yet still conventional discussions of 'men's and women's' clothing. The cut of a woman's skirt, its fabric and tassels, may 'symbolize a woman's sexuality', but what is this sexuality? How was it experienced by the women who wore the dresses, by other women who pronounced on the skill and beauty which went into their making, or by yet other women, or men, for whom the dresses excited sexual desire or perhaps a desire for control?

In short, whatever anatomical category people are fitted into, anatomy is not destiny. People differ in their emotional interests, intellectual character, sexual predilections and in the range of their social and sexual choices and activities at different times and in different places. Such differences disrupt local or analytical certainities about gender as the range of practices in any one setting make clear. Thus, among the Durrani Pashtun in northern

Afghanistan it was not unusual for pastoral households with only the labour of young girls available to them, to dress these children as boys and expect them to shepherd small flocks of sheep and goats (N. Tapper 1991). Similarly Rugh describes how rural women living near the town of Balyana on the Nile dressed so that from a distance they would be mistaken for men working in the fields (1986: 129).

Such deliberate play between dress and gendered identities is all too often ignored in accounts of clothing in the Middle East though there are important exceptions. For instance, though Wikan (1977) may be mistaken in discussing the Omani *xanith* as a representative of a 'third-sex', her account of the *xanith's* dress,

> They all wore pastel-coloured *dishdashes*, walked with a swaying gait and reeked of perfume (1977: 305) ... [the *xanith*] is treated as if he were a woman. Yet he is referred to in the masculine grammatical gender, nor [*sic*] is he allowed to dress in woman's clothes, ... attempts by transexuals to appear dressed as women have taken place, but were punished by imprisonment and flogging (1977: 309)

reminds us how a gendered identity is embodied, and how carefully an understanding of dress must be related to a particular setting. What makes Wikan's account exceptional is her willingness to attend to the topic in the first place. The same may also be said of Centlivres' paper on Afghan dancing boys (1992; see also Lindisfarne Forthcoming). In this volume, Norton mentions the place of pop singers such as Zeki Müren and other transvestites and transsexuals known as *köçekler* (this volume; cf. Janssen 1992), while Bruce Ingham reminds us of a joke told by some Arab men about others they regard as effeminate:

> Two fashionable young men called Foufou and Fifi from an [unspecified] neighbouring Arab country had gone to Egypt on a Nile cruise. While they were besporting themselves on the sun deck, the boat sprung a leak and began to sink gracefully into the river and Foufou and Fifi ended up in the water. While they were flapping about, calling for help and trying not to get their hair wet, they noticed two crocodiles swimming purposefully towards them. 'Oh look' said Fifi in relief, 'They've got Lacoste lifesavers'.

Whenever 'symbols' of anatomical difference are treated as given and self-evident, we are left with problems: either the difficulty of explaining the vast range of different ideals, expectations, practices and experiences with which clothing and sexuality are associated; or, the nice irony that, if differences are fixed and clearly marked, why they should then be 'symbolised' at all.

There is, however, an alternative approach: it is to ask how embodied identities and performance construe sexuality and desire. Put slightly differently, we can ask how gendered differences emerge through social interaction, and when and how they are, or are not, marked through clothing styles and other body alterations. Anderson's (1982) discussion of how veiling practices in Afghanistan affect 'men's' identity and behaviour as well as 'woman's' is a good example of this process. Or these issues can be tackled in terms of who veils in front of whom. Presently within some Arabian Gulf communities, women avoid appearing in front of their male peers even totally veiled unless they are related to them in specific ways. Sometimes however, women may appear before quite other non-kinsmen only partially veiled. This is usually because these other men are regarded as social inferiors and are either actual or potential servants or employees. These days most such men are of southeast Asian or Indian origin, or of other Arab nationalities. As servants, they will live in their employer's household and it is felt to be impractical for women to veil in front of them all the time. Here then, dress, and more specifically veiling behaviour, marks both gendered and ethnic differences in such a way as to emphasize inequality and its association with an impotent, or inferior, masculinity. Conversely, by a kind of social shorthand, women tend to veil in front of all men who wear the style of Arab dress conventional in the Gulf since these men are, within a wide bracket, approximate social equals.

A revealing illustration of these processes occurred when Bruce Ingham, dressed on that particular occasion completely in Arab clothes, was driving in Qatar with an Arab friend. As they were travelling, Bruce's companion noticed a car obviously in trouble on the other side of the road. He recognised the car as belonging to one of his sisters and he swerved round to see what was the matter. Bruce stayed in the background as was proper, though his companion was amused to see that his sisters immediately covered their faces with their black head shawls.

'Don't worry', the man explained, 'It's only the Doctor and he isn't an Arab, so it doesn't matter'.

'Ah, yes, but he's wearing Arab clothes. So it does matter', the sisters replied.

Lorius' work provides another example of how differences emerge through interaction. As Lorius argues in her paper, 'Desire and the Gaze: Spectacular Bodies in Cairene Elite Weddings' (1996), while a bride's clothed body is the designated repository of sexuality during a wedding, so too is a dancer's body such a location while she is performing an eastern dance at a wedding. In such an argument, two quite different issues become salient: the particular ethnography of dress and sexuality on the one hand, and an analytical strategy for tackling 'sexuality' on the other.

Lorius describes how, for an Egyptian audience, 'sexuality is assumed to be a thing, an essence, which inheres in the body of the dancer rather than reflecting the attitudes of her spectators'. Yet, because Lorius is also concerned to describe how notions of sexuality can vary through time and from place to place, her analytical focus is not on the immutability of sexuality, but on the ways in which sexuality is construed through the dance performance itself, and the ways dance is framed in other discourses. As Lorius' study makes clear, gendered and sexualized identities constantly shift in response to the immediate expectations and demands of others. Equally, gendered and sexualized experiences and attributes also change throughout the course of an individual's life (cf. Kandiyoti 1994; Lindisfarne 1994). By accepting that the ascribed relations between dress and identity are fluid, and that every interaction allows for a variety of interpretations, it is possible to challenge essentialist categories of 'women' and 'men', the politics of dress and the generalizing descriptions of all Middle Easterners, or all Muslims.

## Transactable Identities

Given the political implications of essentialist categories, we may ask who uses such categories to describe whom, in what contexts? Certainly, as we know from many comparative examples, it is usual for the greatest social inequalities to be explained and justified in naturalizing terms. Thus, in so far as a female – male gender dichotomy has the effect, as it does in many parts of the Middle East, of benefitting most men and some women, it is not surprising that this dichotomy is made to seem unalterable. What makes the cultural categories so convincing is the way they form part of a circular system. To take a European example, the particular attributes of gentleness, or the emotionality of women, for instance, are deemed intrinsic by association with the anatomical features (the womb or breasts) which are represented as their cause (cf. La Fontaine 1981; Lindisfarne 1994; and with respect to dress, see Gaines 1990, or e.g., Callaway 1992).

There are other ways too in which people understand that clothing transforms or alters identity and behaviour. Clearly this is an issue relevant to any aspect of identity, though here we will pursue our focus on gendering. A first step is to dissociate notions of gender or sexuality from personhood. Thus, following Strathern (1988), it is preferable to treat gender heuristically, as an open-ended category based on Wittgenstein's idea of 'family resemblances'. Strathern understands gender as 'the categorization of person, artifacts, events [and] sequences ... which draw upon sexual imagery [and] make concrete people's ideas about the nature of social relationships' (1988: ix). Thus,

> while it seems that the use of sexual imagery is common to human beings everywhere, ... neither the character of such images nor their relation to social experience are fixed or universal. Within any local setting, sexual

images are only one among many sets of metaphors of identity and their use is both unpredictable *a priori* and ever-changing from the point of view of those who use them (Cornwall & Lindisfarne 1994: 40).

Such a perspective has hardly begun to be considered by Middle Eastern ethnographers; that it has the potential to alter radically our understandings of dress and identity in the area cannot be doubted. It is a perspective which insists that identity does not inhere in actors in some fixed, automatic or inert way. It encourages us to investigate the particular cultural sites of identity and the metaphors by which transformations are understood to take place. By treating the imagery of dress and identity as independent of persons, it is possible to consider how people change by changing their dress. The work of three anthropologists, Kurin, Gell and Pollock, is particularly instructive here.

Kurin's paper (1983) explores the ways in which food, material items such as scarves and flowers and human bodies are understood to become imbued with blessing, *baraka*, from a saint's shrine in Karachi. Kurin's method is to focus on the idioms and metaphors (such as 'hot and cold', or 'having a clear heart') which the pilgrims themselves employ. He also considers in detail the mechanisms (including the offerings made at the shrine) through which the transmission of blessing from the saint to human supplicants is understood to be effected. Though few other Middle Eastern ethnographers have been so meticulous (but see e.g. Good 1977, 1993), Kurin's attention is on the particular and his study is exemplary as a model for understanding how, for example, gendered or other identities are understood to be transformed by items of clothing: whether it be the red bridal veil of the Shahsavan (see Lindisfarne-Tapper, this volume), a Turkish boy's red circumcision cape (see Fig 6) or his sister's white wedding dress (see Tapper 1985–1990/1), a bandoleer (see Chenciner, this volume), or a *'agāl*, head-rope (see above, p.6 and Ingham, this volume).

Moreover, if the gendered imagery of dress is seen as an attribute of identity, this allows us to explore how a basic aesthetic is established, communicated and varied within a range of possible forms. Gell, writing about masking and dance styles in New Guinea (1985), and Pollock, who writes of masking among two native American communities (1995), both consider how transformations occur through the management of a performative aesthetic.

Gell offers a structural analysis of a transformative set or system of ritual masks and dancing performed in Umeda village in Papua New Guinea. It is an observer's model meant to complement or enhance indigenous accounts of the rituals. Following Leach in *Rethinking Anthropology* (1961), Gell suggests that analyses of ethnographic data are best treated 'as a problem akin to the topological analysis of figures drawn on rubber sheeting' (1985:190). Through the use of film and computer graphics, Gell describes

**Figure 6** A Turkish boy dressed for his circumcision in a smart new suit and ready-made 'ermine edged' red cape, hat and red sash which reads *maşallah,* 'Praise Allah'

Drawing by Edward Lindisfarne from a photograph taken by Nancy Lindisfarne-Tapper in 1983

the leg movements salient in a set of dances, arguing that dance meanings originate when non-dance movements are

> seized upon, stereotyped ... and set within a particular context. The logic of dance is ... akin to the logic of play; the message 'this is dance' ... is a metamessage (1985: 192)

which draws on everyday differences between women's and men's styles of walking to explore the paradoxes of Umeda gendered identities.

The relationship Gell emphasizes is important because it opens a new range of inquiry into dress styles and the aesthetics of good and bad taste. He writes,

> If dance style is essentially a product of the deformation or modulation of embedded motor patterns, then it can only be described by setting the dance movement against the template of the underlying nondance schema. The situation, in fact, is not very different in poetry. The meaning of a poem is its paraphrase (what it says about the world, just as the meaning of a dance is what the dancer would be doing in the world were he not dancing), but what

dignifies a poem is the difference between the paraphrase and the poem itself, and it is with this that the translator will have problems (1985: 203).

In short, Gell argues that it is deviation from 'the norm of expression that enhances expressiveness' (1985: 204), suggesting that the aspect of the aesthetic which participants and outside observers appreciate is the tension or gap between the dance movements and the underlying schema which anchors meaning to everyday experiences in the world. In this gap, individual performers both create and confirm social identities which may be evaluated and contested by others.

Like Gell, Pollock too is concerned with *how* masks are able to convey meaning and identity and he too seeks to explain how masking is effective in producing and altering social identities (1995: 584). Pollock extends his study of masks to include a much wider range of signalling systems in what might be called a 'semiotics of identity' in a particular culture. As he notes, anthropologists have expended much energy describing what masking (or clothing) does 'symbolically' and how they transform identity, but they have taken little time to consider precisely how these effects or functions are performed or achieved: to consider 'how masks 'work', or 'how form and function, so to speak, become linked in the mask' (1995: 581).

Semiotic analyses distinguish between iconic and indexical associations (contrasting forms of association which have elsewhere been labelled by other terms, as, for instance, Sir James Frazer's 'sympathy' verses 'contagion', or 'metaphor' verses 'metonomy'. An iconic relation is one where a sign is understood to resemble its object, just as a photograph of a landscape is held to resemble the landscape itself. Another iconic relation is that between a woman's modest 'religious' dress and what it is understood to stand for, or betoken: her lived modesty and pious actions in the world.

By contrast, an indexical relation is one in which the sign is related to its object 'by virtue of being really affected by that object' (Peirce, as quoted in Pollock 1995: 582); for instance, *how* a thermometer works is directly related to what it shows. Or a woman's headcovering may be understood actually to draw on dimensions or extensions of notions of modesty or piety and to alter the woman's experiential relationships. In an argument that acknowledges Gell's earlier insights, Pollock suggests that masks work <u>both</u> iconically and indexically, and are 'analogues of the means – such as hair styles – through which social status is expressed in everyday life' (1995: 585). They work

by concealing or modifying those signs of identity which conventionally display the actor, and by presenting new values that, again conventionally, represent the transformed person or an entirely new identity. Although every culture may recognize numerous media through which identity may be presented, masks achieve their special effect by modifying those limited number of conventionalized signs of identity (1995: 584).

Thus, as Pollock describes, for Euro-Americans the eyes are perhaps the most important site of identity, and even the most token masking of the eyes signals both a moment of play and the suspension of disbelief, offering the opportunity and scope for creating another identity. Yet in exploring the Euro-American example further, it seems that though a disguise may be effected by masking the eyes, it is typically a costume, rather than a mask, that is understood as actually transformative (1995: 584–5). Indeed, it may well be this Euro-American disposition to treat clothing in this manner which goes far to explain the character of travellers' and academic descriptions of dress in the Middle East.

Elsewhere, both the semantics of identity and understandings of the process of transformation are different. Among the Kwakiutl of the Pacific Northwest, masks exploit the mouth as the most salient icon of identity and the chest as the locus of a transformed personhood, while the metaphors of possession or containment bespeak the process of change involved. By constrast, for the Kulina of western Amazonia, it is not the face which is a focus of identity, but aural and oral skills; that is, social identities have to do with hearing and speaking (1995: 590) and their transformation is signalled on the surface of the body by smell.

## Considering Social Change

The processes of social change which we have discussed in terms of transactable bodies and clothing styles are, in effect, similar to social changes of other kinds. In each case, it is the processes whereby change is understood to be effected, and the consequences thereof, which are important. To see why this is so, it is perhaps useful intially to consider changes in clothing fashions from a more distanced perspective. For instance, we are all aware that dress styles have their own histories and that the dynamics of changing styles also vary from periods of considerable creativity and vitality to others where change is less evident.

Charsley (1992), beginning from a position reminiscent of that of Hobsbawm and Ranger in *The Invention of Tradition* (1983), considers aspects of innovation in ways which are useful to our discussion of dress in the Middle East. His starting point is that cultural objects (like the wedding cakes in Britain which are the focus of his study, or clothing, the focus of ours) tend to condition their use, and 'objects and uses together condition the meanings that may be attached to them' (1992: 132).

Indeed, most objects or behaviours derive their social value from the context of their use, so that the ways certain items of clothing are worn, for instance, may be more important than the actual pieces of clothing themselves. Or the way something has been acquired cannot be easily separated from use, and use itself cannot be separated from effect, from the ways in which others react to it (Bourdieu 1984: 21–22). Yet, as Charsley insists, over time, the form of objects, their uses and the meanings attributed to them may all evolve in different directions and at different speeds.

The problematic of Hobsbawm and Ranger's title, *The Invention of Tradition* (1983), has become well-known to cultural historians, not least for their distinction between 'custom' and 'invented tradition'. However, most later critiques, including Charsley's, argue against such a divide, insisting that cultural styles everywhere are continuously modified by innovation. What does vary, though only in degree and not in kind, is the inventiveness associated with any one event. Thus, as Charsley points out,

> where events are frequent and not of any great moment [such as dressing for work each day], arrangements for them may undergo a continuous and often unremarked process of innovation, by modification and drift (1992: 135).

By contrast, however, infrequent events, such as weddings or other life course ceremonies (and thus, for our purposes, the special clothing people may wear at such times) force people to consider cultural styles and rework component parts. In this process, an object, (or uses and meanings) can change and become 'marooned': that is, 'deprived of much of its context, [becoming] to a degree mysterious and open to interpretation' (Charsley 1992: 133). If this happens, aspects of a tradition may be picked up and reworked to blossom in the most elaborate ways. Such is the case with Islamist veiling customs. Or, a marooned tradition may well be termed 'expressive' or 'symbolic' (see above, p.19).

### Folkloric Dress

Examples of the process of 'marooning' can be found in attitudes towards what is, in any setting, known as 'folkloric' or 'traditional' dress. Unfashionable, often rural, clothing styles closely associated with particular settings and ethnicities (and assumed to have been worn since time immemorial) are often labelled 'folkloric' by city people or those of wealth, while the people who wear such clothes are stigmatized and/ or patronized as quaint ethnic or rural bumpkin (see Yamani, this volume). The labelling is about inequality, but the processes involved are complex. For instance, as national governments have tried to create a uniform citizenry, regional or ethnic dress has often been decried as 'backward' or 'primitive', while from the point of view of political dissidents, wearing such dress was often an act of defiance, pride and local integrity and a sign of commitment to at least a degree of regional or ethnic autonomy.

The range of such responses to dress is suggested with respect to some tribal identities in Iran. Beck, writing of Qashqai dress (1986), describes how, though Reza Shah outlawed 'ethnic dress' in 1928, various items of men's and women's clothing, particular the *dogushi,* 'two-eared' Qashqai men's hats were worn as statements of revived Qashqai power, autonomy and identity (see Fig. 7 and Lindisfarne-Tapper, this volume).

The enforcement of dress conformity could often be used as a penalty for intransigent behaviour among rebellious subjects. Within the Arabian Peninsula the wearing of braids (*gurūn'*, lit. 'horns') was normal among many bedouin groups until the early twentieth century and was thought to be a mark of manhood. One branch of the Shammar tribe, the Āl Jarba, were at some point in the early 19th century ordered by Ibn Sa'ūd to shave their heads to prove their loyalty. However the *gurūn* were accorded such importance by the Bedouin that the Āl Jarba left their homeland in Najd and went to live in Iraq never to return. This event is remembered in the epithet *sūdān arrūs,* 'black-haired', which often occurs in connection with the name of the Jarba.

This example points to the way centralizing states are typically gendered in their effects and it is often men, rather more than women, whose dress is directly controlled. This may happen most obviously through military service, through it may be an effect of men's greater mobility and the extent to which, through movement, men become more liable to state control (cf. Yamani, this volume). Thus, contrary to what Rugh says about Egyptian

**Figure 7** A Qashqa'i camelherder wearing a *dogushi* hat and smoking a water pipe

Drawing by Edward Lindisfarne from a photograph by Lois Beck (1986: *op. cit.,* following page 199)

men's 'folk dress' as distinguishing 'a much more limited range of meanings [than women's folk dress]' (1986: 113–4), it is much more likely that women's dress, by default or choice, signals identities which are forbidden or precluded to men.

Where such differences occur, women may continue to wear 'traditional' dress long after men have adopted more metropolitan or cosmopolitan styles. The effects of this may be double-edged: women in their 'traditional' dresses may be described by all and sundry as more backward or primitive than their menfolk, but they may also – and even simultaneously – be honoured locally as the repositories of 'older' and more particular identities. In this respect, the case of particularly women's dress and embroidery among Palestinians is well known (see Weir 1988; Warnock 1990: 170–172). Again the underlying lesson, however, is about relationality: that the dress of all the people in any social setting must be seen as part of a single system (cf. also Tapper, N. & R. Tapper, 1987).

Such processes, and the intersection between dress, gender and state control, are also important for an understanding of how women and men generally, and veiled women in particular, are felt to embody the identities of a religion or a nation as a whole. Thus, Thaiss (1978) describes the metaphors of colonial penetration which were prominent during the Islamic Revolution in Iran, when the country as a whole was feminized and said to be both a 'sister/ mother/ wife' who needed protection from the rapacious west and a whore which had prostituted herself for western goods and power. In each case, of course, the practices of veiling become obvious extensions and elaborations of the metaphors. In a rather similar case, Haifa Al-Ankary considered the changes in veiling laws and their interpretation in Saudi Arabia, finding a relation between the perceived character of external threats to the Saudi state and the control of veiling among Saudi and foreign women within the country (Personal Communication; see also Doumato 1992 ).

Elsewhere, particularly when ethnic or parochial clothing styles are no longer worn as a matter of course, such clothing may nonetheless be worn in quite other contexts. For example, it seems quite common that a history of ethnic difference within a nation-state may be acknowledged through the use of 'folkloric' costumes while simultaneously denying either that such diversity has present relevance or any political import. Thus on various holidays during the year, Turkish school children wear 'folkloric' dress during school celebrations. More or less randomly, the children don contrived, and often radically simplified and stylized costumes: some children will wear clothing representing the peoples living near the Black Sea and do dances associated with that region, while other children from the same classroom may dress in the fashion of Bursa or Antayla. Such an admixture serves to create an image of a state which tolerates diversity

**Figure 8** Turkish school children from southwestern Turkey dancing during the public celebration of a national holiday. They are wearing the 'traditional' dress of Trabzon in the extreme northeast of the country, though it is notable that the Turkish flag they carry is more prominent than their 'folkloric' costumes

Drawing by Edward Lindisfarne from a photograph taken by Nancy Lindisfarne-Tapper in 1983

while in fact undermining difference in an effort to create a uniform identity among its citizenry (see Fig. 8; cf. Kideckel 1983).

Equally, national or 'folkloric' dress may be worn in the Olympic Games or for other international or touristic purposes. In this respect, the dual vision of the veiled woman and women in picturesque 'folk' costumes continues to prevail in the west. This is so in spite of the fact that western fashions which had been followed by the elites for years had also become, by the 1920s and 1930s, widely popular with Middle Eastern women at home (See Baker, this volume; cf. Graham-Brown 1988: 126). Further, as Graham-Brown remarks, contrary to Western ideas, it was also the case that

> women who wore 'modern' clothes had automatically become 'just like Western women' ... although style of dress had considerable importance as an indicator both of people's self-image and of their aspirations, it did not necessarily translate simply into a desire to be 'westernized' (1988: 132).

For the women reformers, education and changes in women's legal status were often far more important that removing the veil (*ibid*. 140). The same can be said of many Muslim and Islamist women today.

## Innovation and Ostentation

More generally, Charsley writes,

> Where the past is positively valued and precedent is clear it may seem important to people to follow it ... [sometimes leading to] a conscious struggle to preserve as much of established tradition as was possible. ... Where adequate precedent is not immediately available, a creative reworking of whatever record there may be is possible ... But even if the past is not given any special value, there is only one other option for events of importance. That is to find something new and special, to exceed the past. A potlatch effect is very familiar to anthropologists in exchange institutions around the world. Particularly in periods of expanding resources and technological advance, but even at other times ... there are striking instances of the way in which periodic rituals may be made special by new additions.... Both the new and traditional may of course be called on in the same event (1992: 134–5).

Yet extravagance on the part of elites or others is by no means inevitable. A variety of mechanisms, including the deliberate display of talismans to ward off the attention of devils, jinn or other rapacious spirits, are available to control display, while precautions against the evil eye (including accusations of the evil eye) also serve as a leveling device. Indeed, a reluctance to display wealth or good fortune anywhere other than within the privacy of household was widespread in the Middle East and remains a behaviour strongly sanctioned in some places. Thus modest, as opposed to ostentatious, dress is one rationale given for women's adoption of the Islamist veil. Contrarywise, others may explain that a woman who chooses to veil (whether in a more traditional or a new Islamist style) is doing so as an effective means of hiding poverty and/or avoiding competitive consumerism.

Escalating potlatches seem to be associated with periods when former hierarchies of prestige and material wealth are in a state of flux. During such periods, which might include much of the twentieth century for many new elites in the Middle East, the most immediate and reliable index of worth is money itself. At its most crude,

> Economic power is first and foremost a power to keep economic necessity at arm's length. This is why it universally asserts itself by the destruction of riches, conspicuous consumption, squandering, and every form of *gratuitous* luxury (Bourdieu 1984: 55).

However, the mechanisms of ostentation and emulation in stratified societies are complex, and much depends on the time frame in which, for example, clothing styles are judged.

As Bourdieu (1984) has described among aristocracies of taste, people in secure, established hierarchies invest in prestigious styles which can only be acquired over a long time, in styles which become naturalized as aspects of 'good breeding' or a 'good education'. Their investment avoids the ephremerality of fashion (cf. Harmon 1995: 8) and is a kind of 'cultural accumulation and a certain image of cultural accomplishment' (Bourdieu 1984: 25). For example, Yamani (this volume) shows most clearly how ostensively 'gratuitous knowledge' also applies to dress. Indeed, we would argue that a knowledge of styles and the ability to achieve a stylish appearance is of considerable social value everywhere. What may differ is the extent to which people in established hierarchies value 'conspicuous formality' over apparently less mysterious and more expressive taste. But what Bourdieu has called 'aesthetic distancing' is also likely to play some part everywhere (1984: 34). As Mary Douglas and many others have insisted, social distance and hierarchy and physical distance and control are likely to be parallel indices of prestige (Douglas 1970).

Yet rarely if ever can status competitions be reduced to a single dimension. Certainly in the Middle East they are likely to be significantly gendered or use age as an important marker of difference. Consider again what Veblen called 'vicarious ostentation': when men who may appear as near equals in terms of their own clothing display their wealth and confidence in themselves through their wives' appearance and dress (see above, p.7), allowing women and men to suggest that women are 'naturally' responsible for back-biting or other forms of competition. In the Middle East such vicarious consumption also had other purposes: Atatürk successfully used his adopted daughter as the embodiment of dress reforms, but when women of the immediate family of King Amanullah of Afghanistan appeared in Kabul unveiled, their action was the spark which started a popular rising and led to the King's exile. Again, context and the wider web of relations must be taken into account.

## A Damascene Example

In Damascus in the early 1990s, bridal fashions were a telling index of social class, good taste and social acceptability (see Tapper 1988/9; Lindisfarne-Tapper 1991). Women of the new elites sought to buy their white bridal gowns in Europe, from *haute couture* houses if possible. Other, less wealthy women had Damascene dressmakers translate and elaborate European patterns into garments made more lavish by the addition of thousands of hand-sewn sequins or seed pearls. Ready-made gowns were also available in boutiques and in the *souq*. These were elaborated, less with hand-sewn ornaments than with fabric, such that no flounce, ruffle, pleat, button or bow was omitted if room could be found for it on the dress. As one woman said, 'There's no place in Damascus now for classic simplicity,' though in fact, wedding dresses available for hire were sometimes of simpler, earlier styles.

But the variation did not stop there. For women who embraced a new Islamist identity, there were dresses which conformed through 'reinventing traditions' with the local expectations of modest covering, *hijab*. The most lavish and expensive of these were brought from Cairo, where dress designers, drawing on Arab historical film romances among other sources, created fantastical dresses, an orientalist's delight: dresses with turbans and tulle for a modern-day Sheherazade (see Fig. 9).

From these brief examples it is clear that women's fashionable dress is an important medium which associates the owning class in Damascus with all that is 'modern', western, wealthy, sophisticated and international. Yet these same dress styles encourage the creation of a specficially Syrian dimension to these affluent associations. Such Syrian specificities lie in both the neo-Arab/Islamist fashions and in the degree of ornamentation of contemporary evening dresses. Yet because indigenous canons of fashion and good taste are complex and ambiguous, fashonable dress, particularly that displayed at the wedding receptions, is a contested arena and competition is rife. Through the idiom of fashion, personal preference and individuality, gendered differences and unequal social privilege all find dramatic visual expression.

In this setting, which is described by Damascenes as one of rapid change, both women and men have an interest in promoting the potlatch of conspicuous consumption which unites fashonable dress and the rituals of marriage. Those women, and there are many among the owning class, who are prepared to accept a secondary role to men economically have a vested interest in a system which celebrates the family: it is a system which disguises women's domestic power and their patronage activities, while affording them extraordinary wealth and leisure for creative self-beautification. Stylish dressing and elegant social performances are an aspect of their active participation in a system which allows them conspicious leisure and considerable informal influence; they are an aspect of their 'bargain with patriarchy', as Kandiyoti puts it (1988). For men, a system which treats women as elegant commodities to be exchanged in marriage provides them with an index of relative wealth and power, while reinforcing 'neo-patriarchal' (Sharabi 1988) authority in domestic, national and transnational activities.

However, fashion discourses in the late twentieth century are self-conscious and fashion has the capacity to unmask hypocrisy. And though women sometimes play the jester's role, it would be quite mistaken to see them as fashion-victims. Members of the owning class may laugh at the kitschy fashions of the urban poor but, in their own fashion competitions, they also self-consciously prick the moral balloon of the regime's legitimacy (cf. Wilson 1985: 10). Women and men are both well-aware that ultimately money values are an important source of taste and they can be scathing about the illicit sources from which that money derives. Dressing over the

**Figure 9** A wedding procession in a five-star hotel in Damascus. Note the contrast between the dress of the bridal couple and the 'traditional' paraphernalia of the turbaned drummers, sword-bearers and the hotel servants who carry flaming torches in brass containers

Drawing by Howard Tangye from a photograph by Nancy Lindisfarne-Tapper taken in 1989 top, whether in diaphanous extravaganzas or in designer jeans is both a joke and a necessity. Few miss the link between fashion and morality, though few escape the system.

Because of the relation between the owning class in Damascus and the ruling clique surrounding the President, it is unlikely that wealthy Damascenes will accept curbs on their spending, though they may institute sumptuary laws among subordinates. However sumptuary laws, as Lurie has remarked, are difficult to enforce and do not last long (1982: 115). Yet media coverage can itself sometimes act as a censor and wedding extravagance, for instance, can be publicized far and wide and have immediate repercussions both informally, and in terms of formal political institutions.

Or the impetus for change may come from other sources. When class differences in Britain were particularly sharp, agents of the upper classes sought to ensure conformity with their wedding customs and eliminate those which they deemed unsuitable (Charsley 1992: 136). Such a process, while not as direct or formalized as the dress reforms in the Middle East, is nonetheless an aspect of the same effort to discipline and control subordinates by excising customs which might signal real differences between their interests and those of the owning classes.

A comparable example is described by Agius (this volume) for Malta where differently coloured veils distinguished social classes. As these class differences were altered by increasing access to wealth other sartorial distinctions were sought. Lurie has described this process in general terms.

> what came to designate high rank instead was the evident cost of a costume: rich materials, superfluous trimmings and difficult-to-care-for styles; ... As a result, it was assumed that the people you met would be dressed as lavishly as their income permitted (Lurie, 1983: 115–6).

Yet, as Charsley has suggested, though practices identified as of high status have been important in determining cultural styles, top-down changes of custom are by no means the only direction or impetus for change (1992: 137). Indeed, because objects, usages and their meanings may all change independently, it is ultimately impossible to treat social change in terms of objective measures. It is more instructive to talk comparatively about the degree and speed of change from the perspective of the players.

In short, dress is a starting point. Our approach though holistic does not aim to be encyclopaedic in thematic or regional terms, nor can we provide in this brief volume an historical atlas of Middle Eastern clothing. Rather, each study considers aspects of dress conventions in a particular setting, each illustrating the intimate relation between aspects of clothing technologies, language use and social relations. What counts as important varies throughout the region and perceptions of difference alter over time.

Some changes and some clothing values, such as those signaled by lexical and phonological shifts, suggest yet other dynamic patterns and time frames for understanding social change.

## Notes

1 By focusing on clothing, we also displace other related questions which can only be briefly mentioned here, concerning raw materials and textile production in the Middle East (see e.g. Mitchell on Egyptian cotton 1988: 15–16), the preparation of textiles by dyeing, spinning and weaving (Cordwell & Swartz 1979; Schneider & Werner 1991), the advent of the Singer sewing machine in the Middle East and other processes of clothing manufacture (see, for example, White 1994, on women home-workers in Istanbul), as well as the relation between fabrics used for clothing and other textiles (e.g. Spooner 1986, on carpets; Messick 1987, on weaving and R. Tapper, Forthcoming, on felt-making).
2 With some exceptions (see Stauth & Zubaida 1987; Middle East Report 1989: 159 on popular culture), there have been few detailed studies of these issues in the Middle East.

## Bibliography

Abu Lughod, L. 1986. *Veiled Sentiments: Honor and Poetry in a Bedouin Society.* Berkeley: University of California Press.

Al-e Ahmad, J. 1982 (orig. 1962). *Gharbzadegi* (*Weststruckness*) (trans. John Green and Ahmad Alizadeh). Lexington: Mazda.

Anderson, J. 1982. 'Social structure and the Veil: Comportment and Composition of Interaction in Afghanistan'. *Anthropos*, 77(3–4), 397–420.

Appadurai, A. 1990. 'Disjuncture and Difference in the Global Cultural Economy'. In Featherstone (ed.) *op. cit.*, 295–310.

Atay, A.T. 1994. *Naqshbandi Sufism in a Western Setting.* Unpublished University of London PhD Dissertation.

Barnes, R. & J. B. Eicher (eds) 1992. *Dress and gender: Making and meaning in cultural contexts.* London/New York: Berg.

Barthes, R. 1983. *The Fashion System.* New York: Hill and Wang.

Beck, L. 1986. *The Qashqa'i of Iran.* New Haven: Yale University Press.

Bordo, S. 1993. 'Feminism, Foucault and the Politics of the Body'. In C. Ramazanoğlu (ed.) *Up Against Foucault.* London: Routledge, 179–202.

Boddy, J. 1989. *Wombs and Alien Spirits: Women, Men and the Zar Cult in Northern Sudan.* Madison: University of Wisconsin Press.

Bourdieu, P. 1977. *Outline of a Theory of Practice.* Cambridge: Cambridge University Press.

—— 1984. *Distinction: A Social Critique of the Judgement of Taste.* Cambridge, Mass.: Harvard University Press.

Callaway, H. 1992. 'Dressing for Dinner in the Bush: Rituals of Self-Definition and British Imperial Authority'. In Barnes & Eicher (eds) *op. cit.*, 232–247.

Carrier, J.G. 1992. 'Occidentalism: The World Turned Upside-Down'. *American Ethnologist*, 19/2, 195–212.

Centlivres, P. 1992. '*Le Jeu des Garcons*'. In Hainard, Jacques & Roland Kachr (eds) *Les Femmes*, Neuchatel (Suisse): Musee d' ethnographie, 55–80.

Charsley, S. R. 1992, *Wedding Cakes and Cultural History*. London: Routledge.
Cordwell, J.E. and R. Swartz (eds) 1979. *The Fabrics of Culture*. The Hague: Morton.
Cornwall, Andrea & Nancy Lindisfarne (eds) 1994. *Dislocating Masculinity: Comparative Ethnographies*. London: Routledge.
Doumato, E. 1992. 'Gender, Monarchy and National Identity in Saudi Arabia. *British Journal of Middle East Studies*. 19/13–47.
Douglas, M. 1970. *Natural Symbols: Explorations of Cosmology*. London: Barrie-Rochliff.
Eicher, J. 1995. *Dress and Ethnicity: Change Across Space and Time*. Oxford: Berg.
Eicher, J. B. & M. E. Roach-Higgins, 1992. 'Definition and Classification of Dress: Implications for Analysis of Gender Roles'. In Barnes & Eicher (eds) *op. cit.*, 8–28.
Eickelman, D. F. 1989. *The Middle East: An Anthropological Approach*. Englewood Cliffs, N. J.: Prentice Hall.
Fawzi el Solh, C. & J. Mabro (eds) 1994. *Muslim Women's Choices*. Oxford: Berg.
Featherstone, M. 1990. 'An Introduction'. In M. Featherstone (ed) *Global Culture: Nationalism, Globalization and Modernity*. London, Newbury Park, New Dehli: Sage, 1–14.
Fiske, J. 1989. *Understanding Popular Culture*. Boston: Unwin Hyman.
Gaines, J. & C. Herzog, (eds) 1990. *Fabrications: Costume and the Female Body*. New York, London: Routledge.
Gaines, J. 1990. 'Introduction: Frabricating the Female Body'. In Gaines & Herzog (eds) *op. cit.*, 1–27.
Gell, A. 1985, 'Style and Meaning in Umeda Dance' in Paul Spencer, (ed.) *Society and the Dance: The Social Anthropology of Process and Performance*, Cambridge: Cambridge University Press, 183–205.
Gerholm, T. 1980. 'Knives and Sheaths: Notes on a Sexual Idiom of Social Inequality in North Yemen'. *Ethnos*. 1–2, 82–91.
Gilsenan, Michael, 1991. 'Whose Honour? Whose Shame? Reflections on the Politics of Humiliation'. *Journal of the British Association for Social Anthropology in Policy and Practice. 9/* 6–8.
Good, B. 1977. *The Heart of What's the Matter: The Structure of Medical Discourse in a Provincial Iranian Town*. PhD Dissertation: University of Chicago.
—— 1993 *Medicine, Rationality and Experience: an Anthropological Perspective*. Cambridge: Cambridge University Press.
Graham-Brown, S. 1988. *Images of Women: The Portrayal of Women in Photography of the Middle East, 1860–1950*. London: Quartet.
Hale, S. 1996. 'Modernism and Middle Eastern Womens Studies: *Muslim Women's Choices: Religious Belief and Social Reality*'. *Middle East Women's Studies* X1/2, 1–3.
Harmon, C. 1995. 'The Battle of the Looks'; a review of Aileen Ribeiro, 1995, *The Art of Dress: Fashion in England and France 1750–1820. TLS*, 1/12/95, 8–9.
Hegland, M. 1995. 'Shi'a Women in Northwest Pakistan and Agency through Practice: Ritual, Resistance, Resilience'. *POLAR: Political and Legal Anthropology Review*. 18/2, 65–79.
Hobsbawm, E. & T. Ranger, (eds) 1983. *The Invention of Tradition*. Cambridge: Cambridge University Press.
Janssen, T. 1992. 'Transvestites and Transsexuals in Turkey'. In Schmitt, Arno & Jehoeda Sofer (eds), *Sexuality and Eroticism among Males in Moslem Societies*. New York: Harrington Park Press, 83–92.
Kandiyoti, D. 1988. 'Bargaining with Patriarchy'. *Gender and Society*, 2/3, 274–90.

—— 1994. 'The Paradoxes of Masculinity: Some Thoughts on Segregated Societies' in Cornwall & Lindisfarne (eds) *op. cit.*, 197–213.

—— (ed.) 1995. *Gendering the Middle East: Emerging Perspectives*. London: I.B. Tauris.

Kanafani, A. S. 1983. *Aesthetics and Ritual in the UAR: The Anthropology of Food and Bodily Adornment among Arabian women*. Beirut: American University of Beirut.

Kennedy, J. G. 1978 *Nubian Ceremonial Life: Studies in Islamic Syncretism and Cultural Change*. Berkeley/ Cairo: University of California Press/ American University of Cairo Press.

Kideckel, D. 1983. 'Introduction: Political Rituals and Symbolism in Socialist Eastern Europe'. *Anthropological Quarterly*. 56/2, 52–54.

Kroeber, A. L. 1919. 'On the Principles of Order in Civilization as Exemplified by Changes in Fashion'. *American Anthropologist*. NS 21, 235–263.

Kurin, R. 1983. 'The Structure of Blessedness at a Muslim Shrine in Pakistan', *Middle Eastern Studies*. 19/3, 312–325.

La Fontaine, J. 1981 'The Domestication of the Savage Male'. *Man*, 16/3, 333–49.

Lane, E. 1923. (orig. 1836) *The Manners and Customs of the Modern Egyptians*. London: Dent.

Leach, E. R. 1961. *Rethinking Anthropology*. London: Athlone.

Lindisfarne, N. 1994. 'Variant Masculinities, Variant Virginities: Rethinking "Honour and Shame"' in Cornwall & Lindisfarne (eds) *op. cit.*, 82–96.

—— 1995. 'Review of Fawzi, C. el-Solh & J. Mabro, (eds) *Muslim Women's Choices* (*op. cit.*) in the *Journal of the European Association of Social Anthropologists*. 3/2, 170–172.

—— Forthcoming. 'Questions of Gender and the Ethnography of Afghanistan'. In Jacques Hainard (ed.) *Festschrift for Pierre Centlivres*. Neuchâtel (Suisse): Musee d' ethnographie.

Lindisfarne, N. 1991. 'In Spectacular Fashion: The Aesthetics of Privilege at Wedding Receptions in Damascus'. Unpublished paper presented at the BRISMES Annual Conference, SOAS, London.

Lorius, C. Forthcoming 1996. 'Gaze and Desire'. *Women's Studies International Forum*. 19/3–4.

Lurie, A. 1981. *The Language of Clothes: The Definitive Guide to People-watching through the Ages*. London: Hamlyn.

Makhlouf, C. 1979. *Changing Veils: Woman and Modernization in North Yemen*. London: Croom Helm.

Mascia-Lees, F. & Sharpe, P. 1992. 'Introduction: Soft-Tissue Modification and the Horror Within'. In Mascia-Lees, F. & Sharpe, P. (eds) *Tattoo, Torture, Mutilation, and Adornment: The Denaturalization of the Body in Culture and Text*. Albany: State University of New York Press, 1–9.

Messick, B. 1987. 'Subordinating to discourses: women, weaving and gender relations in North Africa'. *American Ethnologist*. 14/2, 210–225.

*Middle East Report*. July/ August 1989, 159.

Mitchell, T. 1988. *Colonizing Egypt*. Cambridge: Cambridge University Press.

Moors, A. 1991. 'Women and the Orient: A Note on Difference'. In Nencel, Lorraine and Peter Pels (eds) *Constructing Knowledge: Authority and Critique in Social Sciences*. London: Sage, 114–122.

Nader, L. 1989 'Orientalism, Occidentalism and the Control of Women'. *Cultural Dynamics*, 2, 323–355.

Pollock, D. 1995. 'Masks and the Semiotics of Identity'. *Journal of the Royal Anthropological Institute*, 1/3, 581–598.

Rugh, A. 1986. *Reveal & Conceal: Dress in Contemporary Egypt.* Syracuse: Syracuse University Press.

Said, E. 1978. *Orientalism.* London: Routlege and Kegan Paul.

Sanders, P. 1991. 'Gendering the Ungendered Body: Hermaphrodies in Medieval Islamic Law'. In Nikki R. Keddie & Beth Baron (eds) *Women in Middle Eastern History: Shifting Boundaries in Sex and Gender.* New Haven: Yale University Press, 74–95.

Scarce, J. 1987. *Women's Costume of the Near and Middle East.* London: Unwin Hyman.

Sciama, L. 1992. 'Lacemaking in Venetian Culture'. In Barnes & Eicher (eds) *op.cit.,* 121–144.

Schneider, J. & Weiner, A. (eds) 1991. *Cloth and Social Experience.* Washington, D.C.: Smithsonian Institution.

Sharabi, H. 1988. *Neopatriarchy: A Theory of Distorted Change in Arab Society.* Oxford: Oxford University Press.

Spooner, B. 1986. 'Weavers and Dealers: the Authenticity of an Oriental Carpet. In A. Appadurai (ed.) *The Social Life of Things: Commodities in Cultural Perspective.* Cambridge: Cambridge University Press. 195–235.

Stauth, G. & S. Zubaida, (eds) 1987. *Mass Culture, Popular Culture and Social Life in the Middle East.* Boulder, Colorado: Westview Press.

Strathern, M. 1988. *The Gender of the Gift.* Berkeley: University of California Press.

Tapper, N. 1985. 'Changing Wedding Rituals in a Turkish Town'. *Journal of Turkish Studies,* 9, 305–313.

—— 1988–9. 'Changing Marriage Ceremonial and Gender Roles in the Arab World': An Anthropological Perspective'. *Arab Affairs,* 8, 117–135.

—— 1990/1. '"Traditional" and "Modern" Wedding Ritual in a Turkish Town'. *International Journal of Turkish Studies.* 5/1–2, 135–154.

—— 1991. *Bartered Brides: Politics, Gender and Marriage in an Afghan Tribal Society.* Cambridge: Cambridge University Press.

Tapper, N. & R. Tapper, 1987. 'The Birth of the Prophet: Ritual and Gender in Turkish Islam'. *Man,* 21/1, 69–92.

Tapper, R. Forthcoming. 'Introduction', in R. Tapper & K. McLachlan, (eds) *Material Cultures of the Middle East.*

Thaiss, G. 1978. 'The Conceptualization of Social Change Through Metaphor'. *Journal of Asian and African Studies.* 13/1–2, 1–13.

Thomas, N. 1992. 'The Inversion of Tradition'. *American Ethnologist,* 19/2, 213–232.

Torab, A. 1996. 'Piety as Gendered Agency: A Study of *jalaseh* Ritual Discourse in an Urban Neighbourhood in Iran'. *JRAI (NS)* 2/2, 1–18.

Veblen, Thorstein, 1898, *Theory of the Leisure Class: An Economic Study of Institutions.* New York: Macmillan.

Warnock, K. 1990. *Land Before Honour: Palestinian Women in the Occupied Territories.* London: Macmillan.

Watson, H. 1994. 'Women and the Veil: Personal Responses to a Global Process' in Ahmed, Akbar & Hastings Donnan, (eds) *Islam, Globalization and Postmodernity.* London: Routledge, 141–159.

Weir, S. 1988. *Palestinian Costume.* London: British Museum.

White, J. B. 1994. *Money Makes Us Relatives: Women's Labor in Urban Turkey.* Austin: University of Texas Press.

Wikan, U. 1977. 'Man becomes Woman: Transexualism in Oman as a key to Gender Roles'. *Man* 12/2, 304–319.

Wilson, E. 1985. *Adorned in Dreams: Fashion and Modernity.* London: Virago.

—— 1990. 'All the Rage'. In Gaines & Herzog, (eds) *op. cit.,* 28–39.

# Chapter Two

# Mens Dress in the Arabian Peninsula: Historical and Present Perspectives

*Bruce Ingham*

In this paper, men's dress in the Arabian Peninsula is examined in terms of its historical origins, evolution and geographical connections with other areas. Some reference is also be made to the social meaning of dress and how it marks group identity. My remarks on the history are based on the works of earlier travellers. For the modern period I rely on my own observations made within what might be called the 'local', or, in an even more general sense, 'tribal' milieu, i.e. in the majlises of members of the Āl Thāni in Qatar, the Āl Sudair in Saudi Arabia and among tribal people in Saudi Arabia, Qatar, Kuwait, Khuzistan and to a lesser extent also Iraq. Other dress styles exist in the area among 'non-local' Arabs and may exist among locals also, but I do not deal with them here.[1]

## The Origins of Arab Dress

It is impossible to talk about dress in Arabia without first touching on Arab identity, since in the Arabian Peninsula the two are intimately connected. Although the word 'Arab' in an international sense denotes a person from one of the Arab states, being those states in which Arabic is the state language, in a more local sense in northern Arabia and even in Egypt, it usually denotes someone from the Arabian Peninsula, local tribal Arabs or in western terminology, 'Bedouins'. As the term is used in Alexandria for instance, it refers either to people from the Gulf States or to local eastern Saharan tribesmen like the Awlād 'Ali and Murābiṭīn[2]. It therefore excludes urban populations of Egypt and the Fertile Crescent. This represents a survival of the older sense of the word, which is both linguistic and ethnic and has often been intimately connected with the wearing of Arab clothes (see Fig. 1).

The beginning of Arab identity, according to one theory,[3] has its roots in the contact of Arabian camel-herders with more advanced civilizations

**Figure 10** Standard North Arabian dress
Drawn by Sean Bowen from a photography by
Bruce Ingham taken in 1988.

particularly Persians in the Fertile Crescent. This produced a society of camel-herders accustomed to fighting as cavalry; people identified in Dostal's (1979) terms as the progressive north Arabian 'proto-bedouin' group who appeared from around the 2nd millennium BC onwards, using lances instead of bows and riding on the hump of the camel, and from the 3rd century BC onwards, using the saddle arch. This progressive northern group are identified with the Aribi who disseminated the Arabic language southward displacing the other related languages which were perhaps spoken there and finally replacing even the Ḥimyaritic languages, so that now only isolated pockets of these remain in southern Arabia.

Thus contact with the more advanced Iranians turned the Aribi, originally 'simple herdsmen', into a ruling class which expanded and formed the foundation of the Arabs as we now know them. This led in the 2nd/3rd century AD to what Dostal calls the 'full Bedouin phase' which was associated with the weakening of the north Arabian city states and the development of a strong north Arabian nomad pastoralist society. Dostal also suggests that the present north Arabian dress of *thōb* and *sarwāl,* was introduced from Persia at the same time as the rigid camel saddle,[4] which itself evolved under Persian influence. North Arabian friezes of the early Christian era show men wearing a Persian form of dress with trousers and a shirt which comes down to the knees. Previous to this, Babylonian friezes showed camel herders wearing a kilt form of dress very similar to that of some south Arabian populations of today. What is suggested is that the present form of dress resulted from a gradual lengthening of the shirt. This gives a picture of early Arab 'identity' being manifested by the elements of language, technically advanced camel nomadism and a specific mode of dress.

The possibility of a foreign origin for the mode of dress corresponds to what we see in general regarding material culture in central Arabia, where very little seems to be produced, but where items are introduced from outside and then adapted to meet local conditions.[5] Traditionally some items were made in Arabia, including sandals made in Najd, coffee pots and simple iron work, 'agals and also some very fine summer cloaks made in al Ḥasa. However the great majority of items of clothing, fabric and also fine quality arms and armour such as firearms and watered steel sword blades were imported.

The earliest reference to dress in the north of Arabia that I have found in the modern era comes in De la Roque (1742: 214–20 ) referring to a visit to Syria in 1660. His comments seem to refer to the North Arabian dress for the ordinary people, while the shaikhs and more important persons were said to be wearing Turkish dress. De la Roque is quoted in full below (pp.51–2) in the section on earlier descriptions of Arab dress.

## Variations in Dress and Arab Identities

If we accept that the mode of dress is an important element of Arab identity, it is interesting to look at variation in dress in different regions of Arabia as a correlate of the expanding and contracting of Arabian identities vis à vis peoples of the surrounding lands: Turks in the north, Persians in the east and Indians and Indonesians in the south. Three brief examples of the contact and cultural change are given below; in two of these I have been able to refer to dress and its connection with identity.

### (i) The Hwilah of the East Coast

In the 16th century in the time of the prosperous Zand dynasty and probably even earlier, many Arab families from the east coast of Arabia travelled to the Persian side of the Gulf and settled there. They became considerably Persianized in the process and would seem to have intermarried with the Persian population also. At a later date, after the eclipse of the Zand, many of these came back to the Arabian side of the Gulf. However their Persian connection is still recognized and some families bear names which signal an earlier Persian location. Many such families are found in the Gulf states and al-Ḥasa⁶. As a group they are known as the Hwilah (sing Hōli) and are distinguished both from Arab populations who do not have such a connection, and from the 'Ajam, members of a Persian population of long standing living on the Arab side of the Gulf. These identities are marked sartorially, but in a variety of different ways related to the complex local politics of the ethnically heterogeneous population of the different Gulf states.

### (ii) Assimilation of Persian elements in Khuzistan

During the Safavi period a family of Sayyids from Mecca, chieftains of Wāsiṭ in Southern Iraq, became Wālis of Ḥuwaizah in Khuzistān in southwest Persia. This ushered in an era of Arab domination of the area. At the end of the 17th century the Arab tribe of the Bani Ka'b (often referred to as the Chaub) moved into Khuzistan and took over the area from the Afshar Turks, becoming clients of the Wāli of Ḥuwaizah and later themselves becoming rulers of the area. Layard who visited the area in the early 1800's (Layard 1846: 29,45) mentions that many refugees from the principal towns in the province had settled within the territories of the Arab tribes⁷ and that it had become a common place of refuge for political offenders. He also mentions that 'the Arab language is generally understood, although the Persian prevails, and the Arabic dress is at the same time affected in preference to that of the Persian' (*ibid*: 29). We thus see a picture of what seems to be gradual Arabization of elements of the Persian population in which language and dress are relevant features. Another traveller, Stocqueler, refers to the clothing of the Chaub in some detail:

> 'The costume of the Chabeans is like their language – a mixture. They wear the Persian kabah, or green tunic, loose trousers and slippers, the cummer, or girdle, and a lilac cloth turban of the same form as the Arab's. The sheikhs wear crimson and gold dresses on extraordinary occasions, but for ordinary use content themselves with crimson chintz, variegated with yellow flowers in imitation of gold' (1832: 80).

### (iii) South Arabian links with the East

The people of Hadramout and Oman had strong sea-born links with India and Indonesia. The rulers of Makalla, for instance, regularly supplied troops for the army of the Sultan of Hyderabad. This eastern connection is shown very plainly in the elaborate nature of the clothing of some of the ruling families such as that of Lahej shown in Hunter (1877:156), with its brocade tunic and turban. Also shown is a distinctive type of sword with what seems to be a vestigial dragon's head and is similar in many ways to the Indonesian sword and kris design (see above, p.9, and Fig. 3).

## Variation in dress across the area

In the Arabian peninsula there are considerable differences of climate mainly as regards the northern versus the southern regions. From a practical point of view, this is relevant to the type of clothes worn. In the south for most of the year protection from the cold is not necessary during the day, but some form of sun protection for the head is useful. In the north the weather is quite cold in winter. In part these differences of climate can be seen to underly different types of clothing worn in these regions, which we have also seen have ethnic relevance. In the south a kilt or sarong (*wizār*) is general and is a widespread form of dress in an area bounding the Indian Ocean. This may be worn with a jacket or with a cape or shoulder scarf. In the north the minimum dress is a long shirt (*thōb*), worn over trousers called (*sarwāl*) from the Persian *shalvār*. In addition various forms of coat or cloak can also be worn. The southern kilt is worn in Oman and Greater Yemen and by some sections of the population of Bahrain (the *bahārinah*). In the Emirates it survives as the undergarment to the *thōb* in place of the *sarwāl*; I am told that in Qatar the *wizār* was worn as the undergarment as recently as twenty years ago. In the Yemen wearing of the *wizār* forms a link, along with other clothing features, to the dress of north-eastern Africa. In Oman it forms a link with the *lōngi* of the East Indies (also used in Persia under the name *lōng* as the robe worn in the public baths or *hammām*), being produced of the same material, a very light plaided cotton fabric.

It is possible to regard the basic southern form of the *wizār* as being a more primitive form of dress in requiring less technology in its production; it is most probably the older form. This form is probably also reflected in the *ihrām*, the prescribed dress of the pilgrim to Mecca. The *ihrām* consists of two plain pieces of cloth, one worn around the waist and another around the shoulders. A survival of the kilt form is still to be seen in Bahrain: as originally mentioned by Palgrave, 'its white silk-fringed cloth worn Banian fashion around the waist, and its frock-like overall' (1865 ii, 177, 235). The cloth worn around the waist is still seen in Bahrain and is characteristic of seafarers, being the same item as the *lōng* mentioned above. It can be worn either in place of, or over, the *thōb* .

Various other features of material culture correspond to this difference in dress. As formal weaponry, one is the wearing of the curved ornamental dagger (*jambiyyah*) in the south versus the curved sword in the north. Equally, the evolution of the black goat hair tent (*bēt sha'ar*) in the north may be compared with the rather more rudimentary shelters used by nomads in the south.

The above mentioned differences are not necessarily coextensive but do indicate two main cultural foci of which the northern is now dominant and is encroaching on the southern. This we can see as the tail end of the process initiated by the evolution of full Bedouin culture in the north in the early Christian era. Linguistically, the same pattern is evident. Again one can point to the area of the South Arabian languages versus that of North Arabian, i.e. Arabic proper has now taken over from South Arabian in most of the south although the south Arabian (Ḥimyāritic) substratum is still apparent in many southern Arabic dialects.

## Head wear

In the north an innovation has occurred in the form of a head cloth called variously *ghutrah* (from the Arabic root *ghatar* 'to cover'), *shmāgh* (from the Turkish *yashmak* 'cover') or *kaffiyyah*. This is held in place by a head rope ('*agāl*) derived it seems from the camel hobble rope (cf. the verb '*agal* 'to hobble'). Although the present day '*agāl* is is usually a purpose-made headrope, of which some such as the type favoured by the ruler of Baḥrain are quite elaborate affairs, one still sees examples of the primitive type which is a plain piece of rope. Thesiger (1959: 193) shows an example of this as worn by a Ṣai'ar tribesman of the southern Empty Quarter. The more elaborate type sometimes called *mugaṣṣab* is seen in older pictures of the shaikhs of the Gulf and in the older dress of the Ḥijāz. The *ghutrah* and '*agāl* is now in a general sense the 'uniform' of Saudi Arabia and the Gulf States. A variation on the *ghutrah* is the *shāl* which is a Kashmīr shawl with a decorated border, worn unlike the *ghutrah*, with the edges outside the *bisht* or cloak.

We do not know when the *ghutrah* and '*agāl* became respectable headwear since earlier illustrations, such as the Persian miniatures, always portray the Arabs as wearing turbans. This does not mean that they did wear them necessarily, only that we have no early reference to the present headwear. Even today it is not universal in Arabia. Other styles are worn, such as the turban style of the Hijaz villages shown in Katakura (1977: 78) and the straw hats resembling Mexican sombreros worn in the south west in 'Asīr and Yemen. The *ghutrah* and '*agāl* are reported in the north Arabian desert from at least the early 18th century; the earliest reliable picture we have is of the Imam Abdallah Ibn Sa'ūd, appearing in Brydges (1834; ii: frontispiece; see Fig. 11) and seeming to represent him at the time of his execution in Istanbul in 1818. This headwear is now general in the centre and north.

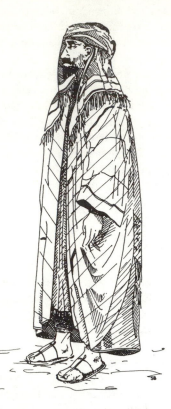

**Figure 11** Imām 'Abdullah Ibn Sa'ūd
Drawing by Sean Bowen after Brydges (1934: 6)

A quite widespread distinction is between a type of headwear originally characteristic of the Persian Gulf coast, Oman and Khuzistan and a type characteristic of Najd and the interior. The coastal people wore the Omani turban while the people of the interior wore the *ghutrah* and *'agāl*. The turban is now only seen in Oman and occasionally in the Emirates, but was in the past more widespread. It was worn by the Ka'b of Khuzistan (Wilson 1911: 117, also de Bode 1845 ii: 188) and photographs of Shaikh Khaz'al of Muḥammarah show him wearing this as late as the early 20th century. Palgrave, who visited the area in 1861–2 reports that Muḥammad bin Thāni of Qatar wore 'a Bengalee turban' and speaks of the 'the light garments of Baḥreyn, its blue and red turban'. The wearing of the turban seems to be a manifestation of closer links with the more prosperous culture of India, while the wearing of the *ghutrah* and *'agāl* can be taken as indicative of links with the 'bedouin' culture of inner Arabia.

The turban style may also be a marker of the old Greater Baḥrain area which stretched from the Shaṭṭ al-'Arab to the borders of the Emirates before the emigrations of the 'Utūb from central Arabia in the 17th century, which led to the formation of the present Gulf States. A transitional style is seen also among riverine people of the Shaṭṭ al-'Arab region both on the Persian and Iraqi side. Here a white *ghutrah,* called there *chaffiyyah,* is worn without a headrope with the two side corners thrown back over the head, one across the other to hang down behind the head; these look from the front rather like a turban. This style is due, I imagine, to the extreme humidity of the climate in that area, making it uncomfortable to have the head surrounded by the *ghutrah.*

A glance through the books of earlier travellers in Southern Arabia such as Thesiger (1959) and Thomas (1938) show a turban-style headgear among the Āl Rāshid of the Empty Quarter and also among the Āl Murrah and the retainers of the Shaikh of Abu Dhabi. As far as I know this type of headgear is no longer worn on formal occasions by the Āl Murrah, although the *ghutrah* may be wound around the head like a turban while travelling. This is presumably because it is cooler or more convenient. Although the turban style is not usually seen in the Emirates nowadays, on Dubai television I recently saw no less a person than Shaykh Zāyid of Abu Dhabi appear in public at a reception wearing the Omani turban style. I have no information on the present dress of the Āl Rāshid or other Bedouin of the southern Empty Quarter.

## The *bisht* or cloak

The cloak, which is basically of a rectangular, sleeved, flat pattern construction with piping going down the top seam of the sleeve, around the cuff and in a wider band down the front lapel as shown in Tilke (1956: 15) is usually worn over the shoulders without the arms going through the sleeves. Winter cloaks called *bisht* or *mishlaḥ* are functional in nature and made of a rough and very hard wearing, sack-like fabric which will even keep off rain for a considerable time. They can be worn while standing, sitting or driving and can be used as a cover over the whole body while sleeping. I have noticed among northern Bedouin that it is quite acceptable for a man to sleep thus covered in the company of others who are sitting round talking in a majlis or at an encampment. Presumably the great mobility of life in nomadic society means that a man may arrive after a hard journey at a time when every one else is awake, but when he is in definite need of rest. On these occasions he will simply pull one corner or sleeve of the cloak up over his head and lie down on his side, facing towards the company, with his whole body covered in the cloak. In this way, his face will be covered, which is important; if his mouth gapes open, it will not be seen. These winter cloaks are universally dark brown.

Summer cloaks are more ceremonial and may be black, brown or even fawn in colour. They are made of very light, fine, sometimes semi-transparent material. The piping may be of gold thread; this is known as the *bisht zari* 'gold embroidered cloak'.

When walking, the cloak may either be allowed to drape from the shoulders or the sides may be gathered up slightly and held under one arm so that the ends do not get caught; this allows faster movement, although in general rapid movement is impractical and inelegant when wearing ceremonial Arab dress. When entering a majlis or receiving a guest, the right-hand side of the cloak may be taken off the shoulder and brought round under the arm to be held together with the left-hand edge under the left arm. This leaves the right hand free for shaking hands. In Khūzistān in the summer it was the custom on ceremonial occasions not to wear the *bisht*, presumably because of the heat; then the *bisht* was carried neatly folded over the left shoulder.

## Sheepskin cloaks and brocade jackets

An item often seen in northern and central Arabia, but less so in the south or on the coast because of the warmer climate, is the fur lined cloak or *farwah* (see figs 12 and 13). This serves as an overcoat and bedcovering during the cool nights. The design is universally the same, although the colours differ and one sees dark brown, navy blue, beige and even maroon base colours with braids of either black or gold down the front edge and on the cuffs and back. The design of these is very reminiscent of 19th century military uniform and I think they were introduced from the north. They are now made mostly in Damascus.

Equally interesting is the *jūkhah* (also *jōkhah* or *chōkhah*). I have never seen one of these, but have often heard of them referred to in stories as worn by important people, and described as long coats or tunics of a material called *jūkh,* a kind of brocade or silk elaborately embroidered, sometimes with broad bands running horizontally down the front. The *jukhah* was buttoned up at the front and was worn over the *thōb* and under the cloak or *bisht*. This was worn by shaikhs or famous warriors. Musil describes it as 'a woollen jacket lined with silk worn by cavalrymen. In olden times such a jacket was a mark of rank and distinction' (1928: 387). This item of clothing would seem to have been introduced from the north, perhaps in Ottoman times. A similar item called *chōkha* is universally worn as an item of national dress in the Caucasus (cf. Hewitt and Khiba, this volume). This is an outer garment, like an extended jacket with long sleeves, in black, with cartridge cases on the breast. The word *chōkhah* has no meaning in the Caucasian languages, but *çöhe* denotes 'heavy felt' in Turkish. A dress of a similar type to the *chōkha* is also worn in India, known there as *chōgān*.[8]

**Figure 12** A fur-lined cloak, or *farwah*, worn when travelling
Drawing by Sean Bowen from a photograph by Bruce Ingham taken in 1982

## The social function of dress

Men's dress is an important aspect of Arab identity in the area and specially in the Bedouin context. This is obvious, but it is interesting to look at which foreigners wear 'Arab' clothes on occasions in an institutionalized manner. In the Bedouin milieu I have noticed more readiness to accept certain types of foreigner in Arab dress rather than others. In particular Pakistani manservants working in the *majlis* often wore full Arab dress. In Qatar the distinction is highly blurred since men of Persian and Baluch origins, of long standing in the area, all wear Arab clothes and usually speak Arabic well. More recently arrived Sri Lankans and Bangladeshis do not wear such clothes, but neither do they speak Arabic. In Qatar the unspoken rule seems to be that to wear Arab clothes one must be able to behave in the Arab manner, both by speaking Arabic and by following local rules of etiquette. A correlate of this is that the wearing of European, instead of Arab, clothes can in some cases allow one to break what can be loosely called the 'rules of purdah', since a man not wearing Arab clothes does not count in the 'local' milieu as a man of equal status and thus may be allowed to be in the company of women to whom he is not closely related by blood or marriage.

**Figure 13** A fur-lined cloak, or *farwah,* worn when seated
Drawing by Sean Bowen from a photograph taken by Bruce Ingham in 1984

This applies to domestic servants, drivers and traders, non-Arabs and non-local Arabs alike, but the rule may also apply to western guests.

It is true to say that the clothes described so far are minimal formal wear. Anything less is regarded as informal and unsuitable for public appearances. Here again 'public' means anything outside the confines of the private apartments of a family home. The 'public' part of the home, *i.e.* the *majlis* in which guests are received, demands this type of dress and in most circles a man appearing bare-headed in a *majlis,* even his own, is regarded as improperly dressed. In the context of formal dress, the 'head cloth' (*ghutrah* ) is obligatory, but the *'agāl* 'head-rope' is not. This rule of head covering applies also to those wearing clothing styles local to other parts of the Middle East, including, for instance, Sudanis, Pashtūns and Baluchis. These latter would also be expected to wear the appropriate head covering.

Those wearing European clothes are to some extent outside the system and no particular rules apply, whether the wearer is European or Middle Eastern. A further element of formality can be introduced by the wearing the *bisht* or cloak and, in particular, the *bisht zari* 'cloak with a gold braid bordering' (see above, p.48). These can be worn at any time, but are particularly worn at special occasions such as weddings and on the 'Īd al-Fiṭr and may also be worn when on important visits.

Interestingly, footwear is almost immaterial. One can appear at even the most important functions wearing either shoes or sandals or even bare-foot. Visits to Europe are to some extent regarded as 'informal occasions' when people can wear non-local clothing to which the local standards of formality do not apply. However even in Europe, if local (i.e. Arab) clothing is worn, it must be worn in accordance with the standards of proper dress.

## Earlier descriptions of Arab dress

Even in the early twentieth century dress was far more elaborate than it is now. The colour and design of cloaks, *thōbs* and head cloths were more varied. Striped cloaks were common and patterned *thōbs* were also worn. Illustrations in Williams (1948) and Asad (1954:169, 199) show beautiful examples of flowered and Paisley-patterned robes. The pictures in Williams are from the 1940's and those in Asad from the same period. It would seem that probably the gradual opening up of Saudi Arabia in the post-war period brought in ideas of modernisation in dress which produced simpler and less exotic designs (but compare Lindisfarne-Tapper, this volume, on the uniformity introduced in men's dress in the twentieth century). The elaborate colours only survive in the dress of what one might call 'court officials', i.e. incense bearers who will often precede the entrance of members of the Āl Sa'ūd at official functions. These individuals often wear quite elaborate jackets, which may be survivors of the old *jūkhka*, as well as bandoliers and ceremonial daggers.

A number of excerpts from the writings of earlier travellers illustrate the elaborate nature of earlier forms and show how they underly the present form which is in fact simplified and standardized from earlier styles, rather in the same way as modern European dress represents a simplification of later 18th and 19th century European dress. De la Roque (1742: 214–20) in *A Voyage to Arabia Felix* (Travels of the Chevalier d'Arvieux in Syria, 1660 214–20) writes of the Arab 'habits':

There's but little difference between the Dress of the Turkish Quality and that of the *Arabian Emirs*. Their habits are commonly of Cloth and Silk and there's nothing but the opening of the sleeves that distinguishes 'em. Those Princes and principal Cheikhs have for their Winter-Dress a pair of Linen-Drawers, and a fine Shirt the Ends of the Sleeves of which cut out in a Peak hang down to the Ground; a Caftan also of Sattin or Mohair, made like a Cassock that goes half-way down the Leg, with large Sleeves, it is ty'd with a Leathern-Belt about half a foot circle, imbroidered with Gold and Silk and beutifi'd with Plates of Gold with Clasps or Chains to fasten it or let it out; they hang to this a short Knife adorned with Jewels. Under the Caftan and over the Linen-Drawers they put a *Chakchier* or Pantaloons of Red Cloth, the Foot of which is of Yellow Spanish Leather. These Pantaloons are always to be of Red, Purple of Violet and never of Green, because as Mahomet admir'd that Colour and his descendants wear a Green Turbant, it would be thought a Profanation of it to put it to such a use.

Instead of a Cloke, they have a long Cloth Vest with Sleeves, furred with Beautiful Sables of Fox-skin, and sometimes without Furr, when it is not very cold. They have sometimes some *Aba*'s of Red, Green or other-colour'd Cloth, trim'd upon the Shoulders with Gold and Silver *Galloon*, and with imbroider'd Roses and Buttons before.

Their Turbant is a piece of Muslin done round a Cap of Crinson Velvet run with Cotton, the Ends of which wove with Gold or Silver hang behind the Back, and form a kind of Plume.

The common Arabs whole Cloaths consist only of a coarse Shirt with long Sleeves, a Pair of Linen Drawers, a coarse Callico Caftan and a Leathern Girth, where he sticks a Poniard of the same Figure as the Prince's, but there is no other Ornament about it than some little pieces of Silver Money nail'd round the Hilt, and the scabbard is of plain Shagreen. Their Cloak is a Barracan *Aba*, strip'd with black and white. In Winter they wear likewise some *Turemaux* Furs, which are Vests made of several Lamb-Skins, dy'd with a sort of *Italian* Glove-colour and sew'd together; when it is warm they turn the Nap inwards, and when it rains, outwards:

They also have large Gowns of very white Linen, made like Shirts, which they put over the other Cloaths in Summer when it is very hot.

Their usual Head-Dress is a Turbant of white Muslin that goes around a plain little Red Cloth Cap, one end of it hangs like a Plume, and the other which is abundantly longe is done about the Neck to keep it from the Heat of the Sun; they often wear this Turbant along with a *Bustaman* we spoke of at the Beginning.

Heude writing in 1819 describes the Bedouin in Muscat as follows, 'The wild bedouins may be distinguished – by a striped kerchief surrounded by lashes of whip-cord, and flying loosely round his head; by a course shirt, a square striped *cumlin* over his shoulders and a *chubook*' (p.22).

David Roberts travelling in the Holy Land in the early 19th century describes a Bedouin guide:

The principal figure is Besharah, an intelligent native of the Bani Said tribe who accompanied Mr. Roberts from Egypt to Mount Sinai and Akaba. The dress of all the Arab tribes who were met with on the route to Petra is nearly the same. Where the person is of rank, as in the present instance, the turban is worn; but in general, a kerchief of gay colour, folded diagonally, is bound around the head by a filet of dark worsted, or a cord, leaving the corners to fall over the neck and shoulders. A course shirt, with loose sleeves, hanging to the knee, is gathered round the waist by a leathern girdle; over this is worn a long mantle of woollen stuff; striped in bands of white and brown. The legs and feet are generally without covering, but some wear sandles of fish skin. They are all armed with a broad, crooked knife, about eighteen inches long, and a matchlock gun of the rudest construction. (1842–9: iii, Edom, 1 Tribe of Beni Sa'id; though Roberts himself, when dressed as an Arab wore far grander garb).

Baron de Bode, who met some 'Arabs near Shūsh in Kurdistan writes, 'The white turbans negligently twisted around the heads of the men contrasted boldly with their dark complexions and jet black hair ... while their broad striped abbas, or cloaks hung loosely on their shoulders in plait [sic] ... These arabs appeared to be more opulent, or at least more attentive to their dress, than the generality of the Iliyat tribes of Persia.' (1845 ii; 188–189).

## Notes

1 This paper represents a development of a paper previously read at the BRISMES conference held at SOAS, University of London, July 1991.
2 Some of these also wear a form of dress similar to the that of the Arabian Peninsula. See for instance illustration of a 'Bedouin' of the Western Desert of Egypt in Tilke (1956:32, 5).
3 These remarks are based on Dostal (1979:130–5), and also on Caskel (1954: 39–41).
4 The earlier Arabian camel saddle referred to by Dostal (1979:132) as the *ḥawlāni* type consists of a non-rigid pad tied behind the hump, whereas the rigid saddle or *shadād* type is formed by a wooden frame fixed above the hump. The *ḥawlāni* type is still used in the south (amongst the Āl Murrah for instance). See also Bulliet (1975 *passim*) and Caskel (1954).
5 An important historical exception seems to be the goat hair tent, which was disseminated in North Africa and the Middle East from Arabia.
6 Lorimer (1986) 8, ii: 754 under 'Hūwalah or Hūlah.
7 This accretion of foreign elements into Arab tribes is not unknown even in more recent times. In the first half of the 19th century at the time of the first Turkish domination of Eastern Arabia after a battle fought between the Turks and Arab forces, a number of children who had been with a defeated Turkish force were captured by the Dhafīr tribe. It is only remembered that these were blond and Christians, and must probably have been Armenian or Circassian. These were adopted into the tribe and eventually given Dhafīri brides. Their descendants, numbering around forty families, are known as the Anṣār 'Christians', although now Muslims. They are still recognizably foreign-looking because of their ruddy complexion while now counted as Dhafīris and Saudi citizens. See Ingham (1986: 38).
8 Oral communication from Miss Kiran Velagapudi.

## Bibliography

Asad, M. 1954. *The Road to Mecca*. Barnet, Herts: Stellar Press.
Brydges, Sir H.J. 1834. *An Account of the Transactions of his Majesty's Mission to the Court of Persia in the years 1807–11, to which is appended a brief History of*

*the Wahauby*. London: James Bohn.

Bulliet, R.W. 1975. *The Camel and the Wheel*. Cambridge, Mass: Harvard University Press.

Burckhardt, J.L. 1831. *Notes on the Bedouins and Wahabys*. London: Association for Promoting the Discovery of the Interior of Africa.

Caskel, W. 1954. 'The Bedouinization of Arabia'. In G.E. von Grunebaum (ed.) *Studies in Islamic Cultural History*. Memoirs of the American Anthropological Association 76: Washington DC, 36–46.

De Bode, Baron C.A. 1845. *Travels in Luristan and Arabistan*. London. 2 Vols.

De la Roque. 1742. *A Voyage to Arabia Felix (Travels of the Chevalier d'Arvieux in Syria 1660)*. Paris.

Dickson, H. R. P. 1949. *The Arab of the Desert*. London: George Allen and Unwin, Ltd.

Dostal, W. 1959. 'The Evolution of Bedouin Life'. In F. Gabrieli (ed.) *L'Antica Societa Beduina*. Rome: Entro di Studi Semitici, Instituto di Studi, Orientali-Universita, 11–33.

—— 1979. 'The Development of Bedouin Life in Arabia seen from Archeological Material'. *Sources for the History of Arabia, 1, Studies in the History of Arabia*. vol. 1. Riyadh: Riyadh University Press, 1, 125–44.

Heude, W. 1819. *Voyage de la cote de Malabar à Constantinople fait en 1817*. Paris.

Hunter, F.M. 1877. *Account of the British Settlement in Aden*. F. Cass: London

Ingham, B. 1986. *Bedouin of Northern Arabia: Traditions of the Al Dhafir*. London: Kegan Paul International.

Katakura, M, 1977. *Bedouin Village*. Tokyo: Tokyo University Press.

Layard, A. H. 1846 'Description of the province of Khuzistan'. *Journal of the Royal Geographical Society*, 16, i.

Lorimer, J. G. 1986. *Gazetteer of the Persian Gulf, Oman and Central Arabia*. 1–9, Gerrards Cross: Archive Editions. (Originally published 1915, Calcutta: Superintendent Government Printing).

Musil, A. 1928. *The Manners and Customs of the Rwala Bedouins*. New York: American Geographical Society.

Niebuhr, C. 1780. *Voyages en Arabie et en autres pays circonvoisins*. Paris, 2 vols.

Palgrave, W. G. 1865. *Narrative of a Year's Journey through Central and Eastern Arabia (1862–3)*. 2 vols. London and Cambridge: Macmillan.

Philby, H. St J. 1955. *Saudi Arabia*. London: Ernest Benn.

Roberts, D. 1842–9. *The Holy Land*. 3 vols. London.

Stocqueler, J.H. 1832. *Fifteen Months Pilgrimage Through Untrodden Tracts of Khuzistan and Persia*. Saunders and Otley, London.

Thesiger, W. 1959. *Arabian Sands*. London: Longman Group Ltd.

Thomas, B. 1938. *Arabia Felix*. Oxford. London: Jonathan Cape.

Tilke, M 1956. *Costume Patterns and Design*, London: Zwemmer.

Williams, M. O. 1948. 'Saudi Arabia, Oil Kingdom', *The National Geographic Magazine*, 43: 4, 497–511.

Wilson, A T. 911. 'Precis of the Relations of the British Government with the Tribes and Shaikhs of Arabistan'. Bushire.

# Chapter Three

# Changing the Habits of a Lifetime: The Adaptation of Hejazi Dress to the New Social Order

*Mai Yamani*

Clothes are an important aspect of everyday life. However, their importance varies from one society to another, from one occasion to another, from one era to another and from one section of society to another.

Dress must be distinguished from 'appearance', 'costume', 'apparel', 'clothing' or 'fashion'. Eicher and Roach-Higgins (1992) explain the different nuances of these words. Dress is distinguished from appearance because appearance includes features of the undressed body such as facial expressions and gestures. 'Costume' by contrast, suggests extraordinary social roles or activities. Costume is dress for the theatre, festivals, ceremonies and rituals. 'Apparel', like the word 'clothing' and unlike dress, emphasizes garments which cover the body, omitting any idea of modifications.

For each society clothing introduces different personal and social values. For example if it covers certain parts of the body it is 'good', if it does not cover certain parts it may be deemed 'immodest' and 'bad'. However, what is believed to be modest dress varies from society to society. Social, economic and political changes in any given society influence the way people dress and can be noted in the changing modes of dress for men and women over time, while 'fashion' more widely refers to prevailing customs and can include different kinds of shapes and forms of material and non-material culture including clothing, jewels, furniture, architecture, music, etc.

Moreover, dress includes a long list of possible modifications such as coiffed hair, coloured skin, pierced ears and scented breath as well as garments, jewellery, accessories. Furthermore, as Barnes and Eicher in their book *Dress and Gender* (1992) explain, dress is not only visual, it may also include touch, smell and sound. In short, the dress of an individual is an assemblage of modifications of the body and/or supplement to the body.

In short, clothing has social, economic, political and religious connotations. Here I explain these variations within the context of Hejazi men's and women's dress. To do so, it is appropriate to give some historical background to past and present concepts of dress in this part of the Middle East.

The country which is now Saudi Arabia was, prior to 1932, formed of different provinces; the Hejaz, the Najd, the Ahsa and the Asir. Despite attempts to create national homogeneity, expressions of regional and class differences still persist in various forms. The women and men on whom I focus belong to today's Hejazi elite. My paper focuses on men and women who are residents of Jeddah, Mecca and Medina in the western part of the country. They constitute a number of families I have described as 'The Families' and perceive themselves, or are perceived, as an elite in the region. Although most of my ethnographic material is from these families, I will also offer, where appropriate, relevant examples from other Arab, Muslim, or Western countries, since members of this elite do not live in isolation, but share aspects of dress culture with others internationally.

Social boundaries are defined among this group through a distinctive dialect, religious practices, food rituals and restrictive marriage practices. These boundaries are also defined by a form or style of dress that, for them, satisfies requirements related to their situation in terms of origins, regional distinctiveness, status and perceived respectability. Their history expresses itself in dress. From my studies it is evident that there are a wide range of social situations that are relevant to the understanding of the evolution, change, modifications and adaptation of dress in Saudi Arabia during this century. For example, women's dress generally has changed from traditional local to Western forms, yet the black veil has remained as a cover for Yves St Laurent creations.

A broad history of dress in Saudi Arabia would include those events which have altered people's perception of their social status and identity. These include the unification of the country in 1932 which led to a development of a sense of national cohesion and homogeneity of dress; the period from 1945 to about 1970 which was characterized by growing contact with people from Egypt and Lebanon; 1970 to 1980 during which the impact of enormous wealth from oil was greatest; from 1980 the combinations of cosmopolitan fashion and various local, regional, Arab and Islamic 'models' were explored. It is noticeable that the relation between a process of combining national homogeneity with western international influences has both sharpened Saudi national solidarity and introduced a new ambivalent dimension.[1]

In the urban Hejaz, prior to 1932, there was an apparent distinction in profession based on the clothes men wore. For example, the *tujjār* merchants dressed differently from the *'ulama'* (see Fig. 14), religious teachers, the *muṭawwifīn*, guides to the pilgrims, the *ashrāf*, descendants from the Prophet's lineage; the ruling class at the time from *za'īm al-ḥāra*, the head of the district, the common people (*'āmmat an-nās*), and *shabāb*,

**Figure 14** The dress of merchants, *tujjar*

Drawing by Sean Bowen from a photograph in the author's personal collection

the young men.[2] Urban Hejazi men wore a long white garment with trousers underneath, and a belt. These were worn under an outer garment, while the head was always covered by the *'amāma*, turban; distinctions of dress were mainly based on the manner in which the headdress *'amāma* was tied, in the type and colour of the material used, in the width of the belt, as well as the length of the *sirwāl*, the trousers which were worn under the outer garment (see Maghrebi 1982; see Fig. 15)

All women on the other hand wore a long, fitted dress, *zabūn*.[3] Under this was a blouse or bodice, *sidriyya*, which was seen through the opening in the *zabūn*. The blouse was fastened with six buttons of silver, gold or diamonds depending on the wealth of the women. The hair was centre-parted and partly covered by the white head cover, *midawwara*. Women of high status prided themselves on the art of wrapping the *midawwara*. Older women explained to me that the style of the headcovering showed the degree of elegance possessed by a woman. There was and is an elaborate vocabulary to describe the elegance of a woman and her dress.

Some have argued that depriving the people of their ethnic dress identity amounts to a transformation to be compared to the changes dictated during the colonial era. In other words some people feel that such radical change underlines the political dominance of the ruling elite. At the time of the

**Figure 15** A Meccan physician
Drawing by Sean Bowen from a photograph in
the author's personal collection

unification of the Kingdom in 1932, one way the ruling elite endeavoured to control the vast country was through eliminating ethnic differences. Thus, the founder of the Saudi Arabian Kingdom, Abdul Aziz al-Saud, decreed that all men serving in government positions must wear the Najdi Bedouin dress, the clothing seen widely in Saudi Arabia today. With the exception of the clothing of a few old men, the development almost made regional dress extinct.

The change of women's dress from an ethnic to a western form was more gradual. There was no political pressure nor urgency to follow the footsteps of the men's dress transformation. The *zabun* dress is still seen today, though it is only worn by older women. On a younger woman, the ethnic Meccan dress would be considered ridiculous and she would be criticized for wearing it, while on the older woman it is seen to be dignified.[4] Hence, younger women only wear the ethnic dress to express their 'Saudi Arabian heritage' at parties held by, for example, charity organizations.

Prior to 1932, the Hejaz (see Baker 1979) was the most prosperous urban centre in the Arabian Peninsula with trade based on the Red Sea port of Jeddah (see Al-Ansari 1982) and exposure to other Muslim cultures through the pilgrimage to Mecca and Medina. Jeddah was distinctively heterogenous, a melting-pot of races and cultures. It was not until the unification of the Kingdom of Saudi Arabia that a sense of regional distinctiveness developed. Furthermore, it was not until the 1950's, after the discovery of oil and the impact of oil revenues, that regular contact was made with Western cultures. People studied, began to travel to Europe and to the United States, and some even studied there. At this point women's dress, behaviour and way of life were transformed.

The 1950's saw the change of the Hejazi women's dress to a form of western clothing, copied from Egypt. However, the new western dresses were only worn inside the home, since all women remained totally veiled when outdoors. The importance of the veil increased because the Saudi state religious teaching, Wahhabism[5] is specifically strict on the issue of women's modesty. Traditionally, Hejazi women wore veils of a pale colour when going out. However, since the unification of the Kingdom, it has been made clear that black veils are preferable. Hence, the standardization of the veil (to the one seen in Saudi Arabia today) marked another move toward national homogeneity.

Two aspects of this process are worth emphasizing. The first relates to wearing clothes at home, where the influence of western clothes is clearly to be seen and where young women, for instance, can wear jeans and sweatshirts comfortably. This contrasts with the women's outdoor appearance, which is marked by a severe black veil. However, this does not represent merely a whimsical or capricious mode of life, but rather an officially sanctioned move away from regional ethnicity. Moreovoer members of 'The Committee for the Order of the Good and the Forbidding of the Evil'[6] make sure that in all public places women are veiled properly. Failure to do so results in a serious reprimand or even punishment. Nevertheless, differing attitudes toward the veil, as between the more strictly religious and the less so, remains a subject for empirical research. An Hejazi woman in her thirties recounted to me with enthusiasm her recent encounter with a member of this committee in the shopping mall. She said that as he ordered her to cover her face she replied 'No, by Allah! I shall not cover my face, my grandmother did not cover hers, nor did my mother, why should I do so?'

Dress has become a significant status indicator. All men of high status such as ministers and other high government officials wear the *mishlaḥ*, the cloak. Among the elite studied, young men only wear a *mishlaḥ* on formal occasions such as the *milka,* the men's wedding party, or the *'aza* of condolence. For these occasions a black cloak is worn for it is more formal, while beige is less so. During a wedding the groom stands out in a white *mishlaḥ*. The older men wear a *mishlaḥ* on all formal occasions, for example, for dinner parties, as well as when they go to the mosque. Equally, in the 1970's with the advent of vast amounts of wealth due to the oil boom, certain nuances of western dress became indicative of women's social status. This was so not only for the women studied but for all Saudi Arabian women. Nevertheless, the competition based on women's dress was particularly fierce among the Hejazi women, perhaps in part because in a situation of increased social and geographical mobility they needed to maintain status and respectability.

Thus today, a woman must always wear a dress that is 'suitable' for the social occasion, to the status of the hostess and her guests and, most important, to express her own social status. However, dress is not only an individual matter, but one that concerns the whole extended family, women as well as men. Men actively participate in the choice of a dress 'their' women wear because it reflects their social position and financial capabilities.

The older women of a family also have the responsibility to guide the younger in matters of dress. When a younger woman is correctly dressed, she is encouraged by a senior member of her extended family, who will say '*bayyaḍti wajhana.*' 'You have whitened our face.' There is a popular Arab saying that everyone repeats '*kul ma yuʻjibak wilbas ma yuʻjib annās.*' 'Eat what you like, but wear what will please people.'

The dresses the elite women have worn at formal gatherings since the 1970's were generally from leading western designers and preferably haute couture. That is, specially and individually designed by the top maison-de-couture of Europe such as Sherrer, Yves St Laurent, Valentino, Christian Dior, Givenchy, Ungaro and Chloe. In this way, elite women feel they are distinguishing themselves from other sections of the society as well as identifying themselves, in some ways, with the international jet-set society. At less formal gatherings elite women may wear 'boutique' dresses, that is, ready-made (*prêt à porter*) dresses from the designers just mentioned. Other non-elite women may wear the 'clothes hanging in the souks'. Although the latter are still western in style they are mass produced.

Women usually go on special trips abroad, preferably Paris, to shop for dresses for the coming social season. If a trip is not possible then, they content themselves with ordering a few dresses from the local couturiers, for example, from the Lebanese couturiers who live in Jeddah and offer the latest collections of fabrics and styles. The latter are as expensive as their counterparts in Europe.

Women from this elite not only wear the most fashionable western dresses but pride themselves on their knowledge of the slightest change in fashion. These well-travelled women, merely by seeing a dress, can identify not only the designer but also the collection – autumn or spring, winter or summer – from which it has come. They acquire this knowledge from the fashion magazines – special issues of *Vogue*, *L'Official*, and *Elle*, from America, Italy, France and England[7] and from video tapes distributed by the famous designers to their important customers, as well as from the regular fashion shows that are held in Jeddah. Invitation cards are sent out to wealthy women informing them that, for example, 'Yves St Laurent's latest spring fashion collection will be shown at the Hotel Sheraton at 7 pm.'

Since national homogeneity in dress had removed ethnic differences, elite women have found new ways of establishing status and spending vast sums to do so. And western designers have responded by catering for the Saudi clientele. They make clothes to suit the wealthy Saudi Arabian and Gulf taste and requirements. These garments are designed to display the insignia of the designer prominently and this is a source of great pride to the wearer. Thus, western designers combined high fashion with the demands of custom and tradition thereby contributing to defining ethnic chic for wealthy Saudi women from the Hejaz. Nicholas Coleridge (1988) has commented how in recent decades Islamic taste first imitated Western high fashion and then modified it in striking ways and to an extent undermined it.'

Explicit borrowing surrounding dress is considerable. Elite women consider the dresses designed by famous European designers suitable for formal occasions provided that they are modest, *muhtasham*, and not 'naked', *'aryān*. These women pride themselves on their knowledge and adherence to religion and consequently their modesty in dress. During the 1980's with a general return to 'tradition' and to a strict Islamic practice, women became more conscious of modesty in dress. They quote the Qur'anic verse 'You have your religion and I have mine.'[8] By this they explain that in the West people have their own way of life while they have theirs. But when the women studied are abroad, it is noteworthy that some younger women wear short dresses and the women do not veil.

Today in Saudi Arabia there are well defined codes of dress. A modest dress is one which covers the ankles, with long sleeves and preferably a high collar and is considered elegant. The collar also keeps the chin high and thus looks 'dignified'. Petticoats are worn even if the dress is not transparent. While the dress is modest in the sense of not exposing the body, it must be well-tailored and fitted to the point of being tight, following the lines of the body and especially the waist, *mikassam*. Since a slim waistline is thought desirable and, indeed, is celebrated in poems and popular songs, many women wear corsets. For formal occasions, the material of which the dress is made must be expensive: heavy damasked satin or patterned brocade. Preferably it should be hand-embroidered, either with silk for older women, or with gold or silver threads for younger women. The desirable dress for a wedding should be 'heavy', *thagīl*. The wedding dress encompasses the maximum expression of status and wealth. The more embroidered the dress, the more it is considered of importance and suited to a wedding party.

Within these dress and new ethnic parameters, colours are significant. For example traditionally desert people from the heart of the peninsula, wear brighter stronger colours, reds, purples and yellows, while urban people, for example, from the western province wear muted greys, blues, greens or beige. Older women explain that it is more 'elegant' to wear quiet, subdued colours with smaller motifs. They may also add that it is only the Bedouins who wear loud colours with bigger patterns.

Since the 1930's all Saudi brides have worn white, whereas previously brides wore other colours especially red embroidered with silver or gold.[9] Nowadays, guests at a wedding wear dresses of all colours except white so as not to 'cover the appearance of the bride.'

Black at weddings is considered elegant for all. However, unmarried women would not wear it as it is considered too 'heavy' for a young person. Black is never worn for a hospital visit, as it is considered a bad omen. Today, Hejazi women wear black for condolence ceremonies, while Najdi women perform condolences in colours. This is because the Wahhabis believe that people should not mourn or cry excessively as death is the will of Allah. Thus people ought to wear their normal clothes. Red and the various shades of pink would not be worn by older Hejazi women as such colours are thought to be lively and sexually suggestive. An older woman wearing red or pink would be criticized as being 'light', not poised, *makhfūfa*. Generally older Hejazi women wear pale colours, light grey, mauve, pale green or blue. Younger women wear darker and more vivacious tones. Hence, a woman not only dresses according to her status and region but also according to her age. The social sanctions against dressing like another generation are strict.

During the early part of the century, it was common practice for jewellery to be borrowed, or rented, on the occasion of a wedding and worn by the bride and her family, as well as by the guests. The more jewellery the bride had on, the more it was appreciated and admired. Her jewellery and everyone else's in those days was eastern in origin and made in India and Indonesia. There are stories about how young brides swooned under the weight of the jewels in the intense heat. This was a matter of pride as it reflected the wealth of the family (even if most of the jewels were rented), as well as showing the youth and delicacy of the bride.

Members of the 'old', but poorer, patronymic groups among the elite still rent or borrow jewellery in order to go to weddings or big dinner parties and appear to be of the appropriate status. This is not because they do not own jewellery, but because the standard jewellery required for the occasion of a wedding is often too expensive to purchase. Moreover the new rule of conspicuous consumption is that sets of jewellery should complement the dress one wears.

Jewellery continues to be an essential part of dress expressing social status. Again for the elite women studied, it is preferably 'western designed': Boucheron, Harry Winston, Van Clef et Arpel, Cartier, Bulgari and Bucellati are some of the famous jewellery houses that cater for these extended families. Representatives of these companies make regular visits to Jeddah bringing their latest collection, coming to homes to show their jewellery. However, there are some local designers, who are acceptable as they are equally expensive and aspire to the same standards. For example, these are Fitaihi, the Saudi Arabian jeweller, and Mu'awwad from Lebanon who have opened branches in Jeddah, Riyadh, Paris and Geneva. Wearing of Western 'designer' jewellery confers on women a distinction over those with less wealth, and distinguishes them from other elites and from, indeed, the nouveaux riches. In this domain as in others, the rule of conspicuous consumption prevails: to wear what is more expensive and from countries which are considered more advanced. No member of the elite appearing at a formal gathering such as a wedding would wear the type of jewellery 'hanging in the souks' made in India and Bahrain and eastern in style, consisting of bangles, chains or multi-layered necklaces.[10] Though the women studied would never wear such jewellery at a formal gathering, they do sometimes wear it in the privacy of their own homes and among relatives. It is interesting that, in the 1980s with the desire and attempts to return to 'tradition', these women find jewellery that 'looks eastern' but which is made in Europe by the famous designers, attractive and appropriate to their status.

Facial make-up is also greatly influenced by Western, cosmopolitan trends. The women follow the latest cosmetic trends from season to season (colours of facial make-up and eye-shadows). The traditional oils used on the face and kohl to line the eyes are seldom worn today. This move towards a modern cosmopolitan face is not peculiar to the women studied or to Saudi Arabia, for the model's face on *Vogue* or other magazines has become an inspiration for many women internationally.

It is not only the clothes, the jewellery and the make-up that must be suitable to the occasion and the status of those involved, but also hairstyles, since these also follow the latest Western fashions. For the weddings of some members of the elite, top hair designers are flown in from Paris to do the hair of the bride and of her family. Other, less wealthy guests get their hair set and modelled at local hairdressers. Where they have it done, whether at home or at the hairdresser's is another indicator of their status.

An interesting 'invention of tradition' is the *thōb* which became a feature of national dress for women during the early 1970's. It appeared first amongst some women of the elite, then throughout urban areas. The new form of dress is a long, relatively loose garment, usually with some embroidery on it. The *thōb* that women have started to wear resembles the men's garment except that it is more 'feminine' in appearance, primarily because it is cut to be more close-fitting,[11] and, secondly, because it can be in different colours (especially those considered particularly feminine: pinks, reds, greens, purples, yellows). During the hot weather masculine colours are white or pale cream and beige, brown, grey, black and navy blue during the winter. For the men's *thōb*, cotton or wool material is acceptable, but never as silk, as this is considered a sin, *ḥarām*. There is a known *hadīth*: 'It has been forbidden, *ḥarām*, for the males of my nation, *umma*, to wear silk and gold which is permitted for the females.'[12] Women may wear any colour, whatever the season. The women who initially started the trend of wearing the men's *thōb* were considered 'intellectual' since at that time they were relatively better educated and well-travelled than others. They appear to have taken the custom from Western women who wore the men's Saudi *thōb* as 'ethnic' dress.

The *thōb* today has become a kind of national dress for women. While the dress that they put aside indicated their regional identity, as a Meccan or woman from Taif, the new dress, the *thōb* indicates a woman's identity as a Saudi Arabian, and a wider one still – as an Arab. The latter is because the recent form of the garment combines aspects of Arab dress in general, whether it is Palestinian, Jordanian, Syrian, Lebanese, Egyptian or North African. The *thōb* is worn by all women from all regions and from different sections of the society.

The recent version of the *thōb* is mostly imported from Morocco, Egypt, the Philippines, Hong Kong and now even from Korea. This new version of the *thōb* is today believed to be a 'traditional' dress. It is worn frequently, since it is comfortable and easy to care for, being straight-forward and without difficult pleats. Most elite women wear it at home, when amongst the extended family and close friends, and they also wear it under the veil when going shopping to the *souk*, and while visiting relatives and close friends. Although there are more expensive versions of the *thōb*, it is not considered suitable for formal gatherings, and especially not for a wedding. The *thōb* is a dress that has become popular like the rest of the ordinary Western clothes 'hanging in the souks'. Hence women of the elite would not ask a famous European designer to make a *thōb* for them for fear that it would be mistaken for just another *thōb*, and as women explain, a waste of money.

J.K. Galbraith has commented that the possession of great wealth is not a disadvantage and that efforts to prove the contrary have usually been unsuccessful. It would, therefore, be surprising if among the group studied there was not evidence of the enjoyment of the wealth available to them. What is striking, however, is the way members of the elite have responded to different pressures: of fabulous wealth, of the need to observe the proprieties variously defined according to origin, family status, religion, age-group and region, and of the need to remain 'the glass of fashion and the mould of form.' How long the marriage of convenience between 'traditional' Hejazi dress and Yves St Laurent will last now that the transitional period is nearly over and the last generation who wore the Hejazi ethnic dress is fading away, no one knows. It may be that the end of the Gulf War marks a new turning point in dress code for the wealthy, for the religious fundamentalists and for the masses at large.

# Notes

1 For a more general historical view of Saudi Arabia see Almana (1980).
2 See Maghrebi (1982).
3 See illustrations of this dress in Binzagr (1979).
4 Cf. Lurie (1981: 49).
5 Wahhabism is an interpretation of Hanbali Law by the Imam Muhammad bin Abdul Wahhab (1703–87). 'Wahhabism' is not a term which is used by his followers.
6 See Al-Yassini (1985).
7 These magazines pass through the censors' procedures organized by the morals committee whose title is sometimes also translated 'Committee for the Propogation of Virtue and the Suppression of Vice'. However, as Coleridge notes 'the private customers still manage to receive the magazines as evident in the response to the merchandise' (1988: 196).
8 Quran, Sura CIX, *al-Kāfirūn*, verse 5. Trans. Yusuf Ali.
9 See illustrations in Binzagr (1979) and descriptions of brides' dresses in Hurgronje (1970).
10 This jewellery is bought not only by other Arabs but by foreigners, mostly American and Europeans, who view it as 'ethnic' jewellery.
11 It has taken not only the shape of the men's garment but also its name. However it is thought of as a woman's dress, not a man's, for the attempt by women to resemble men in dress is disapproved of by the Prophet and forbidden, *makrūh*. According to al-Bukhari, 'the Prophet cursed women who take the appearance of men, and men who take the appearance of women'. Cited by Amrou (1985: 323).
12 According to Abu Daoud: cited by Amrou (1985: 214).

# Bibliography

Almana, M. 1980. *Arabia Unified: A Portrait of Ibn Saud*, Hutchinson London: Benham.

Amrou, M.A.A. 1985. *Dress and Adornment in the Islamic Shari'a* (in Arabic, *al-Libās wal-Zīna fil-Sharī'a al-Islāmiyya*). Amman: Dar al-Furqan.

Al-Ansari, A.Q. *The History of the City of Jeddah*. 1982. (in Arabic, *Tārīkh Madīnat Jiddah*), Cairo: Dar Masr lil-Tiba'a.

Baker, R. 1979. *King Hussain and the Kingdom of Hejaz*. Cambridge: Oleander.

Barnes, R. and Eicher, J. 1992. *Dress and Gender: Making and Meaning*. London: Berg.

Binzagr, S. 1979. *Saudi Arabia: An Artist's View of the Past*. Lausanne: Three Continents.

Carter, J.R.L. 1979. *Leading Merchant Families of Saudi Arabia*. Scorpio Publication.

Coleridge, N. 1988. *The Fashion Conspiracy: A Remarkable Journey through the Empires of Fashion*. London: Heinemann.

Eicher, J.B. & Roach-Higgins, M.E. 1992. 'Definition & Classification of Dress: Implications or Analysis of Gender Roles'. In Barnes & Eicher (eds) 1992, 28.

Gill, E. 1931. *Clothes*. London: Cape.

Hogarth, D.G. 1978. *Hejaz before World War I*. Cambridge: Falcon-Oleander.

Hurgronje, C.S. 1970 (orig. 1888–89). *Mekka in the Latter Part of the 19th Century*. Leiden: Brill.

Jabar, A. 1983.*Wedding Customs and Traditions in the Western Region of the Kingdom of Saudi Arabia: A Modern Anthropological Study* (in Arabic, *'Ādāt wa Taqālīd al-Zawāj bil-Manṭiqa al-Gharbiyya min al-Mamlaka al-'Arabiyya al-Sa'ūdiyya*) Jeddah: Tihama.

Lurie, A. 1981.*The Language of Clothes*. London: Heinemann.

Maghrebi, M.A. 1982. *Features of Social Life in the Hejaz in the 14th-Century Hijrat* (in Arabic, *Malāmiḥ al-Ḥayāt al-Ijtimā'iyya fil-Ḥijāz*). Jeddah: Tihama.

Al-Yassini, A. 1985. *Religion and State in the Kingdom of Saudi Arabia*. Westview Special Studies on the Middle East: Boulder.

# Chapter Four

# The Dress of the Shahsevan Tribespeople of Iranian Azerbaijan

*Nancy Lindisfarne-Tapper*

I first visited Iranian Azerbaijan in the summer of 1965, and during the summer of 1966 I carried out a field study among the Shahsevan in conjunction with Richard Tapper's far more comprehensive research (see N. Tapper 1978; R.L. Tapper 1979, 1994). Here I have used material drawn from both our fieldnotes to describe Shahsevan dress, while my use of the ethnographic present tense refers to the fieldwork period. Richard Tapper and I returned briefly to visit the Shahsevan in 1973 and Richard Tapper has made several more recent visits.

In the 1960s the Shahsevan – the name attaches to the confederation of some 40-odd tribes numbering some 40,000 people living in 5,000 to 6,000 tent-households – were nomads migrating between winter pastures on the Mughan plain along the Soviet border and summer pastures high on the slopes of Mount Savalan. This annual migratory cycle, dictated by their pastoral economy and, in the past, by political considerations, meant that the nomads' material possessions are eminently portable. Shahsevan aesthetic and emotional sensibilities were focused on their felt tent homes, on a variety of textiles including kelims and woven rugs made using the sumac techniques and on women's dress. The textures, colours and designs of all these items are important as means by which major values of Shahsevan life are expressed.

Recently, the 1987 nomad census reported 5,800 families (42,000 people) of Shahsevan 'nomads' in Ardabil-Meshkin-Moghan, while in 1995 there were 7,800 families registered with the Organization of Nomadic Affairs. Very many of these were more or less 'settled' in the Dasht-e Moghan, and in the cities of Ardabil, Tehran and elsewhere. That is, they had settled bases, but qualified as nomads because of their interest in pastoralism. However, in 1995 there were still over 5,000 families pursuing a pastoral life in the Moghan and Savalan region (Richard Tapper, Personal communication, 1996).

What is notable, given conclusions I suggest here about dress and Shahsevan tribal identity in the 1960s is that the clothing styles of the tribespeople have changed so little. Richard Tapper has commented,

> Older men and women, including the middle-aged, are wearing much the same clothes now as they were thirty years ago, though the materials and patterns of shirts and dresses have obviously changed somewhat. Younger men and women are however less easily distinguished sartorially from their non-tribal counterparts. In particular, younger women, those who have attended school, for example, often wear much the same as local village, or urban, educated women: a long skirt, blouse, pullover, jacket or possibly an overcoat and a head-scarf, while very few wear a chador or other 'Islamic' headcovering (Personal communication, 1996).

In a regional context, in the 1960s, earlier and now, the Shahsevan to a great extent share language, culture and probably origins with the sedentary Tats of the area. It is the criterion of nomadic pastoralism which defines the boundary between them; the Shahsevan tent is the prime symbol of this boundary. Within the tribal confederation itself, other boundaries are important. Tribes are essentially political groups each owing allegiance to a chief; they are territorially distinct in winter and summer pastures. On other occasions – during the migration and during the celebration of marriages and circumcisions – tribal identity is signalled by, for instance, the patterns of bedding bags and other woven goods which are often particularly visible. Each tribe further subdivides into local-descent groups, communities each numbering around thirty households led by an Elder or *aq saqal*. Within these communities the status of a household and its relationships with others are judged, among other ways, by the dress, grooming and demeanour of the household women. Dress is also an indicator of a woman's personal standing among other women and a statement of her individuality and mood. The dress of both men and women is part of other cultural systems too, distinguishing stages in the life-cycle from birth to death, marking gender differences, religious status and relations with the supernatural.

Men's clothing expresses most clearly the relations of the Shahsevan as a tribal confederation with the wider political and social environment. Towards the end of the last century and presumably before, Shahsevan men wore white or dark blue belted shirts and brown cotton *şalvar* trousers tied at the ankles with cotton; in winter they wore long yellow ram's wool fur coats with long sleeves (Ogranovich 1891:80–82). Such garments were similar in many respects to those worn by men throughout the region (see Trofimova 1979; and cf. Fig. 20).

More distinctive were their waistcoats and jackets (*penjek*), decorated red ones were worn by young men and green ones by older men. Both red and green are key colours for the Shahsevan. Among them, as among other

Muslims of the Middle East, red is associated with virility, sexuality and life blood and with individual social power and reproduction, while green has a broader eschatological association linking the fertility of the earth with man and God. The most distinctive and spectacular items of men's clothing were their hats (see Fig. l6) by which men expressed simultaneously status differences among themselves as well as the common bond of their tribal identity as Shahsevan. The Shahsevan hats set them apart from non-Shahsevan as effectively as the hemispherical felt *alaçiğ* tents set the nomadic communities apart from their sedentary counterparts.

In the early 1920s when Reza Shah Pahlevi began to extend the control of the central government over disparate ethnic and regional groups in Iran, among other measures he instigated in the 1930s a brutal and ill-judged sedentarization programme which forced the Shahsevan and other nomadic peoples to abandon their tents and distinctive life style until the outbreak of the Second World War afforded them a chance to return to transhumant pastoralism. It is no accident that at much the same time, in his efforts to mould the populations of Iran into citizen/ participants in a new political system modelled on European nation-states, Reza Shah also implemented a series of clothing reforms. The imitative political structure of the state was reflected in the new laws which forbade men to wear anything but 'modern' European-style clothing in public contexts. Such clothing had many of the characteristics of a uniform – dark woollen trousers and jackets were worn over tailored white shirts – and signalled that all men, whatever their ethnic or tribal origins, were to have a similar status vis-á-vis the state. The authoritarian nature of the political system was also suggested: not only was the distinctive clothing which previously had marked ethnic and other divisions of the population eliminated, but so too was their flamboyance in colour and style – the European-style clothing was sombre and constricting (cf. Baker, this volume).

Such clothing reforms were intended to weaken a sense of identity based on membership of discrete social and religious communities. In this respect the forced abandonment of distinctive headgear was particularly effective. The head and face are focal points of a system of body symbolism among Shahsevan and many other Muslims. The head is the seat of reason and will and the face is closely associated with many aspects of a man's honour – a value system put in jeopardy by the reforms. Beards were cut and head hair was uniformly close cropped, traditional hats were discarded and new European hat styles introduced. Initially the Pahlevi cap, or *kepi*, was worn by the Shahsevan and others but, after the second World War, younger tribesmen, men whose fathers were still alive, began to wear the peaked *jämşidi*-style cap, while older men, who were heads of households or local leaders, wore *şäpo* felt Homburgs. (Though forbidden to do so, a few old men persisted in wearing the black cloth *dörgä*, one of the least spectacular of the traditional Shahsevan hats.) The new hat styles reintroduced a status

**Figure 16** Traditional men's hats and hairstyles, as drawn by a Shahsevan chief, 1965

with mirror on top
↓

*tejanpapak*
lambskin hat worn
by old men and
shepherds

*dörgä* with *yaylık*
cloth hat worn
by young men

*şekasri*
lambskin hat
worn by young
men and chiefs'

*şeypuri*
felt hat worn
only by chiefs

*çerkes*
expensive lambskin
hat worn by young
and old

*käkil*
hairstyle worn
by young men

*yan-birçek*
hairstyle worn
by old men and
shepherds

*oyma-birçek*
hairstyle worn
by chiefs

distinction between younger and older men. Moreover the *jämşidi* is nowadays regarded by the Shahsevan as a distinctively tribal hat (though in Tehran it is known opprobriously as a village hat), unlike the felt hats which are worn throughout the region by men of consequence whatever their ethnic origin. It is notable, however, that only younger men, who areunlikely to have significant economic or political dealings with non-Shahsevan, express their tribal identity sartorially (see Fig 17).

Since their introduction the European-style clothing for Shahsevan men seems to have changed little. Fashions have not been further elaborated to express Shahsevan tribal identity, but rather increasingly reflect social differentiation and the development of a class structure within the region. Ordinary men's jackets and trousers are nowadays made by local town-based tailors, while their hats and shirts are factory-made as is their underwear which normally consists of a Western-type vest and pyjama trousers. Socks and shoes, whether plastic or leather, are similarly mass-produced. Shahsevan members of the regional elite, often scions of the

**Figure 17** A young Shahsevan family. The husband wears a peaked *jamşidi*-style cap

Drawing by Sean Bowen from a photograph taken by Nancy Lindisfarne-Tapper in 1966

chiefly families, have followed European fashion trends more closely and sometimes wear expensive hand-made clothing bought in Europe or at least Tehran, while younger men of this elite have ceased to wear hats altogether as a gesture which is seen as expressing their personal emancipation from tribal and religious customs.

Though Reza Shah Pahlevi also introduced anti-veiling laws, these were aimed principally at townspeople and had little direct effect on the dress of Shahsevan women. In spite of the fact that Shahsevan women's clothing would seem to have changed considerably in the past 100 years, women's dress today remains tribal in style and has in fact become a key symbol of the continuing importance of Shahsevan identity for both men and women. In 1870 Ogranovich described Shahsevan women's clothing: it consisted of a

> long blue shirt, trousers (*şalvar*) and a light silk caftan (*arxalix*), a blue shader and woollen stockings and saffron slippers; well to do people wear a coloured dress and fur coat. They wrap a hankerchief around their head and place gold and silver ornaments on top (pp. 80–82).

Today the women's dress consists of four main elements: a full-length shirt-dress (*könek*), a tailored waistcoat (*yel* or *jilitkä*), several wide full-length underskirts (*dizlik*) gathered at the waist, and a small skullcap (*äräxçin*) and two-head scarves (*yaylik* and *käläyaği*) (Ziapur 1967: P.A. Andrews & M. Andrews 1990; see Fig. 18).

It is in their shape that women's clothes have changed most dramatically since the time of Ogranovich's description. I would suggest that it is no coincidence that nowadays in Shahsevan eyes the most distinctive and important element of women's clothing is the overall bell-like silhouette of the ensemble. The shape of women's clothing from the waist downwards echoes the hemisphere of the Shahsevan tents with which it is associated (see R.Tapper 1996). It would seem that when Shahsevan tribal identity as represented by their nomadism and tent homes became increasingly threatened by the central government, elements of the women's clothing, which was remote from such interference, were exaggerated to express tribal identity. In this context it is important to note the essential conservatism of women's and men's attitudes to women's clothing. Though there is some scope for expressing personal choice in terms of the patterns and quality of the dress materials used, the appropriateness of the shape and style of women's clothing is very carefully defined and judged and the smallest innovation or deviation often becomes the subject of adverse comment.

Nowadays the women's shirt-dress is made of some six meters of floral printed cotton (see Fig. 18). The dress has long sleeves set in at the shoulder which are gathered into a narrow buttoned cuff at thewrists. The dress material is doubled to form a quasi-yoke, narrow at the back and roughly square in the front where it is decorated with simple hand or machine stitching. The yoke stiffens and gives a definite line to the top of the dress which otherwise drops straight from the shoulder to the ground. To

**Figure 18** Shahsevan women's clothing
Drawing by Nancy Lindisfarne-Tapper

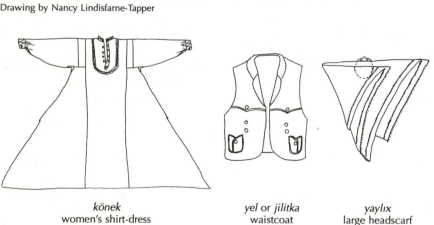

| *könek*<br>women's shirt-dress | *yel* or *jilitka*<br>waistcoat | *yaylıx*<br>large headscarf |

accommodate the voluminous underskirts, the side seams are open from the thigh downwards. A neck opening, fashioned like a collarless man's tailored shirt, extends nearly to the waist; it is fastened with buttons and easily opened when a woman is nursing. The pieces for this shirt-dress are measured by the women in straight lengths for the sleeves and from shoulder to ground; all are rectangular and are simply ripped to the correct dimensions. Women usually sew the dresses by hand, but sometimes when for a large wedding a tailor with a small portable machine may be fetched from town to make new trousers and jackets for the men, he may also machine sew the women's dresses for a small sum. Apart from new clothes sometimes made for weddings or other celebrations, all members of a household are provided with a complete new set of clothing for the New Year celebrations at the spring equinox.

Dress colours, particularly those of the shirt-dress and top undershirt, vary according to the age and marital status of a woman and her personality. The background colours of unmarried girls' shirt-dresses are light, and sometimes even white, while these become less bright and gaudy as a woman grows older until, after menopause, a woman's clothing may be virtually black and the small floral patterns of the cloth all but invisible from a distance. At this time a woman may also wear very dark purple or black headscarves. An understanding of the meaning, colouring and patterning of women's clothing is shared by men and women and used to regulate interaction between them, but the actual choice of cloth does ultimately depend on the men's perception of women's status since it is they who buy cloth and scarves for the women of their households in the local markets. This is one way household wealth and status is directly expressed through women's clothing. Though cotton shirt-dresses are worn by all women in everyday contexts, other, more expensive fabrics may be chosen for wear in more festive contexts. Thus for weddings in the mid-1960s, a few older established married women in affluent households wore printed rayon shirt-dresses, while younger married women of wealthier households followed the then new fashion and wore shirt-dresses made of a printed synthetic tulle (*plastic*) in light, bright pinks and yellows. Women of wealthier households may also wear special *yaylik* headscarves on those occasions when they dress up (*bazanmak*); these are usually white and are of a finer silk that those for everyday use.

Girls and women wear a sleeveless bolero-like waistcoat over their shirt-dresses. The waistcoats of young girls are often made of synthetic velvet materials of dark red and decorated along the front and bottom edges of the garment with gold braid, buttons and pierced, jangling coins. Indeed these decorations are nowadays virtually the only jewellery worn by Shahsevan women apart from a simple gold band worn as an engagement ring. Unlike the decorated waistcoats of marriageable girls, the two front pieces of the waistcoats of married women are made of sombre woollen cloth which is otherwise used to make men's suits. These latter waistcoats have lapels and interior breast pockets and are lined in front, though the lining material alone is used to fashion the back of the garment (See Fig. 18). The married women's waistcoat bears witness to her domestic responsibilities, not only in its colour and style, but because a woman attaches to it a chain carrying the keys to domestic storage bags and trunks, while her pockets hold a knife and box of matches and her lapels, needles and pins. In winter, girls and women wear a tailored jacket over their waistcoat. The same distinction is made between the jackets of young girls, made of dark velvets, and those of married women which are made of woollen suiting.

The bell-like shape of the women's dress is achieved by wearing at least two or three full-length underskirts, though on festive occasions even staid middle-aged women may wear up to five underskirts, while young, marriageable girls may wear ten or twelve such garments. The underskirts are made of ten meters of bright, floral-patterned cotton. The cloth is cut in straight lengths from waist to ground and gathered just above the hips with a cord. The skirts are finished at the bottom in a narrow black piping. The underskirts are all hand-sewn by the women using a simple running stitch, though women of wealthier households may ask the wives of their husband's shepherd or other employees to help them in this time-consuming task. Women wear no other undergarment apart from these underskirts; their socks and shoes, like the men's, are mass-produced and bought in the local markets.

Fashion-consciousness focuses very much on the overall shape of the dress and the characteristic walk determined by the heavy, full-length skirts. This walk is considered provocative by men. Indeed young men often form romantic attachments after having seen a young girl from a distance at a wedding or on the spring migration. If such initial impressions and an attraction between young people (girls notice the stature and stylishness of a young man's gait too) do not conflict with the plans of their respective families, a marriage may follow.

Shape is also a crucial element in the arrangement of a married women's headdress; stylishness is again directly related to the silhouette which is achieved. As was the case with men's hats in the past, women's headdresses are at once the most visible and the most complicated part of their attire. Formally women's headdresses communicate their sexual status, but a wide variety of idiosyncratic statements are introduced through nuances of style. Two scarves are used to fashion a woman's headdress: both are of hand-printed silk and bought in the focal market towns or from itinerant traders who visit the nomadic camps. The larger scarf (*yaylik*) is some two meters square and found in a variety of colours, but particularly white, yellows and oranges patterned with darker colours, greens, purples or black in arabesques or bold geometric designs. The smaller scarf (*käläyaǧi*) is less than a meter square and is almost always the darker of the two. The smaller square is rolled diagonally and tied tightly over the larger scarf and skullcap to hold them in place (see Fig. 19) The shape created by the arrangement of the smaller scarf is a key to a woman's personal status among other women in a camp, while the larger scarf can be adjusted in various ways. Three main distinctions are made: between the *bürük* style in which the eyes and most of the face of a bride are veiled; the *yaşmak* style most often worn by younger married women in which the nose and mouth are covered (see Fig. 19); and the *şatda* style worn by all established married women in domestic contexts in which only the neck is covered. In general these adjustments are used to signal social distance between a woman and other women or men. A woman's reticence with strangers and her avoidance of men's affairs are referred to her supposed natural feelings of embarrassment and shame. All married women also have a *çadir* or the full-length all-enveloping veil worn by Iranian townswomen (see Scarce 1975). However these veils, for which the Shahsevan often use a dark heavy unpatterned cotton, are only rarely worn in the Shahsevan area. They are used as prayer cloths by the women or as carrying cloths for children or other bundles or, when wound round the waist, as aprons (sometimes men when milking also use them in this way). Only on those occasions when Shahsevan women visit the local town or go on pilgrimage do they don the chader thus partly disguising their tribal identity and confounding the townspeoples' stereotypes of tribal women as bold and immodest.

**Figure 19** A young married Shahsevan woman wearing a *yaşmak* headdress with its stylish silhouette

Drawing by Sean Bowen from a photograph taken by Nancy Lindisfarne-Tapper in 1965

Until they are around nine months old, Shahsevan babies are swaddled and both baby boys and girls wear tasselled caps (*papak*) decorated with charms and talismans (*munjuk*). As soon as the children become mobile, both boys and girls wear a cotton dress (*könek*) whose style is similar to those worn by adult women. This garment is ankle length and much impedes a child's efforts to crawl far from its mother's side. By the age of four or five, when it is expected that boys will have been circumcised, they begin to wear full length trousers, a cotton shirt and jackets of woollen suiting. Indeed, in virtually all respects, their dress becomes identical with that of their fathers and elder brothers. At the age of four or five, girls too begin to wear a miniature version of the women's dress, donning an underskirt and waistcoat at this time. From this age onwards, a boy's hair will be closely cropped, while a girl will begin to let hers grow. It will be carefully groomed, washed in *aryan* (watered-down yoghurt) and henna-ed. It is parted in the middle and the back braided into ten or so plaits which are threaded together to hold them in place. Two side locks (*birçek*) are left to hang free in curls visible at the shoulder under their scarves. Apart from the henna which is also used to colour hands and feet on ritual occasions, and kohl which is worn particularly to ward off evil spirits, women wear no make-up. From this time on children, like adults, take regular baths – at least once a fortnight – inside the tent. The women men remove all pubic and underarm hair during a bath when a woman is usually assisted by another woman who will keep the water hot and to pour it over her. Once a week women wash all the household clothing, apart from the men's socks and handkerchiefs which they are expected to, and do, wash themselves.

The similarity between children's dress and that of adults repeats visually the Shahsevan conception of age-based authority and the respect due from all junior to seniors of the same sex. However, some leeway is allowed children until they near puberty and they may be careless about keeping their heads covered. Boys often go hatless and girls wear only the brightly embroidered *äräxcin* skullcaps fastened with a chain or ribbon under their chins (these caps, made by local village women and bought in the local towns, form the foundation of all women's headdresses). As puberty approaches play is segregated and boys and girls become subdued and busy with a variety of chores. Marriageable girls now carefully cover their heads with a single large scarf, the end of which falls attractively down their backs (see Fig. 2).

Marriage, the final ceremonies for which usually occur when a girl is about fifteen years old, marks the most important status change in a woman's life. Circumcision can be seen as a comparable rite of passage for males and the two are symbolically linked in a variety of ways (see R.L. Tapper 1979: 167ff.). The central part of the wedding ritual occurs when the bride leaves her father's house and, riding a white stallion, travels to the home of her husband where she will remain for the rest of her life. During this journey the bride is betwixt and between statuses and she is held to be vulnerable. Her special and dangerous position is marked sartorially in a way which calls attention to her sexuality and procreative powers and, by extension, to the vitality and social reproduction of the Shahsevan. For this journey the bride wears a light coloured cotton chader on top of which is pinned the red bridal veil (*duax*) of some loosely woven synthetic. The red veil is the symbolic focus of a wedding ritual. For three days it envelops the bride's head and shoulders until it is snatched from her head by her father-in-law and she begins to take up domestic tasks in her marital home.

Red is a colour associated with weddings and marriage in another fundamental way. The most elborate and prized items of a bride's trousseau are the woven rugs (*jejim, ojag-qiragi*), bedding bags (*farmaş*), storage sacks (*çual*) and saddle bas (*xorjun*), almost all predominately red in colour. These woven goods, which are prepared over several years by the bride, her mother and her contemporaries, not only represent the bride's personal commitment to domesticity but, because the patterns are transmitted through women, they represent a kind of history of the marriages arranged within and between Shahsevan communities. The items of a trousseau are particularly visible at weddings and other occasions when a household is honoured by guests, and during the migrations when a nomadic community has a physical as well as conceptual unity.

On her wedding day, hidden under the red veil, the bride wears the distinctive two-scarf headdress of a married woman for the first time. She wears this headdress in the *bürük* style for some two years or until after the birth of child, when she assumes the fashion worn by all established married women from this time until they are old. Once the bride has a child of her own she gains considerable independence from her mother-in-law; her importance in the household and community will increase with the number and sex of further children she bears. To signal such changes a woman will effect slight changes in her headdress and gradually she will become more outspoken among men and women and less conscientious about the modesty of her head cover. Around menopause women again slightly change the style of the headdress and often a second large scarf replaces the neat, smaller *käläyaği*. Though the headdress is still tied in the same way, it now looks, in silhouette, not unlike the felt Homburgs worn by senior men. Indeed, with age men and women begin to be defined similarly in terms of their responsibility to their household and children. At this time too the threats to men's honour and to social order posed by women's sexuality are removed and women may begin to participate openly but informally with their husbands and other men of the local community in economic and political decisions. Leadership is regarded as a male prerogative among the Shahsevan, and to some extent positions of leadership among women echo those in the male sphere (N. Tapper 1978). Formerly a community elder, a grey beard or *aq saqal*, was commonly one of the old men of the group. Nowadays, the old men of the community are still respected as such, but they are called *birçek* (grey hair), and the exacting position of community elder is now ideally filled by a younger man at the height of his influence and power. On the other hand, *aq birçek* when used as a woman's title implies not so much that she is old and past menopause, but that she is a women's leader.

Today clothing styles and the colours used by the Shahsevan are suggestive of their lives and values. Clothing reforms forced Shahsevan men to discard traditional garments which signalled both their individual status and their relation to others in the region. At all levels, distinctiveness was muted and inhibited in public display. Differences between men came to be expressed in terms of the acquisition of material goods such as watches and radios, while the great white felt tents became a principal, and explicit, symbol of tribal identity. Only in women's dress did these aspects of identity coincide. Brightly patterned dress materials, chosen by men, convey a variety of messages about an individual woman's household's strength and wealth, while her dress style, which is new and has taken its present within the twentieth century, is nonetheless held to embody the most precious and honourable aspects of tribal identity. Men's clothes are now predominantly the black and white imposed by the secular authorities – colours also, however, associated with the main religious ceremonies observed by the Shahsevan, the funeral rites and mourning ceremonies during the month of Muharram, and those other times when village mullahs visit the camps. By contrast, the shape of the women's dresses, their bright colours and those of the woven goods in their trousseaux, for both of which the red bridal veil remains a key, suggest values and ideals intimately associated with everyday Shahsevan lives.

# References

Andrews, P.A. and M. Andrews 'Clothing, The Šahsevan and Qaradagi'. In *Encyclopaedia Iranica* (ed.) Ehsan Yarshater. Costa Mesa, Calif: Mazda Publications, 837–838.

Ogranovich, I. A. 1980. 'Information on the Shahsevans.' *Caucasian Calendar for 1871* Tiflis, Pt. ii, 68–84 (in Russian).

Scarce, J. M. 1975. 'The Development of Women's Veils in Persia and Afghanistan'. *Costume* vol. 9, 4–14.

Tapper, N. 'The Women's Subsociety among the Shahsevan Nomads of Iran'. in L. Beck & N. Keddie (eds) *Women in the Muslim World* (Harvard University Press) Cambridge, Mass. & London, 1978, 374–398.

Tapper, R. 1979. *Pasture and Politics*. London & New York: Academic Press.

—— 1994. 'Change, Cognition and Control: the Reconstruction of Nomadism in Iran'. In C.M. Hann (ed.) *When History Accelerates: Essays on Rapid Social Change, Complexity and Creativity*. London: Athlone, 188–211.

—— 1997. 'Felt Huts, Haired Tents, Scene Changes, Thought Structures:

Reflections on Nomad Dwellings'. In Peter A. Andrews (ed.) *Nomad Tent Types in the Middle East*, Tübinger Atlas des Vorderen Orients, Beiheft B 74, Vol 1, 517–27.

Trifimova, A.G. 1979. 'The Garments of the Present Day Azerbaidzhan Province: Traditional and Modern Elements'. In J. M. Cordwell & R. A. Swartz (eds) *The Fabrics of Culture*. The Hague & Paris: Mouton.

Ziapur, J. *Clothing of Tribes, Nomads and Peasants in Iran*. (Min. of Education and Culture) Tehran, 1346/1967 (in Persian).

# Chapter Five

# Felt Capes and Masks of the Caucasus

*Robert Chenciner*

Between the Black Sea and the Caspian Sea, the road south to Azerbaijan passes along the Caspian Sea through the walled city of Derbent, built on a five-thousand-year old settlement, which blocks the narrowest part of the way. A mountainous region about the size of Scotland, Daghestan has absorbed peoples through successive conquests and migrations throughout history. Today thirty-three languages are still spoken locally by two million inhabitants, two thirds of whom live in over 700 mountain, lowland and plains villages. The largest ethnic group are the autochthonous Avars with a population of about 600,000 and the smallest, the autochthonous Ginoukh, with 400 people. This ethnic mosaic is in many ways a microcosm of the former Soviet Union. However Daghestan is different in the virtual absence to date of inter-ethnic violence. Perhaps one reason for this is the survival of mountain village life which is typified by a traditional style of clothing, masks and felt capes which are worn alongside modern dresses, tracksuits and Bonny-and-Clyde style peaked caps.

Daghestan men's dress is a form of display or disguise, and sometimes both, even when its design (as with football gear, prison or army uniforms) lies outside the control of the people who wear it. People use dress both to conceal their individuality and to stress it, and so it becomes a measure of their identity. The cut, the cloth, or the patterning and other embellishments pick out differences of gender, nationality and class. For Daghestanis, in addition to the influence of everyday dress, the felt masks and capes represent a certain style of masculinity.

As herdsmen, traders or fighters, much of men's lives were spent moving about, so all over Daghestan men's clothes had become uniform by the eighteenth century. They wore a tunic-like shirt and full plain trousers. Over the shirt they wore a quilted waisted jacket, the *beshmet*, with long sleeves and a narrow stiff collar. The jacket was embroidered on the breast- and side-pockets; it flared at the knee, shaped by triangles of cloth sewn in below the waist with a three-metre hem. This jacket was considered a light outer garment which a highlander could wear at home, out on the street or to work in the fields. It was made from a variety of materials from rough homespun to satin, taffeta or silk. Over the jacket on social occasions, in public or simply in cold weather, men wore the pan-Caucasian *Cherkess* (see Hewitt and Khiba, this volume) or Circassian coat, made mainly from homespun materials. The coat was similar to the jacket but wider and longer. It fell both below the knees and had wide sleeves of finger-tip length which could be turned up for convenience, also a V neck-line and two breast-pockets, each sewn into small sections for a banderole. The hem, sleeves and pockets were finished off with a braid of silk and golden thread.

An important outer garment for both men and women was the *tsuba* which in winter was worn over the *beshmet* and sometimes even over the *Cherkess*. This was usually made of sheepskin though these coats varied according to the climate and a man's wealth – the finer were of white lambskin or furs from Russia (Gadjieva 1981:125; see Fig. 20).

A hat was essential to the identity of the Daghestan mountain man. He would gladly give away anything that was his, except his hat or his *kinjal* dagger. I was told not to offer to buy men's hats when I caught a glimpse (along the road to Aguali) of an elongated bell-shaped black felt shepherd's hat, carried upside down and filled with food. The *karakul* pelts were from aborted lambs and so the wool was soft, full of shiny lanolin and tightly curled. Two golden *karakul* hats cost 400 and 300 roubles (then 1 rouble=£1) in Makhachkala Market. The golden colour was rarer than the silver. Modern fashion was either a Russian brushed felt hat, a local raked trilby or most popular – the *aerodrome*. This distinctive wide-peaked cap has become the modern equivalent of the Ottoman fez as *the* man's hat in Daghestan and some other Caucasian republics. When I wore one in Moscow, people stared. To go with his hat, the older man would treasure his walking-stick, of cornel or apricot wood decorated with flat metal discs and ribbons, which were clipped and hammered into the shaft. This type of decoration was invented in Untsukul late last century. Nowadays men villagers wear rubber boots or army boots, but until the 1950s it was possible to see archaic Scythian-style over-shoes with upturned-toes, or short-haired leather moccasins, both worn with leather gaiters.

Before the Soviets came, when the Daghestan highlander went to war or looked for loot , he wore his *djigit* dress. The distant glimpse of a black cape on horseback must have induced the same terror as the fluttering pennant of a Japanese *samurai*. The *djigit* or 'warrior' wore his armoury. His hand rested lightly on his *kinjal* dagger and sheath, usually decorated with silver gilt and niello. Occasionally the dagger had a carved ivory hilt and the sheath was damascened in gold with carved ivory plaques. The sheath hung from a narrow leather belt decorated with niello and silver studs or slides,

**Figure 20** Long-sleeved sheepskin *tsuba* worn by both women and men
Drawing by Sean Bowen from a photograph taken in an Avar village in Daghestan, from Gadzhieva (1981: 28)

like a medieval European belt (Gadjieva 1981: 124). On the other side hung his sword, the *shashka* in its sheath. An expensive example would have a steel blade damascened in gold with a leather-covered sheath with silver gilt and niello mounts. His fire-power was a pair of exotic flintlock pistols and a *miquelet* rifle[1], its lock damascened in gold, with silver gilt and niello mounts. The more important the man, the richer his tackle.

Under his weapons, his black wool cloth *Cherkess* coat with its woollen cloth *bashlik* hood, worn in cold weather, were standard dress for over two hundred years until the 1930s. The sixteen cigar-shaped pockets across the breast of the *Cherkess* coat were filled with decorative *gazeri*, or charges from a bandoleer, wood tubes with silver and niello caps. Always ready to ride, he wore black breeches, narrowing at the knees, kept tight with a loop under the instep, covered with his tall black soft leather boots, which would rest on stirrups of iron, damascened in gold. His saddle was also decorated, the woollen-cloth cover embroidered with laid and couched gilt-wrapped thread.

Male and female participants in the Khunzakh and Shamilkala festivals certainly enjoyed dressing up in traditional costume. The men and boys always dressed as *djigits*, and the most important ones paraded as the heroes Shamil or Haji-Murat. In another festival which I attended at Akhty, a torch-lit parade started the spring festivities at dusk. We, the 'important' people, sat on the podium under the statue of Lenin and a slogan saying 'the Party is the mind, honour and conscience of our epoque.' In front of a giant cardboard toothed-wheel, representing industry, the white-robed queen of the festival recited a Lezgin poem to the crowd while the organiser sat to one side, resplendent in his white *bourka*. A husband and wife in costume performed an 'arguing' dance, followed by a satirical song from a horned clown and girls in long pink dresses playing tambourines. The finale was a costume pastiche of all Soviet nations, with the Ukranian, as usual – so I was told – playing the fool. At night, during festivities in Daghestan all men who had firearms went out shooting to frighten off evil spirits·(Alimova 1987: 96; cf. also Vladikavkaz 1927: 8). My host started shooting once when I was at supper in Untsukul. I didn't know what was going on.

Long ago Daghestani men devised ways of masking themselves as totems of macho or animal cults, perhaps in competition with the overwhelming presence of the mountains. According to Bailey (1960), treasured felts were frequently mentioned in the ancient epics about Nart giants, which spread from Iran to Ossetia, and then south to Daghestan, where Narts only appeared in folk-tales, a thousand of which have been collected by A. Abdulrahmanov and A. Adzhiev of the Daghestan branch of the Academy of Sciences of Russia. Two tales from Ossetia are typical. In the first story two wives of a giant Nart are working on a *Nymat* iron making felts for their husbands – felts which were made of a hundred fleeces compared with six fleeces for a real man. In the second story, the more grisly fur coat of Soslan Kartsa was made of beardskins of the men whom he had slain. Two felts were designed for display and disguise – the *bourka* cape and the ritual mask.

## The *Bourka* Cape

The *bourka* is a shaggy, full length cape with wide square shoulders, the traditional all-purpose mountaineer's garment – a symbol of Daghestan. Even today, men, like their ancestors, asked to be photographed in their *bourka* and *papakha* sheep-skin hat. In the second century AD, Ptolemy recorded that the Alans, a tribe which occupied the Caucasus, wore black woolly cloaks (Kalakovski, quoted in Aglarov 1988: 126). The next mention of such capes is in the seventh century, when Moses of Chorene (Dasxurane'i 1961), (uncorroborated by Faustus of Byzantium, whom he usually plagiarised) noted that 'the giant leader of a savage group of Caucasian mountain-men invading Armenia from the north-east was covered in spear-proof felt armour', a description which reminds me of a legendary Nart. A good *bourka* stands up on its own. The armed followers of Shamil, the Djigit warrior (1831–59) (see p.83 above), showed that the cape was also reasonably bullet-proof against the Tsar's army. The black capes can still be seen wrapped around sleeping shepherds on guard against attacks from wolves in the mountains, or folded and tied to the saddle of a shepherd's horse, or sheltering goods or lambs in a shepherd's camp, or on a mountain village bed. The three-inch-long hairs stopped water gathering and penetrating the felt so a mountain man could roll up in his *bourka* and sleep in the open, as I once tried 2500 metres up from Archi, although it was not for me.

The felt cape was endowed with wide-ranging significance and almost accorded supernatural status. Capes were only made full-sized, for men not boys. White *bourkas* were used for festive wear, with black for everyday. A *bourka* was considered the highest present, expressing kinship. Standing under the *bourka* with someone was a further sign of kinship and protection. In disputes, the felt also had its role in a blood-feud. When men fought a duel with *kinjals* or daggers, they stood on a couple of capes and the one who was forced off lost. To stop a knife fight, a friend would put a *bourka* between the fighters. The final job of the black *bourka* was as a cover for the shrouded corpse – male or female – when it was carried on a stretcher to the grave.

The cape also appeared in folklore as a substitute for the hero as victim, enabling him also to escape. According to one story, there once lived a hunter who, before he went off hunting, said to his wife, 'Do you see that fire? Don't throw any raw liver on it!' His wife obeyed him, but after a while she thought, 'What will happen if I do?' So she threw the liver on the fire which hissed and went out. 'Aaah', she thought, 'so that's why my husband told me not to.' As there were no matches in those days, she left her house and looked far and wide for another fire to rekindle her own, and at last she saw a distant light. She went up to it saw that it was the one-eyed cyclops demon – the *valuch-tush*. She was afraid and wanted to run away, but he stopped her and took her into his cave and hospitably cooked some meat for her. While she was too frightened to eat, he ate his meal and fell asleep across the entrance, so she could not escape. In the meantime, her husband returned to find the fire out and his wife gone, so he set off to find her. He reached the cave and saw the demon dozing and, inside, his wife. He signalled her to come out and when she saw that it was her husband, she became brave enough to step over the demon and run off. When they returned home, the hunter scolded, 'You got us into trouble, and now the *valuch-tush* will return for sure and get us both.' And she said, 'Listen, let's close the shutters on the window and get a dog.' The husband smiled and said, 'What are shutters or dogs compared to a *valuch-tush*?' All the same, he raised a tree trunk in his yard with a sabre sticking out from it, point-first, and covered them with his wide-shouldered *bourka*. Then, he hid in a nearby tree with his gun, waiting for the cyclops to come. And indeed, night brought the demon. He took the cape for the man, jumped on it and stabbed himself. Next, the hunter shot him and wounded him again as he ran off. The following day, the hunter set off to see what had become of the demon. He found the *valuch-tush* dead in his cave, leaving a one-eyed child and a woman behind him. He asked her, 'Who on earth are you?', and she said, 'I'm just a woman. Five years ago I was taken off by the demon, and we had a child.' The hunter killed the child as it was cursed with one eye, and took the woman back to her village where her relatives welcomed her home.[2]

I had been told that the craft of making *bourkas* had died out. In spite of the Stalinist Party prohibition of all private production from 1929, I found that *bourkas* were still made by a few families in Gagatl' village, next to Andi. The nineteen-year-old girl I met took a day to make a cape which sold for 90–110 roubles, though a complete lined and embroidered version sells for 300. I told her to put up the price as the dust from the wool made it unpleasant work, which is usually done during winter when the village is snowed up.

Four kilograms of wool were used in a garment. The wool was first carded on a vertical steel spiked comb mounted in a wooden triangle; the work was done by hand, cleaning the brambles and droppings from the wool. The natural coloured dark brown-black wool was then teased with a gut-stringed bow. The wool was laid out to shape on a large coarse black blanket, called a *'palars'*, by four to six women who pressed it with the backs of their forearms and elbows while crouching on their knees. At such a felting party, songs were sung, accompanied by the drums, *pandur* and balalaika. The felt was repeatedly wetted and rolled on a bumpy wattle frame, called *ch'um*. Beside the storage chest where willow-bark for dyeing was kept, my young friend's grandmother stirred the black dye vat where a couple of *bourkas* were simmering overnight, over a cow-dung fire, directly fuelled by the cows who spent the winter in the adjoining byre. Each bourka used up 2 kg of dye and 100 gms of ferrum sulphate ($FeSO4$) mordant, which was bought in plastic one kilogram bags.

The felt was next washed in a pool at the edge of the village, then brought back home and shaken out by two women on the rolled-earth verandah and laid out to dry. A fist-full of stiff linen stems were used to brush out the hair on the *bourka*. A calf, belonging to the houshold, was sniffing at a packet of cow-bone glue powder, which was dissolved in water and sprinkled over the cape to make sure the long hairs did not work loose. The roofs and clothes-lines were covered in drying felts. These locally-made *bourkas* have rounded shoulders, a style popular in north Daghestan, and unlike the pointed-shouldered version made by the factory which they call 'Kabardin', Gagatl' *bourkas* would stand up on their own. Afterwards, the home-made capes were often embroidered, on the inside and at the bottom.

A similar situation existed among the neighbouring Kvarshin, a community of one thousand members, who had been transported down the mountains, north to Vedeno in 1944. Sheep-shearing took place twice a year, producing spring wool and better quality autumn wool. Both wools were used to make a hairy woollen blanket, the *tsakh'a ala*. The example I saw in Archi looked like an unstitched cape. Making a blanket felt was communal women's work, for the autumn wool had to be combed, rolled by hand, washed and spread out to dry. The barter for one such blanket was a cow in calf. For the lining a specialist helped prepare the finest cloth, called *enu* which, it was said, could pass through a finger ring; other men helped with the drying (Aglarov 1988: 124).

*Bourkas* were reputed to have first been made in Andi, where I met the last old woman who knew the secret of making an especially silky long-haired cape. But today, except for Gagatl', they were made by women at the factory in Rakhata, an Avar village near Botlikh not far from Andi. The male technical director believed his method was traditional, except that they used short, machine-carded wool, but there were other differences from the home method too. Long, white, autumn wool was collected from Akwakh, Gumbet, Tsumada and Botlikh flocks. After the long wool was hand-carded, it was taken to the felting room. The long wool was first teased with a strung bow and laid in the shape of a cape, on a linen cloth, on the floor, where it was wetted. A second layer of short wool was laid on top, wetted, and then rolled up by two women workers. For half an hour they repeatedly lifted the roll onto the table, unrolled it, combed the long hairs, wetted, rerolled and pounded it on the floor. It was hard physical work.

Then the felt was dyed black in boiled willow-bark from the forests of Chechenia to the north. Afterwards, the cape was immersed in a water bath outdoors, taken out after a few minutes and held, dripping, by a ring of women who beat it with sticks. The felt was laid on the ground where the hair was steel-wire brushed. It was then dried, sprinkled with cow gum for waterproofing, and further dried in the yard. The felt became a *bourka* when the shoulders were stitched into a square shape. Donkeys carried the folded capes for a last wash in the river and they were finally dried outdoors. As a finish, grey cloth linings were machined-in and black leather piping and two small red triangular tabs were sewn on the lapels. The whole process took about a day and a half. They hoped to make 16,000 *bourkas* (and *arbabash* felt carpets) a year. These were all bought locally, retailing in Daghestan for up to 300 roubles each. One family might own two or three though they were expensive given that the official average monthly wage was 150 roubles. The hairy felt was also cut up for linings for the inside of boots made in Kuban for Siberia. Pilots also wear gaiters (*unty*) with fur on the outside and felt on the inside.

## Masking in Daghestan

Under the totalitarian Soviet state, the mere existence of independent societies was forbidden, let alone the secrecy implicit in the masking activities in Daghestan. Nevertheless in the 1970s, one scholar had the courage to write that in the North Caucasus

> Masks are known to everyone – they are worn in festive performances, New Year carnivals and street processions. But masks have not always been related to joyous occasions. Sorcerers, as resurrected ancestors, wore masks to terrify, and warriors wore masks to protect their faces and scare the enemy. But mostly masks were used in rites to ensure fertility of the land, living creatures and man. And even if, in reality, the mask did not possess the magic powers invested in it by the believer, it still created enjoyment, happiness and hope (Studenetskaia 1980).

By the 1980's however, Caucasian masks were virtually unknown, so I tried to track them down. I was first alerted by the astonishing photographs in E. Schilling's book (1949) about Koubachi (see Fig. 21). During subsequent visits, I photographed three masks there, including one dated 1986, and was subsequently given three more. Eight masks and a hobby-horse, collected by E. Schilling from 1925 to 1944, and eight more from the rest of the north Caucasus are now in the St Petersburg Ethnographic Museum. The late Dr Studenetskaia, for many years Director of the Caucasian Collection, published a tantalisingly brief illustrated booklet on the masks, though her copious notebooks are in the museum. In the museum there is also a photographic collection including a photograph of a posse of seven masked Kabardian horsemen; two brandishing *mauser* pistols, two pictures of groups of horned masked men with a ram from Ikalto in Georgia and others of bear-mask and goat-mask festivals.

A fourteenth-century carved stone relief in a wall in Koubachi seems to portray a man with a mythical *simurgh* bird mask and a serpent wrapped around his waist, running on bird-clawed feet. Iron masks of male faces with moustaches and beards, wearing helmets, usually with plumes, were also widespread. The oldest, from the tenth century, was found in the southern Russian steppes and is on show in the Hermitage Museum in St Petersburg, while other steel masks date from the twelfth century (in the Royal Armouries, Moscow), the sixteenth century (in the Daghestan *Krayechevskii* Museum, Makhachkala) and the eighteenth century (in the Tower of London). And there are further sources. In the mountainous Dargin village of Gapshima, I met old women who were specialists in making felt boots and masks and were still making them in 1992. Sergei Luguev in Daghestan mentioned photos of Shaitli masks taken by Yuri Karpov of the Leningrad Ethnographic Institute. Again from Daghestan, I have Paruk Debirov's drawings of an Itsari devil mask, a goat mask and

**Figure 21** Three masks from Koubachi village, Daghestan
Drawing by Sean Bowen from Gadzhieva (1981; 1985)

goat rider and an Itsari wedding masked dance horseman. There is also Waqidat Shamadaeva's list of Daghestan masks and drawing of the tall bride, while Rasiat, Magomedkhan's wife, has told me that in her Dargin village, Khuduts, there is also said to be a sack mask, though I have not seen it. These examples can only represent a fraction of a tradition which was widespread in the mountains of the North Caucasus. Elsewhere I have seen an example from as far away as Dargin in the north-west.

As felt helmet masks survived in the same village, Koubachi, where the steel helmet masks were made, they seem to be related to the tradition which Schilling (1949) has called 'scare armour'. There were other more ancient local precedents. An early example was Hercules' terrifying lion-head helmet, which also had the magical effect of transferring the power of the lion to the wearer. Hercules was a legendary father of the Scyths, whose arrowheads have been found widely in Daghestan. Sassanian Persians ruled Derbent until the Arab invasions during the seventh century. Rustem, the hero of Iranian legends, also wore the same head-dress. The plumed masks possibly also derive from an earlier re-enactment of the Iranian Zoroastrian creation myth. An ancient Daghestan bronze in the Moscow Oriental Museum also has a broken plume or plant growing out of the top of the two-sided head of a male and female body. These attributes were confirmed in the Zoroastrian scripture account of the creation.[3]

Up to the present, in Koubachi and the nearby Itsari and Tsunda villages, on the second afternoon of the three-day wedding, young male friends of the groom interrupt the feasting with a ritual performance in masks and costumes. In the drama the Cruel Khan (or Shah) kidnaps the Bride, played by a boy, who was rescued by the Rider after a battle in the presence of the Devil (*Shaitan*) or the Khan's servant, who sometimes dressed as an Arab with his face and hands blackened with soot (Waqidat Shamadaeva, Personal Communication). The Cruel Khan sometimes wore the steel mask. However, in 1986, a boy dressed up as the Cruel Khan, wearing an *aksakal* felt mask (see below), steel mail, white Red Army long-johns and a huge white hood with a red tassle and a painted inscription in the Koubachi language. He carried a whip and a binocular case, which was probably meant as a begging bowl. The Cruel Khan was surrounded by his Women also played by young men. The climax was the appearance of Warriors in gruesome painted masks who tried to abduct the Women. A battle followed in which the Cruel Khan was always defeated. In another such fight, there were half a dozen Warriors against twenty Ruffians.

Another sort of conflict performance at weddings occurred in Arakul village, in the Rutul and Lak regions, in the hunt of a mummer, masked as a *tur* goat. Sometimes a character with a hobby-horse, covered in a plastic cloth, was the narrator: the St Petersburg Ethnographic Museum notes call it a 'sham' horse, meaning a minstrel. Avars and Laks also used a pantomime wedding-horse, which in the south, the Rutuls and Tsakhurs turned into a camel (Waqidat Shamadaeva, Personal Commumication). Schilling (1949) wrote that the Koubachi customs had died out before the 1920s, but during the 1950s when Studenetskaia wrote (see Studenetskaia 1980), masked buffoons took part in all the celebrations in Koubachi, including *gulala*, celebrating the last three days of bachelor-hood. They wore mail and aggressive painted felt masks, a reminder of the warlike Union of Men, a local form of militaristic public-school. At weddings, the masked buffoons usually carried a cradle, in which they tried to put a little boy, to ensure a male first-born.

A Rider mask I acquired was of painted white felt, stiffened by a patchwork of diagonal, close-stitched cloth inside, like eighteenth-century Mughal Indian battle helmets. The sides were decorated with a chessboard design, which were cut-out for the ears, and high on the forehead there was a pink star. A red paint stripe on the forehead was once a symbol of beauty and may have derived from an ancient custom of tattooing, which survived in Kazi-Kumukh and the southern Samur districts until early this century. Only the fastening threads remained of the beard and moustache. A second mask in my possession, the black felt Devil or Ram mask from the nearby Dargin village Khudut, has joined stuffed horns like a hold-all bag-handle. The eyes and ear-holes are surrounded by a stitched band of red cloth, setting off the white sheepskin beard and the dark horse-hair moustache and eyebrows. The sweaty plastic-foam inside lining suggests recent use. Another masked character was called *aksakal*, meaning *white beard* or *elder* in Turkish. Two different *aksakal* masks survive. One is entirely a white sheep fleece with a red nose, eyes and mouth and sprouting two barbers-pole hornlets, the other a white felt triangular face with a pointed moustache and beard. The *aksakal* in Daghestan seemed to be the same as the *azhegafa* or billy-goat in Kabardia. My mask was made from a Red Army greatcoat (recognisable from the black metal clip inside the front flap) and decorated with white-painted lines, a white wool sheepskin beard, brown goat-hair moustache and eyebrows, with cut-out ear-holes and a white horse-tail plume.

## Other occasions for masking

In Koubachi at *Bayram*, at the end of the fast of *Ramazan* children competitively collect walnuts and sweets from house to house. Earlier this century, Kumyk children and teenagers also celebrated by dressing up, painting their faces or wearing masks, going from home to home and performing antics in disguised voices, for which they were rewarded by presents (Gadjieva 1989: 7; also Waqidat Shamadaeva, Personal Communication).

One night in 1991, Niamh, my assistant, who was visiting Daghestan to study women's customs, was sitting in the mayor of Koubachi's home when four masked young men burst in, shrieking and ullulating. They leapt into the main room, pelting everyone with walnuts, while the women of the house cowered in the corner. Michael Zand explained later that the walnuts represented fertility and should be thrown at women (Personal Communication), though I am not clear what the villages thought. Everyone was screaming with excitement. The men of the house tried, but failed, to grab the intruders' masks to reveal who they were. The intruders were wearing cylindrical tall grey felt masks, slightly tapering down from the top, without plumes, but with beards and eyebrows. The terrifying masks were painted with slanted white or orange stripes. One also sported short triangular felt horns. Another wore steel mail, and they all wore baggy white Red Army long-underwear. Their loose shirts were held in with belts. One had a bag full of nuts slung on his belt and the others had them over their shoulders. After five minutes they left. Half an hour later, with whooping and screeching, they 'attacked' my assistant's car, bouncing the yellow Volga and trying to turn it over. They mimicked the driver when he offered them cigarettes. One took his mask off when he was trying to get the window open, revealing a handsome clean-shaven face. When the driver wound down the window to push them off, they threw in more nuts and tried to grab Niamh and the others who were all laughing. They then went off to surprise another house.

At the Lak First Furrow spring festival, a man dressed in a wolf mask with a black face chased the masked figure of a ram which was cheered on by the crowd (Waqidat Shamadaeva, Personal Communication). Other animal costumes and masks were probably connected with fertility festivals, such as the Lak ram and cockerel and the Dargin bull and ram. In festivals in Daghestan and Chechenia, masked mummers accompanied the popular tightrope walkers. Paruk Debirov recalled that the mummers usually dressed as a bear, wolf or devil, and that they entertained the audience, while the tightrope walker took a rest. They also collected payment for the performance, teasing and bullying the audience to give more. In Ossetia (cf.Studenetskaia 1980) mummers also appeared on New Year and at weddings, as bears or monkeys. Masked mummers apparently also danced around the sanctuary of St. George in the Ossetian mountain village of Dzgvis on his name-day, called *Georgoba*, though I did not see this when I took part in this festival in November 1991. This may be because I visited Dzgvis only on the Sunday, the main day of celebrating, though the seven day festival appeared to have started on the Wednesday. However the custom has more likely died out. Yet with the current enthusiasm for 'national festivals' it might well make a come back. With the Kabardians, Cherkess and Adyghes also, the *azhegafa*, or ram, played an important role in the festival of the First Furrow. With his band, he went around all the homes of the village, performing his 'death and resurrection' for a reward or ransom paid by the owner of the house, as in the photographs (in the archive in the St. Petersburg Ethnographic Museum) taken in Ikalto village in Georgia at the *Berikaoba*. The resurrection of the ram signified the growth of grain from freshly seeded, once-abandoned, soil (cf. Studenetskaia 1980).

Earlier this century, different masks were used by several of the other peoples in the North Caucasus. The survival of the Karachaev and Balkhar mountain cattle-rearers depended on haymaking for winterfodder. Every group of haymakers chose a strong, clever lad whom they called *aksakal* – white-beard, or *teke*, ram. Wearing a mask, like that of my Dargin *Devil* or Ram, the boy was armed with a felt whip and a wooden hay-fork. He would demand 'tribute' from every passer-by, be he his own brother or a peasant, an official or a prince. His haul included delicacies, cattle or money for the evening's festivities. Then after work, he entertained the harvesters. Whenever he met another *teke*, they fought and the victor, representing the harvest, assured his own people of abundant hay. But at other times, he set an example by his own work, as well as keeping the work standards of others high (cf. Studenetskaia 1980).

In the Caucasus, over the centuries, masked rituals sometimes degenerated into masked amusements, which in turn evolved into satirical performances. Before the Revolution, mummers, like the Ottoman *karagoz* shadow-puppets, derided unfair judges, greedy *mullahs*, Tsarist generals or police officials. Their jokes were often socially or politically unacceptable, so their masks kept them out of trouble. The double identities which had to be adopted during the Soviet period to cope with the hypocrisy of reconciling Party dogma and traditional honour made actual masks unnecessary and masking became a part of the satire of everyday life.

## Notes

1  According to A.R.E. North (Personal Communication), the gun was named after its North African lock mechanism, of Spanish origin, showing how international the arms trade was.
2  Abdulhakim Magomedovich Adzhiev (Personal Communication).
3  In *The Greater Bundahsn*, an encyclopaedia of Zoroastrianism (written c. 800 AD, and translated from the Armenian by Bailey, Ms TW2, Ch.1: 101), it is written,

> It was forty years in the ground. At the end of the forty years it grew out in the form of a *repas*, a red plant like rhubarb, with one stalk and fifteen leaves. Marte – the male – and Martane – the female – grew out so that their hands were placed back to their ears (like many male and female bronze figurines from Daghestan dated variously from 1200 BC to 300 BC) They were joined one to the other of the same stature of the same form. And in the middle of them appeared the *gdh* – perhaps meaning good fortune – of which mankind was created.

## Bibliography

Aglarov, M. 1988. *Village communities in the mountains of Dagestan* (Russian text). Moscow: Nauka.

Alimova, B. M. 1987. *Communal celebrations and ceremonies of the Tabassarans,* (Russian text). Makhachkala, A. Nauk Daghestan: Filial.

Bailey, H. W. 1960. 'Ossetic (Narta)'. In J. Hatto, (ed.) *Traditions of Heroic and Epic Poetry.* Oxford: Oxford University Press.

Dasxurane'i, Movses 1961. *History of the Caucasian Albanians.* Transl. C. J. F. Dowsett. Oxford: Oxford University Press.

Gadjieva, S. 1981. *Dress of the People of Daghestan.* (Russian text). Moscow: Nauka.

—— 1985. *Family and Marriage of the Daghestan people in the 19th and early 20th Century* (Russian text). Moscow: Nauka.

—— 1989. *Traditional Kumyk Feasts & Ceremonies in the Agricultural Cycle* (Russian text). Makhachkala, A Nauk Daghestan: Filial.

Studenetskaia, E.N. 1980. *Masks of the Peoples of the Northern Caucasus* (Russian text). Leningrad.

Schilling, E. 1949. *The Kubash and their Culture* (Russian text). Moscow: Nauka.

# Chapter Six

# Male Dress in the Caucasus: with special reference to Abkhazia and Georgia

*George Hewitt and Zaira Khiba*

Though today it is sadly not in use, being reserved for folk song- and dance-ensembles, traditional dress for men is a feature which in its essentials is shared by all the various peoples of the Caucasus, whose autochthonous denizens speak some 40 languages.[1] This paper is concerned with one aspect of their common heritage, namely male dress, and concentrates on variations in Abkhazian and Georgian cultures for the simple reason that these are the ones with which the authors are most familiar.[2] Whilst this paper is not primarily addressed to linguists, we have included a selection of native terms for the various articles of clothing described so that readers may gain a flavour of the differences in, for example, vocabulary found across the native language-families. The most numerous of the Caucasian peoples today are the Georgians – along with the Mingrelians, Laz (who predominantly reside in Turkey) and the Svans, they make up the Kartvelian peoples. The North West Caucasians are the Abkhazian-Abazinians, Circassians and Ubykhs – this last group left the Caucasus when the Russians took control in 1864, preferring a life in the Ottoman Empire, where their language immediately went into the decline that makes it today all but extinct. After the Georgians, the Chechens are the most numerous Caucasians today, and their language-group has the three members: Chechen, Ingush and the endangered Bats. All remaining languages referred to below belong in the final, Daghestanian/North East Caucasian family.

The most distinctive component of male dress is the striking tunic, which Cossacks adopted when they were settled in the North Caucasus as the frontiersmen for Imperial Russia's drive southwards. Chechenia, Ingushetia in the North Central Caucasus and Daghestan in the North East were finally subdued with the defeat of Shamil in 1859, and in the North West the Circassian tribes (together with their kin, the Ubykhs, around Sochi, and the Abkhazians further to the south on the Black Sea coast) were conquered in 1864, leading to a mass-exodus to Ottoman lands (principally

Turkey) of all the Ubykhs, most of the Circassians and Abkhazians plus various other North Caucasians. The Turks call the Circassians *Cherkess*,[3] and the pan-Caucasian tunic is generally known by its Russian name of *cherkesska* (see also Chenciner, this volume). Indigenous Caucasians, however, do not use this term. In Georgian it is commonly known as *čoxa* (cf. Turkish *çuha* (cloth)), which root is also widespread, if not entirely universal, in Daghestan (e.g. Avar/Andi *čuXt'u*, as given by Kibrik & Kodzasov 1990: 127) and the North Central Caucasus (e.g. Chechen *čoa*, Ingush *čokxa*). In the North West Caucasus, on the other hand, this root seems to be unattested as the name for the garment in question,[4] for in Circassian we have *ce.y/cə.y< cə* (wool) (Shagirov 1977:124), whilst Abkhaz has *a-k°'əm.ž°ə*, which would seem to contain a stem of uncertain meaning *-k°'am.z-* as seen in the noun *a-k°'əm.z.c°a* (material for cherkesska), where *a-c°a* is (skin, pelt). In Georgian's sister-language, Mingrelian, the term *γart-i* applies to both the article of dress and to the woollen material from which it is made, just as in Georgian too the latter may be referred to by the word *čoxa* (as well as by the full term *sa-čox-e maud-i/šal-i* (material/woollen cloth for cherkesska), which material might have been Georgian, Daghestanian or Ossetian in origin).

Of the native Caucasian languages only Georgian has more than a century's history of writing, and, according to the eleven-volume Georgian Encyclopaedia, *čoxa* is attested in Georgian literature from as early as 9th century texts. The most usual colour for the garment is black, though other colours (such as red, grey, brown and blue) are not unknown, and noblemen might have them in white (see Fig. 22). It is drawn in tightly at the waist, whilst the lower portion extends to below the knee and broadens out with a number of loose pleats (Abkh. *(a-)ay.k°ər.ç*, Geo. *naoč'-i*) at the rear, gathered at the waist. The sleeves are exceptionally long, dropping well below the hands, and are normally worn folded. Fastened at the centre with five fasteners, not buttons (Abkh. *a-ḥ°ənc°'ra*, Geo. *γil-i*) but bobs of braid (Abkh. *a-q'aitan*, Geo. *q'aitan-i*) which fit into cotton-loops serving as button-holes (Abkh. *a-ḥənc°'ra-təp*, Geo. *k'ilo*). Open from half-way up the chest, it has no collar of its own but reveals the collared under-garment beneath; open from the abdomen down, it facilitates the mounting and riding of horses, the standard Caucasian mode of travel. Each breast is decorated with between eight and ten protruding rounded pockets for cartridges (Abkh. *a-ḥazər.tra*, Geo. *sa-masr-e*), which today usually hold plastic imitations. These cartridges are half white, half black – the white end is normally visible, but the black is used on occasions of mourning, when previously even a nobleman would dress only in a black cherkesska. When real cartridges were in use, they might be capped with a silver top, each covering being attached to a silver chain, secured near the shoulder-blade. The garment is lined, apart from the hem at the base, with braid, including the tops and bottoms of the cartridge-pockets. There are usually

**Figure 22** Tbilisi Men wearing cherkesskas

Drawing by Sean Bowen from a studio portrait reproduced in Gersamia (1984)

two vents (Abkh *arq̇'ars.ta,* Geo. *čak-i*) at the base and two side-slits (Abkh. *a-ǰəyba-r.q̇a'*, Geo. *γiob-i*) through which the undergarment could protrude for decoration. The cherkesska was the dress of all Caucasian males, regardless of station in life, a peasant's garment being merely of inferior quality and workmanship. If nobles wore theirs on all occasions, a peasant would don his only when he was going out.

There were, of course, regional variations to the basic theme. Inal-Ipa (1965: 317) quotes 19th century descriptions of Abkhazian cherkesskas as being somewhat shorter than those of the Circassians, though he notes too that in earlier times the Abkhazian cherkesska was longer, citing the measurements of an example from a St. Petersburg museum as being 43 cm. from waist to top, but 66 cm. from waist to base (see Fig. 23). Malija and Akaba (1982: 110–111) present representations of Abkhazian cherkesskas with a collar. If the Abkhazians were generally reluctant to indulge in ornamentation, such was not the case with their Mingrelian and Georgian neighbours. Volume 3 part I of the Georgian series which translates as *Materials for the History of Georgia's Domestic Industry and Craftsmanship* (ed. Iv. Dzhavakhishvili 1983) is devoted to dress in the various regions

**Figure 23** Man wearing a cherkesska

Drawing by Sean Bowen from a 1995 calendar illustrating Abkhazian 'national dress' of the 18th and 19th centuries

of Georgia. For the capital, Tbilisi, a variety of *cherkesska* is described which had no fasteners, as it was meant to be worn open so as to show off the undergarment in its full glory (*ibid.*, p.189). Instead of loose plaits it had between eight and sixteen vents. Instead of cartridge-pockets it was decorated with up to thirty smaller compartments, into which only half a woman's little finger could be poked, which originally will have been designed to contain flint-steel (Geo. *k'ves-i*) and tinder (Geo. *abed-i*) and are thus known as 'flint-steel containers' (Geo. *sa-k'ves-eb-i*). Below them ran two strips of braid-decoration (Geo. *čapariš-i*) with a decorative button-hole (Geo. *munǰ-i k'ilo*) beneath the final flint-pocket. The Georgian Encyclopaedia also mentions a specific type of cherkesska, known as the Khevsurian cherkesska after the remote mountainous region, now virtually deserted, of Khevsureti in north-central Georgia (bordering Chechen-Ingushetia), which was devoid of fasteners but, like all cloth-work in the region, richly ornamented with applied symbolic designs (such as the cross). If the cherkesska itself has a military air about it, it is perhaps because

Khevsurs as late as the 19th century still used to dress in armour (Geo. *čačkan-i*) with chain-mail shirt (Geo. *javšan-i*) to do battle (see Mak'alatia 1984: 146–7), a fact which led to the suggestion that the Khevsurs were descendants of the Crusaders (Geo. *jvarosn-eb-i*). Elaborate embroidery is, of course, characteristic of female Khevsurian attire, such as depicted by Mak'alatia (*ibid.*, 145–6) for the *koklo*, a sort of female cherkesska, though his few coloured plates (the book was first published in the mid-thirties) illustrate the intricate workmanship so typical of this district on other articles of male and female clothing. An illustration by Gogebashvili from the 1912 edition of his *Nature's Door* depicts (1976: 478) a rather ornate cherkesska from the western province of Imereti, with a short and flounced lower portion, whilst for the province of Guria, whence hails Eduard Shevardnadze, to the south-west, Gogebashvili both notes and illustrates (p. 495) a local alternative to the cherkesska, found especially in the southern part of the region towards Turkey, which is called *č'onia*. It comes down only to the waist and resembles a smoking-jacket; according to the illustration, it would seem that it is worn with a sort of heavy cummerbund around the lower waist.

The stylised cherkesska described above will have represented the pinnacle of a long development. An Italian missionary, Don Christoforo De Castelli, spent the years 1628–1654 in Georgia and left an album of drawings showing scenes from Abkhazia, Mingrelia and Georgia proper. These were published in full for the first time in Tbilisi only in 1977 (along with the Georgian translation of the original descriptions of the illustrations in a work edited by Giorgadze), and one can detect, as in Drawing No. 224 of an armed Abkhazian nobleman, a plainer precursor, with nothing on the chest-area, of the dress-like garment that was to become the handsome cherkesska of later days.

The cherkesska is worn together with a special shirt called in Georgian *axalux-i* and in Abkhaz *a-k'aba*, such that both languages refer to the traditional male outfit by employing the combinations *čoxa=axalux-i* and *ak°'əm.ž°ə-y a-k'aba-j* respectively – the Russian term is *bešmet*, the Chechen *γovtal*. The materials from which this shirt might be made include silk, satin, staple, brocade, demi-cotton. As to colour, it is usually white, but black is also possible. Today it extends to below the crotch, but earlier it seems to have been longer. In Georgian the word for a dress is *k'aba*, and in Mingrelian, which language for centuries has been a buffer between the Abkhaz-speaking and the Georgian-speaking areas, *k'aba* is used (in addition to the Georgian borrowing *axalux-i*) to refer to this shirt, which would be natural if at some stage in its development the shirt more resembled a woman's dress. From Mingrelian the word seems to have entered Abkhaz, where the Georgian root is not found.

Like the cherkesska, the shirt is fastened with bobs of braid from the chest up to the top of the straight collar, which itself has two such bobs, as well as around the wrists. Unlike the cherkesska, the shirt has pockets over each breast. The shirt is worn outside the trousers.

A full, dress-length and double-breasted (Geo. *došluyian-i*) shirt is shown (Dzhavakhishvili *op.cit*.: 188) as a garment worn in Tbilisi. Such an elaborate shirt fastened at the side with up to 200(!) bobs of braid (though the winter-variant had shiny black buttons instead) had a border of blue braid, its own loose plaits and vents, and was typically used in association with the open-fronted cherkesska described earlier. The equivalent single-breasted (Geo. *sc'oryulian-i*) shirt fastened in the centre by means of twenty metal fasteners (Geo. *dugma*, Abkh. *a-xapa*) with what are known as male (Abkh. *(a-)arbaŷ*, Geo. *mamal-i*) and female (Abkh. *(a-)arcna*, Geo. *dedal-i*) parts, had a border of gold thread with no loose plaits, though it did have eight vents.

Beneath the shirt a vest may be worn, called in Georgian *p'erang-i* (shirt) (cf. *maisur-i* (vest)), in Abkhaz *a-xarp*, in Chechen *koč*, in Dido *ged*, in Lak *huqa*, and in Russian *rubaška*.

Over the cherkesska was worn (and still is by shepherds out on the mountain-pastures) a voluminous, full-length black cloak of heavy felt (Abkh. *a-wap'a*, Geo. *keca/teka*), with shaggy hair on the outside and extremely broad, straight shoulders (see Fig. 24). It is called in Abkhaz *a-wap'ča*, in Georgian *nabad-i*, in Chechen *verta*, in Circassian-Ubykh *č'a:k°'a*, in Lak *warsi*, in Rutul *lit*, and in Russian *burka*. It fastens only at the top, being held around one, in the manner of a cloak, against inclement weather. As with Caucasian dress in general, it was extremely convenient for use on horseback: Inal-Ipa (1965: 319) describes how an Abkhazian would always have his cloak with him, rolled up and attached to his saddle in good weather, and actually wear it while riding with his right shoulder tucked well into the right side, so that the cloak's centre would be by the rider's left shoulder, leaving the left side of the cloak free to be swung (via the saddle) over the bearer's right shoulder, providing excellent protection, especially for the chest-area. At night-time it served as a warm layer for a traveller forced to sleep beneath the open skies.

Inal-Ipa (*loc. cit.*) also refers to a long obsolete garment, made of felt like the cloak but in shape somewhat similar to a cherkesska, which he calls *a-g°abanak*. Malija (1985) illustrates it . It is a plain brown jacket, fastened from the midriff to the collarless neck, but otherwise open and extending to just below the buttocks – the wearer is depicted wearing a simple, conical hat of the same material. Georgian has the term *gvabanak'-i*, but interestingly Ubykh had *g°əda:k'a*, which Vogt (1963) translated as 'manteau', noting that Dumézil (1931) had defined it as 'la longue chemise caucasienne fermée jusqu'au menton', but adding that two Turkish equivalents had been offered at different times, namely *yelek* 'waistcoat' and *hırka* 'short cloak'. Circassian has *g°abanač/γ°abanač*. The source of these forms is Turkish *kepenek* 'coarse felt cape' (Shagirov 1977: 111). Fur

**Figure 24** Man wearing a heavy felt cloak

Drawing by Sean Bowen from a 1995 calendar illustrating Abkhazian 'national dress' of the 18th and 19th centuries

coats are also found (Abkh. *a-xamə,* Geo. *kurk-i* – cf. Turkish *kürk* – or *t'oloma*) – in Georgian a woman's fur-lined coat is called *katib-i.*

Black trousers (Geo. *šarval-i,* Abkh. *(a-)ay.k°a* or *a-jəyk°a* from Mingrelian *jikva*) were a simple design of light-weight wool, one variety (as worn by the small-traders or artisans of Old Tbilisi, known as *q'aračoɣel-i/q'aračoxel-i,* literally 'the one with black-cherkesska' from Turkish *kara* 'black' even though their open cherkesska was blue in hue, or *k'int'o* for the more uncouth types) was especially capacious down to the knee; below the knee, however, they cling to the calf, fitting inside tight-fitting, black, knee-length boots (Abkh. *a-mag°,* Geo. *čekma/c'aya⁵*) and are secured at the bottom with a single strip of material. When such long boots were not being worn, the trousers would be tucked into leggings (Abkh. *(a-)ay.msə,* Geo. *sa-cvet-i/p'ač'ič'-i/p'aič'-'i*) that covered the shin and were kept in place by a loop under the instep and strapped at the top. Malija and

Akaba (1982: 56) note that in Abkhazia these leggings could be ornamented with gold or silver thread, and they were of cloth for use in the home, but of morocco for outside.

These authors also describe a variety of other footwear (Abkh. *a-ša.c'a(.ṭ°'ə)* or *(a-)ay.maa*, Geo. *pex-sa-c-m-el-i*), such as *a-čabər.ay.maa* 'leather shoes', *a-ž°.c°.ay.maa* (small raw-leather shoes) (Geo. *kalaman-i*) worn without socks, though in winter socks of rough material or morocco (*a-mest*[6]) were worn (woven and often nicely patterned woollen socks are called *a-kalpad,* Geo. *c'inda* – in parts of the Caucasus, such as amongst the Bats who, though they are related to the Chechens and Ingush, today live in a single east Georgian village, patterned (socks) with thick woollen soles double as slippers (Geo. *plost'-i*)). Small shoes for both men and women were called *a-c°.ə.ṣ.ay.maa* (Geo. *čust'-i*) when made of morocco and worn for going out. In addition to leggings covering the shin, one also found 'knee-protectors' (Abkh. *a-ša.m.x.tə/a.r.pa,* Geo. *sa-muxl-e*).[7]

Perhaps the most widespread headgear worn by men as part of their traditional outfit and made by the furrier[8] is what the Russians call *papaxa.* It is quite deep, round and, at a distance, trapezoid in shape, narrow at the base and widening at the top. Made of sheepskin, it has tight curls of black wool (after the fashion of an astrakhan coat) on the outside. Some local designations are – Abkhaz *a-xə.l.pa.r.č,* Georgian *boxox-i,* Andi *raG°ara,* T'indi *q°'apa,* Hunzib *L'oq'ol.* Narrow and tall, cone-shaped variants exist, possibly with a soft interior raised above the curly woollen base.

Other types of headgear occur, some being characteristic of a particular locale. A common type is what the Russians call *bašlyk,* but in Abkhaz it is *a-x.tə/a.r.pa,* and in Georgian *q'abalax-i.* It is made of fine white wool, sitting on the head in a cone-shape with a tassle (Abkh. *a-ča.x°,* Geo. *poč-i*) on the end of a double six-inch thread and braid-bobble with a three-inch vent, held by two looped twisted cords, at the bottom of the head-covering at the back, and with two long side-pieces extending down beyond the knee and each provided with a half-inch hem (Abkh. *a-ç'ə.k°'ə.r.ṣa,* Geo. *koba*). Laid flat with the side-flaps upwards, the hat makes an L-shape. The flaps might be left dangling over the back, folded one over the other but still at the back, or tied in an intricate fashion so that the head then has a rather bulbous covering. Alternatively, the whole head-piece might be girt around one's waist, allowed to rest on the shoulders with the head-part over the small of the back, or draped over the right shoulder, as illustrated by Malija and Akaba (1982: 116–7). This particular head-covering could even be worn over the *papaxa* to lend an even more impressive and weighty appearance to the wearer.

At one time Abkhazian men used to shave their heads apart from strands left to grow from the crown into a long clump resembling a raised pony-tail. In order to accommodate this growth appropriate headgear had to be devised (cf. the illustrations in Inal-Ipa, 1965: 321).

Two distinctive types of headgear that immediately betray their provenance from a particular region of Georgia are those from Svanetia in the mountainous north west and K'akhetia in the east. The Svan hat (Geo. *svan-ur-i kud-i*) is usually grey (though white and brown are also found); it is made of strong, felt-like wool (so strong that it may be used as a cup to drink from mountain-streams) and grips the head like a large skull-cap, being half-spherical in shape. A black lining of twisted cord runs around the base with perhaps a couple of rows of black stitching above it, and a second rim of twisted cord is stitched around the hat some two inches higher; one strip of such cord runs from this over the top from front to back and a second from side to side and, at the meeting-point on top, there is a small bobble. Though not essential, a further foot or so of cord may run down from the interior of the hat at the back, and to this a tassle may be attached. This hat has become very popular even outside Svanetia, and nowadays tourists find it especially attractive.

The K'akhetian hat is made of the same material as a cherkesska and is thus usually black in colour (though one also finds it in white). Again it is essentially a skull-cap but with the material turned up and tucked in to provide a two or three inch border. Two strips of twisted cord again run over the centre-piece from front to back and from side to side but this time, instead of meeting at the top in a bobble, there is a raised, button-like top-point encircled by the braiding. This cord-ornamentation remains black even if the main hat is white.

Though not itself an item of clothing (Abkh. *a-mat°a*, Geo. *t'an-sa-c-m-el-i/t'an-i-sa-mos-i*), no description of male Caucasian dress (Abkh. *a-š.c'a.t°'ə*, Geo. *ča-c-m-ul-oba*) would be complete without noting that no Caucasian would have considered himself fully dressed without his belt (Abkh. *a-maq'a*, Geo. *kamar-i*) and dagger (Abkh. *a-q'ama*, Geo. *xanǰal-i/ sa-t'ev-ar-i*). A top-quality belt, like the scabbard, would be decorated with silver – the silversmiths of the small Daghestanian village of K'ubachi were particularly famous for all types of silver-ware (see, e.g. Chirkov 1971). The scabbard (Abkh. *a-q'ama.t.ra*, Geo. *karkaš-i*) itself was either of leather-bound wood with top and base of silver (Abkh. *a-razna*, Geo. *vercxl-i*) typically ornamented with beautiful black inlay, known as niello (Abkh. *a-p'st'ə.r.k'.ra*, Geo. *sevad-i* <= Arabic *sawād*, blackness), or wholly of silver. The base of the bone-grip would also be decorated with matching silver, incorporating one of the two silver studs over the pins securing the dagger. The belt itself would also be ornamented with a silver buckle (Abkh. *a-pə.ǰ*, Geo. *abzind-i*) and silver studs and silver tips to one or more of the decorative straps hanging from the belt – these ornamentations are known in Abkhaz as *a-q°' əna*, and such an ornamented belt is called in Georgian a *gobak'-ian-i kamar-i*. Various accoutrements could be suspended from the belt, but especially common was a small metal pouch to hold fat (for greasing one's weapons or coins); its name in Abkhaz is *a-k'apa.tra* from *a-*

*k'apa*, 'sheep's fatty tail'. Weapons in addition to the ubiquitous dagger would have included a full-length sword (Abkh. *(a-)aḥ°a*, Geo. *xmal-i*) and pistol (Abkh. *a-k'ara.x°*, Geo. *dambača*).

The oldest description of Caucasian dress with which we are familiar comes from the description of Mingrelia written by one of the early Italian missionaries, Don Archangelo Lamberti, who lived for about twenty years in the region in the second quarter of the 17th century. A Georgian translation of his work was published by A. Ch'q'onia in 1901, and this was reprinted in both 1938 and 1990. We close this article with an English rendering of the relevant chapter (VII) based on this Georgian translation.

Since we have described the population, it is now necessary that we portray how the Mingrelians dress. Concerning the vulgar folk it cannot even be said that they wear any clothing, for their poverty has reached such a pitch that their clothing hardly covers half their body. It is true that male dress is comprised of some woollen strip, which scarcely reaches to the knee, and for a belt they have ordinary string. They have no thought for anything else; they can't be bothered with shirt, trousers, socks and shoes. There are even those who can't obtain even this strip of wool and go about entirely naked. Since the damp air of Odishi [= Mingrelia] does not facilitate the rearing of sheep, and since sheep are expensive, Mingrelians find it difficult to acquire even a modicum of clothing to cover their naked body. It is for just this reason that as soon as Turkish boats approach the shores of Mingrelia (they come every year), the Mingrelians will rush out of their homes and fall upon these boats to buy woollen cloth, but, since they have no money, they will bring out hemp, honey, wax, flax or flax-seed and barter such as these with the Turks for cloth.

It is not only the poor who have string for belts. Every Mingrelian considers string not just useful but an essential necessity, especially on the road. Indeed, if a Mingrelian wants to steal a horse, he needs string. If he needs hay for the horse, he must bind it with string and fetch it; if he wants to lead the horse into water, without string he will be unable to. If he captures a prisoner in war, without string he won't be able to bring him home; if he catches a thief and wants to punish him, he must have string to tie his hands and bind him to a tree. In a word, string is so essential in this land that every Mingrelian has it about his waist and values and glorifies it greatly.

Apart from string, nobles and wealthy peasants have a leather belt girt around the waist which is decorated with silver studs (Geo. *polak-i*). On this belt they will usually suspend a variety of things, such as they may require on the road. On the belt they will hang first a sword with broad thongs, which has a length of three, four or five spans, so that when they walk about, they drag the sword along the ground like a long tail. They will also hang on the belt a knife with its own sharpener, a small money-pouch, in which there is either nothing at all or just a few paltry items. In a second pouch they have flint, steel, matches and tinder; in a third pouch they have needles with different kinds of thread. They have hanging there also a comb, bodkin, a small cord, an implement for bleeding a horse, a really tiny pouch of leather full of pounded salt, yet another pouch with pepper or full of some other kind of condiment. And they have suspended a small wax candle in case they should spend the night on the road and perchance require it. A hundred other nugatory items they have hanging there, but to save space we won't list them. In a word, about their waist is suspended an entire shop.

In Odishi they sew shoes in the main from undressed leather, like our mountain peasants. Many sew these shoes so elegantly that even squires wear them when they go hunting for walking more nimbly. Women and the well-born wear Persian high-heeled shoes (Geo. *koš-i*) with one-inch heels. These shoes are sewn from different coloured leather. From such leather they sew those boots too which women don when riding. These boots are not high-necked ones; the neck, which is decorated with gold and precious gems reaches only as far as the shins. As for poor women, for them dress and blouse are one and the same, the shirt's partner reaches down to their feet, and the feet they have ever naked.

Royalty and the aristocracy dress quite well. They sew shirts (Geo. *p'erang-i*) from different coloured silk. They ornament the neck and hem of the shirt with gold-thread, precious stones and pearls. So that all should clearly notice this ornamentation, they have the shirt flapping outside the trousers. Over the shirt they wear the *axalux-i*, which they have reaching down to the knees. This *axalux-i* is of woollen cloth or silk, and so that it does not conceal the embroidered shirt, it is shorter than the shirt. On it they have sewn from the throat to the waist buttons of wrought silver. About the waist they wear a belt, as we described above, and on the belt there is a Turkish sword suspended, and, apart from this, there hangs the renowned string. Above the *axalux-i* in cold weather they wear a second article of clothing, shorter still, like a Cossack. This second article is of purer wool or silk or velvet and for lining has sable-skin.

The hat of vulgar folk is made of felt and looks more like a goblet than our kind of *chapeau*, since it has no edges at all and hardly covers the head. They give different shapes to this hat. Royalty and aristocrats sew this hat from pure wool or silk; some have it embroidered or decorate it in the Tatar fashion with sable-skin, or have points sewn in the Persian way, like the headgear of the Cappucins and decorate it with silver-coloured sheepskin, which they import from Persia. When I went to that land and the Mingrelians noticed our *chapeau* and became convinced that this *chapeau* is very advantageous at times of rain and sunshine, they conceived a desire to introduce it there. First the priests, then the nobles and finally the peasants too did indeed introduce it. But, since they have no master who can make the material necessary for such a *chapeau*, they adopted its form at any rate, and some have it made from wool and place cardboard inside, some from the bark of trees and fasten over it a waxed canvas, and some have it made from tree-bark shaped on a turner's lathe. This *chapeau* they will never put directly on their head but on top of their own hat; neither do they always wear it, but only when it rains or in sunny weather.

The vulgar folk knit socks from local wool or silk.

Apart from this Mingrelians when feasting or at festival wear another type of dress, which is long down to the feet and whose open sleeves (Geo. *q'urtmaĵ-i*) reach to the ground. This article is especially elegant both in design and the rich material from which it is sewn. They sew this garment from damask or velvet or silk. As lining they give it sable-skin, and from top to bottom it is ornamented with buttons of gold or pearl. Each royal or aristocratic person has several such garments of different material so that according to the circumstance he might don one or another. This garment is common to both men and women.

Although the women are far from our country, they still do not fall short of our women in comeliness, especially in the combing of the hair and in covering the head, which plainly bears witness to the emptiness in their heads. They wish (against Nature) with the help of colouring and fard to shew themselves white to people. But, of course, like our womenfolk they have neither the artistry nor the equipment. They pound the fard and smear it on in such a way that their faces look more like they have been powdered with flour than dyed. As for colour, they do not import material from Spain or Asia Minor but use what comes to hand – for example, lac, vermilion and other dyes. Then they will smear them on their cheeks in such a way that it appears as if they had had them smeared all of a sudden and without any womanly know-how. And their eyebrows they paint with dye from the pyramid cypress in such a way that they lengthen them in both directions almost to the ears and in the middle join them above the nose. With the same dye they paint the eyelashes too. Imagine it – they do not even spare their eyes and yellow even the eyeballs with some sort of ointment. You are lucky to recognise such a bedecked or, better to say, re-coloured woman only by her voice if at all, otherwise it is impossible to recognise her by any other sign. Mingrelians are so enamoured of such plastering and painting that, if a painter paints the portrait of any woman and fails to reproduce her plastered and painted in this way, he quite upsets the woman. It happened exactly so to one artist to whom had been entrusted the painting of the face of a dead queen. The artist was trained in Italy. He painted the queen as she really was, without colouring and fard, but as soon as the women of the court observed the painting, they were so annoyed and so perturbed the artist that he became forced to do the picture all over again according to their taste.

They plait the hair in different ways. Long hair they divide into four plaits, two they will wrap over the ears, and the two which are longer some will toss over the shoulders, and some over the bosom. These latter two plaits have at the ends tassles of black silk, decorated with gold, precious gems and pearls. The rest of the hair, adorned in this same fashion, they will knot over the throat and raise up from the chin to the top of the head, where they will bind it.

On their head they will place a very fine and white veil, cut into three flaps, so that one flap they wear let down on the back and the remaining two on the shoulders. The veil is fastened on the head by a special kind of hat of golden thread of silk, which resembles a crown. To this fancy crown they usually attach a feather or beautiful flower. (Don Archangelo Lamberti, translated in Ch'q'onia 1990).

# Notes

1 The Greater Caucasus mountain range runs for some 500 miles and in this relatively narrow neck of land that separates the Black from the Caspian Sea one finds: (a) the indigenous Caucasian peoples, who collectively speak some 40 languages, divided into certainly three and possibly four language-families (Daghestanian/North East Caucasian, its clear but more distant relative North Central Caucasian, and North West Caucasian, all three of which families possibly derive from a single, very remote ancestor, whilst it is impossible to prove that the final family, South Caucasian or Kartvelian, has any genetic links with any of the northern groups or indeed with any other language-family within or beyond the Caucasus): (b) peoples who speak a number of Indo-European languages (e.g. the Ossetians, Tats, Talysh and Kurds, all four of whom speak languages related to Persian, the Armenians, Greeks, Gypsies, and, of course, the Russians and other Slavs, who first appeared in the Caucasus area only in the second half of the 16th century): (c) a variety of Turkic-speaking peoples such as the Turks themselves and the Azerbayjanis, plus the Karachays and Balkars in the NW Caucasus, and the Nogais and the Kumyks in the NE; to the north of Daghestan are the Mongol Kalmyks: (d) the Semitic peoples (a small Assyrian group in Georgia, and Jews, among whom the Mountain Jews of Daghestan evidently speak Iranian Tat).
2 For a discussion of the history of Georgian costume in the VIth-XIVth centuries see Chopik'ashvili (1964). For details on the specific dress of Daghestanian tribes (both male and female) see Gadzhieva (1981).
3 The debate continues as to whether this term is in any way related to the people on the Black Sea coast who were known to the ancient Greeks as 'Kerketai'.
4 In Abkhaz we have *a-čouḥa* used as in Turkish, i.e. with the meaning '(woollen) cloth'.
5 For a short boot, the word is *c'uya*.
6 In Georgian *mest'-i* is defined as small-collared, soleless footwear of poor-quality sheep-skin or poor-quality sheepskin collarless footwear with sole.
7 The word for cobbler is in Abkhaz *(a-)ay.maa.jax.y°ə*, in Georgian *xaraz-i* (cf. Arabic *xarrāz*) or *me-c'uy-e*.
8 Abkhaz *a-xa.l.pa.jax.y°a*, Georgan *č'on-i*.

# References

Chirkov, D. 1971. *Dekorativnoe Iskusstvo Dagestana* [Decorative Art of Daghestan]. Moscow: Sovietsky Khudozhnik.

Chopik'ashvili, N. 1964. *Kartuli K'ost'iumi (VI-XIVss.)* [Georgian Costume (VIth-XIVth centuries)]. Tbilisi: Academy Press.

Dumézil, G. 1931. *La Langue des Oubykhs.* Paris: Sociéte de Linguistique de Paris.

Dzhavakhishvili, I. (ed.) 1983. *Masalebi sakartvelos šinamrec'velobisa da xelosnobis ist'oriisatvis* [Materials for the History of the Domestic Industry and Craftsmanship of Georgia], III.1. Tbilisi: Mecniereba.

Gadzhieva, S. 1981. *Odežda Narodov Dagestana* [Dress of the Peoples of Daghestan]. Moscow: Nauka.

Gersamia, T. 1984. *Jveli Tbilisi* [Old Tbilisi]. Tbilisi: Sabč'ota Šakastvelo.

Giorgadze, B. (ed.) 1977. *Don k'rist'oporo de k'ast'eli: cnobebi da albomi sakartvelos šesaxeb* [Don Christoforo De Castelli: Reports and Album about Georgia]. Tbilisi: Mecniereba.

Gogebashvili, I. 1976. *Bunebis k'ari* [Nature's Door], facsimile of the 1912 edition. Tbilisi: Ganatleba.

Inal-Ipa, Sh. 1965. *Abxazy* [Abkhazians]. Sukhum: Alashara.

Kibrik, A. & Kodzasov, S. 1990. *Sopostavitel'noe Izučenie Dagestanskix Jazykov: Imja. Fonetika* [Comparative Study of the Daghestanian Languages: The Noun. Phonetics]. Moscow: University Press.

Lamberti, Don Archengelo 1990. *Samegrelos Aγc'era* [Description of Mingrelia]. Translated by A. Č'q'onia. Tbilisi: Aiet'i. First published 1901, reprinted 1938.

Mak'alatia, S. 1984. *Xevsureti* [Khevsureti]. Tbilisi: Nak'aduli

Malija, E. 1985. *Ukrašenie Odeždy u Abxazov* [Ornamentation of Clothing among the Abkhazians]. Sukhum: Alashara.

Malija, E. & Akaba, L. 1982. *Odežda i Žilišče Abxazov* [Clothing and Dwelling of the Abkhazians]. Tbilisi: Mecniereba.

Shagirov, A. 1977. *Étimologičeskij Slovar' Adygskix (Čerkesskix) Jazykov* [Etymological Dictionary of the Adyghe (Cherkess) Languages], in 2 vols. Moscow: Nauka.

Vogt, H. 1963. *Dictionnaire de la Langue Oubykh.* Oslo: Universitetsforlaget.

# Chapter Seven

# Fashions and Styles: Maltese Women's Headdress

*Dionisius Albertus Agius*

Lexical information on the subject of headdress in the Maltese language is limited and the researcher who wishes to pursue this subject in detail is confronted with several linguistic and historical problems. There is no information on the early medieval Maltese attire and it is only from the sixteenth century onwards that travellers to the Maltese islands start to make sporadic comments on dress. Historically, the subject of costumes in Malta was dealt with by Cassar-Pullicino (1966: 149–216) with accessible data drawn from documents, deeds and travel literature. However, an adequate linguistic inquiry on Maltese dress terms, in particular those dealing with head covering is lacking.

It is, therefore, the aim of this paper to investigate these dress-terms in the Maltese language. Though historically evidence points (at least with some terms) to Romance origins, linguistically, our terminology shows, in general, an Arabic rooted base. This could have come from a nomenclature directly linked with North African Arabic or Siculo Arabic, the latter being a language once spoken by Sicilian Muslims and Sicilian Christians and Jews acculturated to Islam during the Arabo-Islamic domination (213–485/ 827–1091) and continued, though with a lesser impact, during the Norman rule (485–681/1091–1282).

## Interpreting Headcovering

Styles of head coverings may be governed in general by climate, available materials, as well as customs and traditions which often come under the dictates of religions. An ancient practice, particularly in the Middle East and North Africa, head covering was a mark of modesty and respect for both men and women; and, for women, it was often not only the head that women covered but also the face.

Styles of head covering around the Mediterranean may have originated from further east. It does seem that this fashion, for whatever reasons, protective or ceremonial or both, has travelled with the spread of Islam from the east to North Africa and thence to Spain and Sicily. In North Africa, Arabs and Berbers, men and women have for centuries worn flowing robes and head coverings that indicated the status of the wearer as well as the tribe that he/she belonged to. The tenth century geographer and traveller al-Muqaddasī (d. 378/988–9) (1906, 239) noticed that Maghribīs followed the Egyptian fashion of dress, which suggests that (presumably al-Muqaddasī is reporting on urbanized *Maghribīs*) all along the North African coast there was a common mode of dress. Up to the present day North Africans have not greatly modified their style of dress since the early medieval period, though social mobility, as Stillman (1976, 583) observed, precipitates changes in attire. Among North African women, dress styles, and particularly the number of headcoverings that exist, have changed less than men's, suggesting the degree of their seclusion or protection (but cf. p.107 above and other arguments (pp.12–13; 29; 71) about women's dress. To an extent, this is also true of the Maltese islands, albeit on a smaller scale, right up to the late fifties Consequently a great variety of terms for mantles, veils and enveloping wraps is represented in the language.

The Maltese islands, consisting of Malta, Gozo *(Ghawdex)* and Comino *(Kemmuna)*, with an area of 122 square miles and a population of less than a quarter of a million, are located 60 miles south of Sicily and about 200 miles north of the Libyan coast. Maltese, the language of Malta shares the morphological features of Arabic (largely the North African dialects) but has also been affected by Sicilian lexically, syntactically and idiomatically.

## Early North African Influences

The ethno-linguistic information found in the travel literature points overwhelmingly to a North African fashion, which reflects the social, economic and religious status of Maltese women; the country women retaining a much more constant and conservative style of dress than the urbanized women who were open to all sorts of influences especially during the rule of the Order of St. John (1530–1798), better known as the Knights of Malta. Throughout the sixteenth and seventeenth centuries, travellers described Maltese women as being veiled (Cassar-Pullicino 1976, 136) and classified them as Moors, such as in the account given by De Nicolay around 1576 (*idem*, 1966, 186). The veil or mantle was worn from head to foot covering their face, a fashion, wrote Davity in 1660s, found among city and country women as well as slaves (*ibid*). What needs emphasizing here is that it was not only their heads that Maltese women were covering in those times but that, as a visitor to Malta in 1677 noticed, one eye only was left free to peep through a small opening (Semprini 1934, 109–10). In general, accounts seem to agree on the fact that women in Malta went about veiled after the 'Oriental fashion', which actually meant in a North African style. A few travel accounts, nonetheless, reported that the women's attire was styled after the Sicilian fashion and that they looked similar to Sicilians in many respects (Cassar-Pullicino 1976: 136). Yet, a general look at how Sicilian women dressed, particularly on the east coast of the island, shows overwhelmingly North African features. Women in Syracuse and Catania, for example, dressed in black and covered their faces with a black peak, the significance of which is that eastern Sicily, up to the late seventeenth century, still followed the North African vogue in style. Eastern Sicily was at a cross road of Byzantine and Arab influences during both the Islamic and Norman periods and the wearing of mantle or veil was a result of merging of cultures.

Historically, the islands of Malta and Gozo shared a common style of dress with North Africans and Sicilians, the latter, seemingly, from the sixteenth century onwards. Sicilian women, in their turn, as contemporary travellers' accounts pointed out, continued to follow the 'Oriental fashion'. In other words, the Maltese fashion of headdress, particularly among urbanized women, though it tended to become Sicilian in style, never lost its distinctive North African features. With country women, the style was predominantly North African. Du Mont, visiting Malta at the end of the seventeenth century, wrote that: 'the peasants are as black as Egyptians ...'. His lively account of Maltese women is quite remarkable:

> In the streets you see nothing but a long black veil instead of a woman, which covers them so entirely from head to foot ... [they] in this city [of Valletta] look just like so many ghosts wrap[ped] in shrouds, stalking about the streets (*idem*, 1966, 188).

Covering the head and face brought about abuses by loose women towards the second part of the seventeenth century. The Maltese *manta* (s.v.), which was in vogue at that time, was prohibited at night by a magisterial *bando* after many reports reaching the Grand Masters of the Order, namely Fra Nicola Cotoner (1663–1680) and Fra Gregorio Carafa (1680–1690), that the Knights, who were under the vow of chastity, were making assignations with women covered with *mantas* (Spreti 1949, 38). This may have given rise to the Maltese proverb *hemm dwieb tal-ghenienel u bil-mantiet* 'there are women of loose morals in every class of society wearing *ghonnellas* [s.v.] and *mantas* [s.v.]' (Aquilina: 1972, 153; Cassar Pullicino: 1976, 150, n. 50).

From the descriptions of eighteenth century travellers' accounts we do not seem to have women going about with downcast heads and wrapped from top of the head to their feet, covering their face except their eyes. The *faldetta* (s.v), a sort of short cloak, and the *ghonnella* (s.v.), a mantle covering the head but not the face, are now being mentioned in contemporary accounts.

The colour of these *ghonnellas* varied from usage in the city, town and country side. For example Agius de Soldanis (d. 1770), a lexicographer and an ethno-linguist (Agius 1990: 172–3), noted that, of olden times, the wearing of white *ghonnellas* was the urban colour compared to green in rural areas. In his times also, black was the colour for both urban and rural areas (Cassar-Pullicino 1966: 189). A blue-coloured petticoat with white stripes was the *geżwira* (s.v.), a variant of the *faldetta*, which was used in doors, while the *ċulqana* (s.v.), another type of *ghonnella* was made of blue cotton covered with white spots (Cassar-Pullicino 1976: 149). From the twenties up to late fifties the black *ghonnella* dominated the streets of towns and villages; country women continued to follow this fashion when the educated class were gradually dropping the wearing of this headdress. After the fifties, it became exclusively a head cover of a laywomen's religious organization, known as Tal-Mużew, who for decades, until the early seventies, kept the fashion alive. The abandoning of the black *ghonnella* and the *velu* (s.v.) came about during a time when the Roman Catholic Church was undergoing changes in accordance with the Ecumenical Council decisions which took place in the Vatican in the early sixties. One change revolutionized fashion in Malta; Maltese women were now allowed to go to church unveiled. In some way the black *ghonnella* and the *velu* symbolized the end of a history of headcovering on the islands.

The eighteenth and nineteenth century Maltese travel literature provides us with information on the use of headdress terms such as *ċulqana*, *faldetta*, *ghonnella* and *geżwira* (s.v.), which are relics of the recent past. Their description is undoubtedly valuable but, for the linguist, this information may obstruct some possible alternative derivations which, because of the late Romance influence or interference, become totally obscure. The investigation into an Arabic origin cannot be sought in the description of Maltese folk life of the early travellers' accounts. Often these sources are lacking terms such as, *mustaxija*, *radda*, *star* and *xedd* (s.v.) and, it is virtually impossible to tell which particular headdress they are referring to, let alone attempt to reconstruct morphologically the history of the terms concerned.

Lexicographical works such as those of Ġan Pjer Franġisk Agius de Soldanis and Mikiel Anton Vassalli (d. 1829), whose systematic approach and detailed information are worth mentioning, present us with an important alternative in tracing the history of these terms (Agius 1990, 172–3). Both Serracino Inglott (d. 1983) in his nine volume *Il-Miklem Malti* (Malta 1975–1989) and Aquilina's two volume *Maltese-English Dictionary* (Malta 1987–1990) have thoroughly researched the lexicographical data left by their predecessors. Their work has opened our way better to understand the historical and linguistic background behind rare terms, such as *futjana, kurkar, leff, mleff, mallut* and *terħa* (s.v.). Their works together with Dozy (d. 1883)'s *Supplément aux dictionnaires arabes* (Leiden 1967, Volumes I-II) and the *Dictionnaire détaillé des noms des vêtements* (Beirut, 1845) are useful tools for comparative research with Arabic dress terms.

## The Terminological Links

What follows is a discussion of terms relating to women's headdress in Maltese, investigating their historical and linguistic links with Arabic and the Romance languages. Each Maltese term, underlined and written in the current orthographic system, is followed by a corresponding phonetic transcription between slashes. Arabic terms are italicized and represented phonetically and other terms, also italicized, are given as found in sources. Abbreviations: a. year; Ar. Arabic; c. about; fl. flourished; Mal. Maltese; p plural; s singular; SA Siculo Arabic, s.v. term listed under the heading; > becoming; < deriving from.

Mal *ċulqana* /čul'āna/ (s), *ċlieqen* /člī'en/ (p) is a long loose garment of blue cotton covered with white spots or sometimes with a flowery design, worn by peasants (Aquilina: 1987: I, 188) on the east coast of Malta. It is probably traced to Graeco-Latin origin *kefalos-kano* 'weather rural cape' (Cassar-Pullicino: 1966: 206) or Byzantine *cefalkana* (*idem*, 1976: 147). Badger (1858: 126) described the *ċulqana* as a headdress worn by country women, generally striped and used instead of a *ghonnella* (s.v.). It is quite possible, as Laferla (1913: 19) noted, that the term originates from Arabic *šarqāna* and then into Maltese */shur'āna/*, giving the present usage, *ċulqana* (where liquids /r/ and /l/ interchange), a word signifying 'eastern or Oriental woman' (Luke 1949: 26).

This head cover may have been an early type of dress which predates the *faldetta* (s.v) and the *ghonnella* (s.v.). What is significant about the *ċulqana* is the colour blue which, compared to the later black *faldetta* and *ghonnella* indicates a possible medieval style traced back as far as the Arabo-Norman rule (870–1282), during the latter part of which Sicily and Malta had strong trade links with, among other places, Fatimid (458–567/969–1171) and later Ayyubid (564–650/1169–1252) Egypt. A striking feature in these times was that Christian women wore blue veiled garments, as al-Suyūṭī (d. 911/1505–6) reported (Stillman 1976, 582).

The point to make here is that occasionally Islamic caliphs or governors did impose on minorities the wearing of different colours to distinguish themselves from the Muslim community. If we assume that villages hold fast to tradition and they are the last to change and adapt newer fashions, the fact that only village women in eastern Malta wore the blue *ċulqana* suggests it is a very old custom. A watercolour by David Rose (d. 1964) illustrates beautifully a country girl who is wearing the blue *culqana* and is standing by her betrothed who is playing the guitar (De Piro 1988, 170, no 3; see Fig. 25).

Mal *faldetta* /faldetta/ (s), *faldetti* /faldetti/ (p), is a term not recorded in Maltese lexica. It is used variably with *għonnella* (s.v.). Originally, it seems that *faldetta*, as early as seventeenth century, meant a skirt (Cassar-Pullicino 1966: 187); it developed into a combined hood and cape by the eighteenth or nineteenth century. It was described as a short cloak gathered into plaits on one side only, completely enveloping the back with a half-moon shape on the right, and held in the left hand (Griffith & Griffith 1845: 105 ). It was only worn when attending church functions (Miège 1840: I, 179), and women of all classes wore this attire (*ibid*). The *faldetta*, historically, was white or green in the countryside and, later, black in the city.

**Figure 25** Drawing by Ruard Absaroka from David Rose (1871–1964) 'The Blue Faldetta', a watercolour of a country girl wearing the blue *ċulqana* headdress with her betrothed (De Piro 170, no 3)

It looks possible that the term originated from medieval Latin *faldilla* or *falda* meaning 'fold of cloth, skirt', but also possible that Maltese /fald-etta/ is connected to Arabic *farda* (with shifting of liquids /l/ and /r/) meaning 'a piece of woollen cloth' (Dozy 1967: II, 251). By extension, it came to mean in Maltese a type of skirt and later came to be understood as a head cover; but equally possible, as Dessoulavy (1938, 20) suggested, that there may be a connection with the Arabic *faḍlā'*, 'a piece of cloth fabricated in Tunisia and Algeria' (Dozy 1967: II, 267), in which /ḍ/ switches with /l/ and *hamza* drops, to produce Maltese *falda*, meaning an elongated part of a skirt trailing behind on the ground (see Fig. 26). A series of watercolours representing women in *faldetta*s by Carlo Camilleri highlights the trailing *faldas*, a feature not well illustrated by his contemporary artists (De Piro 1988: 47, 3–6). It is probable that the train of the woman's dress came to be used as a head covering, hence the term *falda*. A smaller version was called *faldetta*.

A further confusion arose with the Maltese term *faldar/fardal* (note the liquids /l/ and /r/ are common shifts but the final liquid being intrusive),

**Figure 26** Drawing by Ruard Absaroka from Carlo Camilleri (fl. 1900), 'The Faldetta', a watercolour depicting a woman in *għonnella* headdress wearing the *faldetta skirt* and a trailing *falda* (De Piro 47, no 4)

meaning apron. It was worn on top of the skirt which corresponds, to some extent, with the Arabic *faḍla* (without the *hamza*) given to mean clothes in 'addition over and above clothes that are used on various occasions' (Lane 1984: II, 2413); although it is more directly related semantically, but perhaps not morphologically, to the Arabic *fuḍal* meaning 'a smock used for work or home or night' (Pellegrini 1972: I, 176) and loaned into Siculo Arabic *fadali* or *fodali* 'apron, smock' (*ibid*).

Finally, Maltese */farda/ or */falda/ merged with an earlier or later Romance term *falda* and with the Sicilian/Italian diminutive suffix /-etta/ made it into *faldetta*. The Arabic etymology has been proposed as an alternative to the already existing assumption that Maltese *faldetta*, linguistically and semantically, comes from Sicilian/Italian *faldetta*. There are two possibilities. Either the earlier generic Arabic meaning of 'a piece of cloth' referring to some material for making a skirt or dress, the base for the Maltese-Arabic rooted *falda*, merged with Sicilian/Italian *falda*, meaning a fold of cloth and then suffixed to the diminutive /-etta/, or, both terms, Maltese-Arabic */falda/farda/ and Maltese-Romance *faldetta* existed independently of each other and fused ultimately by the seventeenth or eighteenth century, as recorded by our travel accounts, to mean a kind of pleated skirt. Changes may have occurred after the fifteenth century and, as Cremona noted, the Maltese *faldetta* since then underwent some evolution in shape and material (Cassar-Pullicino 1966: 206). What is significant, however, is how the fashion of wearing a styled skirt *faldetta* developed into a head cover.

Mal *futjana* /futyāna/ (s), *futjaniet* /futyānīt/ (p) 'a kind of white-streaked sash worn by country people round their head like a turban' (Aquilina 1987: I, 371). It is also, according to Barbera (1939–1940: II, 380), though his lexicon is to be used with caution, a long embroidered veil worn by women. No mention of *futjana* is found in travel literature. It comes from Arabic *fūṭa*, a kind of turban, according to al-Maqrīzī (d. 845/1441–2) (Dozy 1845: 342), which is traced back to Sindī *pūta* 'waist wrapper' (Lane 1984: II, 2459); see Maltese *terḥa*.

Mal *geżwira* /geżwīra/ (s), *geżwiriet, gżiewer* /geżwirīt/ gżīwer/ (p) 'a woman's long dress wrapped round the body like the sari worn by Indian women' (Aquilina 1987: I, 434). It is a variant of the *faldetta* (s.v.) for use in the house. In his account of nineteenth century Malta, Badger (1858: 125–6) wrote that *gezwira* was worn on particular occasions such as marriage or a christening. He described it as 'a kind of petticoat of blue cotton striped with white, done up in very thick creases round the waist, and open on the right side, where it is tied at different distances with bows of ribbon'. The term is related to the Arabic '*īzār*, one of the meanings of which, is a garment worn from waist downwards, but it also means a woman's long veil which is wrapped around the body (Dozy 1967: I, 19), and Arabic *mi'zar* is a cloak or mantle (Dozy: 1845, 41). Maltese *geżwira* seems to be a diminutive form of the Arabic '*īzār*, assuming the Maltese form */zwayra/.

Some Maltese diminutives employ /w/ as though it were the second radical (eg. Mal /rās/ > /rwaysa/ 'little head', Mal /šitān/ 'devil' > /šwayten/ 'imp'). Diphthong /-ay-/ became an elongated /ī/, and /ʾ/ developed firstly into /we-/ and then /ge-/ (note Mal /gedwed/ 'to gabble, mumble' < Ar *wadwada* 'to hasten, hurry', Mal /gedidu/ 'darling, pet' < Ar *wadūd* '[devoted, friendly]' [Aquilina 1987, I, 429, 436]), giving finally the present word *geżwira* (see Fig. 27); compare semantically Arabic *wizra* given by Hava 'short garment' and Arabic *wazra* by Beaussier 'a small woolen *haïk* with which women wrap themselves when they go out' (*ibid.*, 434). See Maltese *liżar*.

Mal <u>*kurkar*</u> /kurkār/ (s), *kurkariet* /kurkārīt/ (p) 'trailing veil' which female mourners wore in the presence of the deceased (Cremona 1973: 301) from the verb *karkar* 'to drag along' and ultimately from Arabic, according to Beaussier, *karkara* 'to drag, draw, pull along' (Aquilina 1987: I, 623); see Maltese *star, velu*.

Mal <u>*leff*</u> /leff/ (s), *leffiet* /leffīt/ (p) 'a shawl; a garment in which one wraps up oneself' (Aquilina 1987: I, 735; Serracino-Inglott 1975–1989: V, 268)

**Figure 27** Drawing by Ruard Absaroka from Carlo Camilleri (fl. 1900), 'The Country Girl', a watercolour showing a country girl wearing a *geżwira* and a *manta* with vertical blue stripes (De Piro 47, no 8)

from Arabic *laffa* 'to wrap up', also *mleff*, a head cover from Arabic *milaffa*, a woman's veil (Dozy 1845: 403). Note the Siculo Arabic verb *alliffari* meaning 'the way one adjusts the turban' (Pellegrini 1972: I, 220) ; but also, Maltese *leff* could be a derivation from Arabic *lifā'* which is like a long veil that covers the woman's body, similar in meaning to *milḥafa* (Ibn Durayd 1925–1926: III, 127), a term passed directly into Siculo Arabic with the Greek *mélxafen* (Caracausi 1983: 286). A possible example of a *leff* or *mleff* is found in a watercolour of a country woman by Sebastiano Ittar (d. 1847) (De Piro 1988: 122, no 2). The shape and style of the *leff/ mleff* (Fig. 28) is an early survivor of what later was called *għonnella* (s.v.) or understood by some as *faldetta* (s.v.).

Mal *liżar* /lizār/ (s), *lożor* /lozor/ (p) is a long mantle, according to Vassalli (Dozy 1845: 34) deriving from Arabic *'izār*, a long veil or mantle which women wrapped around their body, a fashion, still in use in North Africa (Barbera 1939–1940: II, 643–644). It was survived by the Maltese, *leff/mleff* (s.v.), *manta* (s.v.) and later the *għonnella* (s.v.).

**Figure 28** Drawing by Ruard Absaroka from Sebastiano Ittar (*c.* 1780–1847) 'Donna del Gozzo', a watercolour of a Gozitan woman with a red and white striped *faldetta*, a *faldar*, a possible *leff* (an early survival of the *għonnella*) and a *maktur* (or *mendil/mindil*) (De Piro 122, no 2)

Mal *maktur* /maktūr/ (s), *mkatar* /imkātar/ (p) 'women's kerchief, scarf' (Aquilina 1990: II, 772); also known as *maktur tar-ras* 'a head scarf' that women wore for church (Serracino Inglott 1975–1989: VI, 29). Originally from Sicilian *maccaturi* (Aquilina *op.cit.*). The Maltese *maktur* is probably a later version of Maltese *mendil/ mindil*, the meaning of which was a scarf or veil (Dozy 1845: 415–6); women wearing the headscarf styled *maktur* or *mendil/ mindil* are beautifully depicted in lithographs by Bellanti (d. 1883) (De Piro 1988: 21, nos 4 and 6; see Figs 29 and 30). See Maltese *velu* and *mustaxija*.

Mal *mallut* /mallūt/ (s), *mlalet* /imlālet/ (p) worn in Malta at one time as recorded by Vassalli (Dozy 1845: 412–3); it is a cape with a hood used in mourning or by an old woman, but also worn by a monk (Serracino-Inglott 1975–1989: VI, 32). It may have originally referred to a woman's veil as is the case with the Spanish *marlota* (Dozy 1845: 413). The Maltese *mallut* fell into disuse two hundred years ago (Serracino-Inglott 1975–1989: VI, 32) and may have been very popular during the Aragonese and the Castillian periods (1283–1530) during the time of which political, religious and trade links were strong with Malta, Sicily and Spain. *Mallut* comes

**Figure 29** Drawing by Ruard Absaroka from Michele Bellanti (1807–1883) 'The Cart', a lithograph showing three women on a cart wearing the *maktur* (or *mendil/mindil*) around their neck. The woman, on the right, is probably wearing a later version of the eighteenth century *manta* which then became the *għonnella* (De Piro 21, no 4)

**Figure 30** Drawing by Ruard Absaroka from Michele Bellanti (1807–883) 'Country Woman', a lithograph of a country woman on a horse wearing an *ghonnella* with a dark brown horizontal striped *faldetta* skirt and wrapped in a *maktur* (or *mendil/ mindil*) (De Piro 21, no 6)

from Arabic *mallūṭa* which, in its turn, Dozy seems to think, derived from Greek, mallotè (Dozy 1845: 412).

Mal *manta* /manta/ (s), *mantijiet* /mantiyīt/ (p) is defined by Agius de Soldanis (MS 143: fol. 344v) in eighteenth century Malta as a black silk veil which a woman wore from head to foot covering the face except the eyes. All city women carried a *manta* to which a *pizzo*, 'a piece of lace' was attached protruding in a point form on the forehead. The *manta* corresponds with the Sicilian *manto* which is of 'oriental' origin (Cassar-Pullicino 1966: 162). In some way, both the Maltese *manta* and the Sicilian *manto* resemble the North African and Spanish *ḥayk* or *ḥā'ik* which was a square woollen cloth large enough to envelop the whole figure (Dozy 1845:

147–53). City women put on white mantles in Palermo and country women wore them black, while in Catania women wore embroidered mantles and others wore them black or red. In the countryside around Catania the peasant women generally covered themselves with blue woollen *manti* (*ibid*). Hardly any colour has been mentioned in the Maltese tradition of wearing *manta*s, though, it seems from other types of head covers that the general pattern was white in cities and blue in the countryside, while black was common for both as it was the case in Sicily. One example that depicts a black woollen *manta* in Malta is a pastel of a Maltese lady (Fig. 31) by the Swiss artist Jean Etienne Liotard (d. 1789) (De Piro 1988: 134). Seventeenth and eighteenth century visitors to Malta described the *manta* as a veil after the Moorish (i.e. North African) fashion and a *mantilla* in the Spanish and Sicilian style was worn when Maltese women of higher class went abroad. The visitors were struck by the *pizzo* of the Maltese *manta* jutting out on the women's forehead (*ibid*.: 163). It was the style in seventeenth and eighteenth century Malta for all women to wear the *manta*,

**Figure 31** Drawing by Ruard Absaroka from Jean Etienne Liotard (1702–1789) 'Maltese Lady', a pastel of a Maltese lady showing a short black woollen *manta* (De Piro 134, no 1)

including slaves, the latter being remarkably the only observation that exists, among the travel accounts on Malta, on slaves' style of wearing *manta*s (Cassar-Pullicino 1966: 187). An intriguing water-colour picture by Vincenzo Fenech (fl. late 18th and early 19th century) depicts a Maltese lady with servant and slave, all wearing a long black veiled *manta* (De Piro 1988: 92). The painting refers to an ancient Maltese costume which, according to our travel accounts, can be dated to the sixteenth and seventeenth centuries.

Also found in Maltese is *mantell*, 'a mantle; cloak cape; a woman's long cloak' (Aquilina 1990: II, 779) or *mantilja*, 'woman's cloak (*ibid*); another similar cloak, but worn by men, is the *mantar*, probably directly from Siculo Arabic *mantarru* and the *mantarra* used by women in Corleone and Palermo, both originating from Arabic *mimṭār* 'a garment of wool worn in rain' (Pellegrini 1972: I, 179; Lane 1984: II, 2722).

The term *manta* is a direct borrowing from Latin *mantum*; it seems that the Maltese *manta* replaced the very early use of the *liżar* (s.v.) and *leff/mleff* (s.v.). In its decline, the *manta* was survived by the *ghonnella* (s.v.) or, as it is believed by some, the *faldetta* (s.v.), in the latter part of the eighteenth century. What distinguished the *manta* from other head covers is the lace work involved in the making of the mantle. Not all *manta*s had lace work and the ones that had were used on ceremonial occasions. Today, a version of this headdress is the *mant* which is a small mantle or veil made of black lace, or a bridal veil or a small white veil worn by girls in the first Holy Communion (Aquilina 1990: II, 779; Serracino-Inglott 1975–1979: VI, 42).

Mal *mustaxija* /mustāšiyya/ (s), *mustaxijiet* /mustāšiyyīt/ (p) is a woman's garment which is wrapped around the face and body (Serracino-Inglott 1975–1989: VI, 226), the style of which is that of the Maltese *liżar* (s.v.). It later became to mean a veil, generally made of black silk, better known as *mustaxija tal-għarusa* 'the bride's veil' (Cassar-Pullicino 1976: 23). It is traced by Kazimirski to Arabic *mustaghshiya* (Form X, passive participle) of the verb *ghashiya* 'to cover, conceal' (Aquilina 1990: II, 873; Serracino-Inglott, *ibid*).

Mal *ghonnella* /onnella/ (s), *għenienel*/enīnel/ (p) is described as a '*faldetta*, a rustic headgear of a village woman, now out of use' (Aquilina 1990: II, 1005); the reference to *faldetta* (s.v.) is essentially a skirt and the extra material of this skirt was used to cover the head in particular when women went to church (Serracino-Inglott 1975–1989: III, 228–9). According to Agius de Soldanis, on festive occasions Maltese women wore a *faldetta* and a headgear called *gonnella* (i.e. *ghonnella*). A confusion followed in the use of the terms *faldetta* and *ghonnella*, and it seems that both terms were used variably to mean head cover (Griffith & Griffith *et al.* 1845: 103–5). Badger's (1858: 124–5) detailed description of this head-dress is worth noting: the *faldetta* is a generic term to mean a black silk petticoat often called *nofs ghonnella* 'half *ghonnella*' while the upper part is called the *ghonnella*, the actual head cover. It is made of black silk 'drawn up into neat gathers for the length of a foot about the centre of one of the outer seams. In the seam of one of the remaining divisions is enclosed a thin piece of whalebone, which is drawn over the head, and forms an elegant arch' (*ibid*) (see Fig. 32). An even finer distinction of terms is given by Laferla (1913: 19); *Ghonnella ta' fuq* is the skirt worn over the *ghonnella ta' taht*, the underskirt and *ghonnella ta' fuq ir-ras* (or *nofs ghonnella*) 'the head *ghonnella* (or half *ghonnella*)' is the skirt for over the head; the latter is what has been referred to as the *faldetta*. The *ghonnella ta' fuq ir-ras*, to use the right terminology, took the shape of a black silk mantle reaching to the feet. Caruana Dingli's (d. 1950) oil and watercolour paintings of women in *ghonnellas* (mostly coveted by Maltese collectors) fit well in this description (De Piro 1988: 54–5, nos 1–2). Some *ghonnellas* were embroidered all round with gold and a velvet ribbon tied the edge of the seams below the knees (Laferla 1913: 19).

The colour of this voluminous hood was black everywhere save in the villages of Żabbar and Żejtun in Malta, where it was blue and called

**Figure 32** Drawing by Ruard Absaroka from Albert William Crawford McFall (1862–1923) 'St. John's' a watercolour of Maltese women with whaleboned arched *ghonnellas* at St. John's Cathedral (De Piro 137, no 8)

*ćulqana* (s.v.). In its shape, there is no doubt historically that the *ghonnella* owes its origin to oriental influence. It is assumed that the term came from Italian *gonnella* or Sicilian *unnèdda* (liquid /ll/ becomes post alveolar emphatic /dd/ in several Sicilian words) meaning 'skirt petticoat' (Serracino-Inglott 1975–1989: III, 228–9). The possibility of looking into the Arabic origin for the term *ghonnella* may not be remote if one were to relate it to the word *qinā'*, a 'kind of face veil; a portion of which is placed over the head, beneath the *'izār*, the rest hanging down in front, to the waist, or thereabout, and entirely concealing the face' (*The Thousand and One Nights* I, 190); it seems, according to Arazi (1976: 149) that, the *qinā'* was rectangular in shape (cf. the early Maltese *manta* [s.v.] and the North African *hayk*). It is proposed that Arabic /q/ of *qinā'* became Maltese */'/, pharyngealized at one time but lost over the past two hundred years, though the shifting of Arabic /q/ to Maltese occurs rarely (eg. Ar *qult* > Mal *ghidt* /ētt/ 'I said' [note the pharyngealized long vowel /ē/]. What we have now is a possible Maltese *\*'ina* /īna/ for Arabic *qinā'* (where final Arabic *alif* and /'/ drop in Maltese). A later fusion of Arabic and Italian/Sicilian occurred probably by the sixteenth or seventeenth century with the suffixing of the diminutive /-ella/ to make an *\*ghinella* /īnella/ becoming finally the present *ghonnella*. This development may have occurred in a time when the Italian/Sicilian *gonnella/unnèdda* was imported into the islands during the rule of the Order of St John. Worth noting is the medieval Spanish *alquinal* 'a kind of veil' from Arabic *qinā'* (Steiger 1991: 211).

Mal *radda* /radda/ (s), *raddi* /raddi/ (p) and *raddiet* /raddīt/ (counted plural) 'the black silk edging on a woman's scarf or mantle' (Aquilina 1990: II, 1173), perhaps, as proposed by Dessoulavy (1938: 95), a mantle from Arabic *ridā'* (Dozy 1845: 59): also, found in medieval Spanish Arabic denoting 'veil' (Corriente 1991: 82). A bridal veil with lace sewn round its edge is called in Maltese *mant tar-radda*; see Maltese *star, velu*.

Mal *skufja* /skūfya/ (s), *skufji* /skūfyi/ (p) is a 'cap, coif' (Aquilina 1990: II, 1335), a type of close-fitting hoodlike cap. Prior to the eighteenth century, Agius de Soldanis (MS 143, fol. 455v) remarked, Maltese women used to wear a 'particular coif' which later developed in the style of the Maltese *manta* (s.v.) that city women wore. The term *skufja* may have come from the Tunisian *šqūfiyya/qūfiyya* a 'women's bonnet' (Stillman 1976: 746), but also Arabic *kūfiyya*, which is a rectangular cotton or silk veil pleated diagonally and placed on the head with two pointed corners on each side of the shoulder (Dozy 1967: II, 500); the purpose of these two pointed corners was to raise one or both of them to the face to protect oneself against the sun's rays, hot wind or to cover oneself from being recognized (Dozy 1845: 394). The origin of this dress term looks clearly a Latin borrowing *cūfia(m)*, which, in turn, is of uncertain origin (Zingarelli 1971: 457). It passed on to several European languages and then into Arabic *via* the medieval Mediterranean trade especially during the eleventh and twelfth century (Dozy 1845: 394). But an Arabic origin should not be totally ignored; for example al-Zabīdī (d. 1205/1790) lists the term under the radicals /k-w-f/, signifying 'a thing that is worn upon the head; so called because of its roundness, or its being round' (Lane 1984: II, 3004; Al-Zabīdī 1987: XXIV, 346) with *kawwafa* 'to reel off' and *kawfan* meaning 'circular' (Al-Zabīdī, 345–6).

Mal *star* /stār/ (s), *stari* /stāri/ (p) and *stariet* /starīt/ (counted plural) 'veil' (Aquilina 1990: II, 1277), also 'a small veil; a laced silk veil' (Serracino-Inglott 1975–1989: VIII, 258–9). It is usually used to denote a 'bridal's veil', *star ta' l-gharusa*. Originally from Arabic *sitār/sitr/satara/ʔistār*, this term means 'anything by which a person or thing is veiled; a veil' (Lane 1984: I, 1304). Dozy makes no mention of this dress term in reference to 'veil'. In the Siculo Arabic we find *sytir*, recorded in *a.* 1248 and *a.* 1279 (Caracausi: 1983, 256–7) which may imply that the Maltese term may have been used as early as the thirteenth century; a cognate term is Maltese *velu* (s.v.).

Mal *terha* /terha/ (s), *triehi* /trīhi/ (p) and *terhiet* /terhīt/ (counted plural) is a scarf-like veil vestment which covers the shoulders and hands worn during High Mass in the Roman Catholic tradition as recorded in Qala, Gozo (Aquilina 1990: II, 1425); it also means a band or sash which country men wore at one time around their waist like a belt (Serracino-Inglott 1975–1989: VIII, 392). A reference is made, however, to a *terha mtarrża*, which in style is similar to a Maltese *futjana* (s.v.), a kind of band worn by country people round their head like a turban (*ibid*; Aquilina 1987: I, 371). It comes from Arabic *tarha* denoting a headdress. The custom of wearing this head cover on the shoulders is noted by Dozy (1845: 254). It is found in Arabic sources to mean a woman's veil which is longer than a man's *tarha* (*ibid.*: 257). There is no mention of this word as a woman's veil in Malta and Gozo in any document. However Dapper, around 1686, notes that women wore in the seventeenth century a kind of blue bonnet on top of their hood (Cassar-Pullicino 1966: 187); this may be similar to the dark blue *tarha* made of muslin or flax worn by country women as described by Dozy (Dozy 1845: 261). We find in Siculo Arabic the term *tarca* (note SA /c/ graphemically represents Ar /ḫ/), signifying 'black veil', used once by women as a sign of mourning as recorded in *a.* 1015 (Pellegrini 1972: I, 181; Caracausi 1983: 367–8). This may have been the case in Malta during the Arab and Norman periods. The custom of wearing a *tarha* in nineteenth century Egypt is best described as a 'kind of head-veil worn by women, the two ends of which generally hang down behind, nearly reaching to the ground; but it is often worn in another manner, about a quarter of it hanging down behind, and the remainder being turned over the head, and under the chin, and over the head again, so that the middle part covers the bosom, and both ends hang down behind' (Lane 1984: II, 1837). The Maltese *leff/mleff* (s.v.) could have been a development of a once existing Maltese *terha*.

Mal *velu* /velu/ (s) *velijiet* /veliyīt/ (p) 'veil', a word derived from Sicilian *velu* is normally made of light and usually transparent material worn over the head to protect, conceal or decorate the face (Serracino-Inglott 1975– 1989: IX, 6), commonly used, until the sixties, for church functions; a cognate term of Maltese *star* (s.v.) and, possibly, at one time, Maltese *mendil/mindil*.

Mal *xall* /šall/ (s), *xallijiet*, *xalel* /šalliyyīt/šalel/ (p) 'shawl' which, no doubt, comes from Sicilian *sciallu* (Barbera 1939–1940: IV, 1128), or an earlier version of Siculo Arabic *sciallu* (Pellegrini 1972: I, 180); in any case, the word derives from Arabic through Persian *šāl*, 'a shawl or mantle, made of very fine wool of a species of goat common in Tibet' (Steingass 1977: 724). The Maltese *xall* may have been used as a headdress, an alternative to the *star* (s.v.), *velu* (s.v.) or *maktur* (s.v.) but also, if long, to the Maltese *manta* (s.v.). Nowadays a *xall* is wrapped on one's shoulders, normally used in winter by women and over the head when it gets cold. A cognate term is the Maltese *mleff* from Arabic *milaffa* used as a woman's headdress (*leff* [s.v.]), but today it is used by males and females as a comforter worn around the head and neck (Serracino-Inglott 1975–1989: VI, 180; IX, 62).

Mal *xedd* /šedd/ (s), *xeddiet* /šeddīt/ (p) has the meaning of 'wearing (of dress)' (Aquilina 1984, II, 1554); it also refers to something that fastens clothes which could mean a ribbon or band etc. (Serracino-Inglott 1975– 1989, IX: 76). Traced to Arabic *shadd*, it means specifically a muslin or silk band that is wrapped around the turban (Dozy 1967, I: 736) but is also used to cover the neck like a cravat (Dozy 1845: 214–5).

Mal *xuxa* /šūša/ (s), *xuxiet* /šūšīt/ (p) 'long hair; bareheaded' (Aquilina 1990: II, 1587), also 'tuft of hair' (Dessoulavy 1938: 140) coming from Arabic *šūša* which, in North Africa, meant not only the hair but also a head cover (*ibid*). For skull cap, the word *šāšiya* is used; a band is wrapped around the cap to form a turban (Dozy 1845: 240). In Siculo Arabic *sciacinë* was used in Calabria and *çiçía* in Pantelleria to signify a hoodlike cap worn by night (Pellegrini 1972: I, 180–1). The Maltese *xuxa* may have referred, at one time, to a skull cap and someone going out without a cap was called *bla xuxa* 'without a cap'; semantically, *xuxa* developed to mean 'bareheaded', when the word *bla* dropped.

## Conclusions

The fact that Maltese, over the centuries, has acquired several terms for women's headdress is significant from both the socio-economic and religious points of view. The history of women's head coverings in Maltese, like any other history of dress, is complex. The lack of documentation prior to the sixteenth century leaves the information on the early history of dress terms patchy. On the linguistic level we may only look at existing dress terms recorded in lexica and speculate on possible links with their original source. In our case the headdress terms seem to show, in general, an Arabic root base, even though on the surface some may appear to be of Romance origin.

An area that needs attention in the study of women's head coverings is the number of illustrations found in travel books and old paintings preserved in parish churches and monasteries or small chapels, the interpretation of which must be reassessed in the hope that more light will be shed on details of Maltese costume. The *Cabrei*, the land registers of the Malta Public Library also provide useful material on this subject. Finally, water-colour drawings by artists Michele Bellanti, Carlo Camilleri and Eduard Caruana Dingli, to mention a few, animate the various life scenes of nineteenth century Malta. All these are visual documents which are indispensable to the reconstruction of Maltese head coverings. Images are not a guarantee of historical discovery but they do provide an aperture through which it is possible to answer linguistic clues.

## Bibliography

Note: Names and titles of books in Arabic follow the Library of Congress System.

Agius, D.A. 1990. '*Il-Miklem Malti*: A contribution to Arabic lexical dialectology', *British Society for Middle Eastern Studies Bulletin*, 17, ii: 171–80.

Agius de Soldanis, Ġ.P.F. *Damma tal kliem kartaginis mscerred fel fom tal-Maltin u Ghaucin* MS 143 Malta Public Library, Valletta, Malta.

*Degli abiti, costumi, sponsali, matrimoni e funerali dei Maltesi.* MS 142, Volume V, Malta Public Library, Valletta, Malta.

Al-Zabīdī, Al-Sayyid Muḥammad Murtaḍā l-Ḥusaynī 1987. *Tāj al'Arūs*, ed. Muṣṭafa Ḥijāzi. Kuwait: Maṭbaʻa Ḥukūmat Kuwayt; Vol. XX1V.

Al-Muqaddasī, Muḥammad b. Aḥmad. 1906. *Aḥsan al-Taqāsīm fī Maʻrifat al-Aqālīm*, ed. M. J. de Goeje. Leiden E. J. Brill; first edited, 1877.

Aquilina, J. 1987–1990. *Maltese-English Dictionary.* Malta: Midsea; Volumes I-II.

—— 1972. *A Comparative Dictionary of Maltese Proverbs.* Malta: The Royal University of Malta.

Arazi, A. 1976. 'Noms de vêtements d'après al-Aḥādīt al-Ḥisān fī Faḍl al-Ṭaylasān', *Arabica*, 23, ii: 109–155.

Arē, R. 1965. 'Quelques remarques sur le costume des musulmanes d'Espagne au temps des Naṣrides', *Arabica*, 12: 244–261.

Badger, G.P. 1858. *Description of Malta and Gozo.* Malta: P. Cumbo; second edition.

Barbera, G.M.D. 1939–1940. *Dizionario maltese-arabo-italiano.* Beirut: Imprimerie Catholique; Volumes I-IV.

Caracausi, G. 1983. *Arabismi medievali di Sicilia.* Palermo: Centro di Studi Filologici e Linguistici Siciliani.

Cassar-Pullicino, J. 1976. *Studies in Maltese Folklore.* Malta: University of Malta.

—— 1966. 'Notes for a history of Maltese costume', *Maltese Folklore Review*, 1, iii: 149–216.

Corriente, Federico 1991. El-Léxico Árabe Estándar y Andalusí del 'Glosario de Leiden'. Madrid: Universidad Complutense.

Cremona, A. 1973. 'Maltese death, mourning and funeral customs', *Maltese Folklore Review*, 1, iv: 301–304.

De Piro, N. 1988. *The International Dictionary of Artists who Painted Malta*. Malta: Said International.

Dessoulavy, C. L. 1938. *A Maltese-Arabic Word-List*. London: Luzac.

Dozy, R. P. A. 1967. *Supplément aux dictionnaires arabes*. Leiden: E. J. Brill; a reprint of 1887 edition, Volumes I-II.

—— 1845. *Dictionnaire détaillé des noms des vêtements*. Beirut: Librairie du Liban; first published in Amsterdam.

Griffith, G.D. and Griffith, L.D. 1845. *A Journey across the Desert, from Ceylon to Marseilles, comprising Sketches of Aden, the Red Sea, Lower Egypt, Malta, Sicily and Italy*. London; Volumes I-II.

Ibn Durayd al-Azdī, Abū Bakr Muḥammad b. al-Ḥasan. 1925–1926. *Kitāb Jamhara fī l-Lugha*. Hyderabad: Dāʾirat al-Maʿārif; Volumes I-IV.

Laferla, A. 1913. 'Ancient customs of Malta', *The Malta Daily Chronicle*, (April): 19.

Luke, H. 1949. *Malta: An Account and an Appreciation*. London: Harrap.

Miège, D. 1840. *Histoire de Malte*. Paris; Volumes I-III.

Naselli, C. 1966. 'Manto siciliano e 'faldetta' maltese', *Maltese Folklore Review*, 1, iii: 217–225.

Lane, E. W. 1984. *Arabic-English Lexicon*. Cambridge: The Islamic Texts Society; first published 1863–1893.

Pellegrini, G. B. 1972. *Gli arabismi nelle lingue neolatine*. Paidea: Brescia; Volumes I-II.

Semprini, G. 1934. 'Malta nella seconda metà del seicento (da un manoscritto del tempo)', *Archivio Storico di Malta*, 4, ii-iv: 97–112.

Serracino-Inglott, E. 1975–1989. *Il-Miklem Malti*. Malta: Klabb Kotba Maltin; Volumes I-IX.

Spreti, C. 1949. *Description of the Island of Malta and a Brief Treatise on Knightly Behaviour written in the Year 1764*. Translated by A. Mackenzie-Grieve. Hertford: S. Austin.

Steiger, A. 1991. *Contribución a la fonética del hispano-árabe y de los arabismos en el ibero-románico y el siciliano*. Madrid: Consejo Superior de Investigaciones Científicas; first published 1932.

Steingass, F. J. 1977. *A Comprehensive Persian-English Dictionary*. New Delhi: Cosmo (Original, London 1892).

Stillman, K. 1986. 'Libās: The Muslim West', *Encyclopaedia of Islam*, Volume V: 742–747: new edition.

—— 1976. 'The importance of the Cairo Geniza manuscripts for the history of medieval female attire', *International Journal of Middle East Studies*, 7: 579–589.

*The Thousand and One Nights*. 1979. Translated by Edward William Lane and edited by Edward S.Poole. London: East-West Publications; first published London-Cairo 1838, Volumes I-III.

Zingarelli, N. 1971. *Vocabolario della lingua italiana*. Milano: Zanichelli; tenth edition.

# Chapter Eight

# The Burqa Face Cover: An Aspect of Dress in Southeastern Arabia

*Dawn Chatty*

More than twenty years ago, Hilda Kuper (1973: 348–367) wrote about the indiscriminate way in which anthropologists dealt with clothing. Some focused on the origin of items of clothing, and the modesty and vanity of human beings. Some (Kroeber 1919: 1940) looked at the relationship between changing fashions and social upheavals. Others, in the Malinowski tradition, described the clothing worn by different people in different situations, and the meaning of changes in clothing styles over time in the colonial situation. What emerged from all these writings was a concept of clothing as a 'universal and visible cultural element consisting of sets of body symbols deliberately designed to convey messages at different social and psychological levels' (1973: 348). In short, personal appearance was consciously manipulated to assert and demarcate differences in status, identity and commitment.

In recent years, the renewed popularity of the face covering (*ḥijāb, niqāb, burguʻ*), worn by increasing numbers of women in the Middle East, has received a great deal of attention. Much analysis has lately been directed at linking the face covering with the resurgence of Islam in the Middle East. The actual significance of facial covering in the context of the totality of Middle Eastern societies is being lost in popular justifications and political explanations of social phenomena.

This study begins with a brief historical review of head covering and veiling in the Middle East. A short summary follows of the major trends in the analysis of the phenomena of female covering. This summary primarily draws on the substantial number of studies available on women in Egypt. The centuries of Mamluk rule, and subsequent colonial encounters with France and Great Britain, put Egypt at the forefront of the major historical movements which were to affect women, their status, their dress and their deportment throughout the Arab World. Finally, this study concentrates on face covering in southeastern Arabia particularly among the remote and marginal pastoral populations of the Sultanate of Oman. It will isolate those personal factors that women consider before they decide how to dress and cover themselves. It will also show the significance of their individual decisions on the larger social groups, and will relate these to the major political, economic and social issues facing their society today.

## Historical Review

The origin of face veiling lies obscured in prehistory. What is certain is that it is pre-Islamic in origin, and appears to have been occasionally in use among the peoples of the southern Mediterranean rim from the Greeks to the Persians. The only exceptions to this generalization appear to be the Egyptians and the Jews (Ahmed 1982: 1992).

> The conquest of Egypt by Persians and Greeks ... relegated ... aristocratic Egyptian women ... to an inferior position like their counterparts in Hellenic society: they were introduced to the customs of seclusion and the veil around the third century B.C. (Marsot, quoted in El-Guindi 1981: 475).

All historical accounts point to the fact that women just prior to and in the early days of Islam in Arabia, and in the countries that came under the influence of the Arabs, played an active role in the social and political life of the community (Ahmed 1992). A study of the Koran and the Hadith show that there is no specific injunction indicating that women should be veiled or secluded from participation in public life (Abdel Kader 1984). However, unwritten traditions do indicate that Mohammed asked his wives to wear face veils to set them apart, to indicate their special status, and to provide them with some social and psychological distance from the throngs that regularly congregated at his homes. The spread of the practice of veiling and general seclusion of women was initially a matter of personal choice, in emulation of Mohammed's wives. Although originally a private matter, which some people adopted and others ignored, it became a widespread custom as the number of slaves and concubines increased (Nelson 1973).

It was about one hundred and fifty years after the death of Mohammed that the system of veiling and the associated practice of seclusion of women was fully accepted among the wealthy classes. Seclusion was the practice of confining women, after puberty, to their own company. Thus women as wives, concubines, and slaves were shut away from other households and watched over by eunuchs (Levy 1965). Veiling, the wearing of a head and face cover in public, thereby became the symbolic expression of the seclusion of women. It was more an urban than a rural phenomenon, as only the wealthy ruling and merchant families could afford a system that regarded women as property, a wealth to be hidden away and kept for private viewing and pleasure. The majority of the population, the working classes and the rural, agrarian population, could put neither veiling nor seclusion into practice. Female labour was too important for the survival of the simple family group and neither seclusion nor veiling could be entertained.

What was clearly encouraged in the Koran as regards the appropriate dress of good Muslim men and women was to be modest in dress, and to cover the head. Thus both women and men were enjoined to cover their hair. In addition, women were expected not to reveal their jewellery when out of their domestic environment. For many this meant covering the upper chest, neck and ears which were typically adorned with jewellery. Throughout the centuries and across the Islamic world this tradition was variously interpreted by different cultures and ethnic communities. In some regions a total and all encompassing body covering was required of women. In other areas a full face veil was considered appropriate. In certain areas and at certain times only a lower face covering was required, while in a few places the complete covering of the hair with a totally exposed face was considered normal dress.

## Major Trends in the Analysis of Female Covering

### Social Status and Economic Privilege

During the early centuries of Islam, head covering and seclusion was an overt indication of the economic success of a woman's family. Only the urban rich could afford the luxury of removing their women from economic toil outside of the household, thus creating – if only in image – an 'idle', leisured class of people. Veiling as an element of dress clearly demonstrated elevated social class, and the practice of seclusion, often indicated by the veil, became a custom to which a few upwardly mobile families aspired.

A few centuries later, during the Mamluk era, veiling and seclusion also came to represent a very real political statement. At the head of Mamluk Egyptian society were the ruling families and their Turko-Circassian military defenders. The Mamluk slaves (both men and women) were imported as children from the area surrounding the Caspian sea, and were then brought up as Muslims. The men were trained in military academies and became soldiers in the different private armies of Mamluk princes. Those who showed promise were given positions of importance in the armies and in the government. But is it was not uncommon for a Mamluk to turn against his master. By killing his master, a Mamluk could take control of the master's other slaves and begin to acquire his own.

The Mamluks formed a distinct military caste. Their reign in Egyptian history was distinguished by its brutality and constant internecine fighting (Hatem 1986: 256). It was of utmost importance to maintain their distance from the rest of the population. In order to do so the Mamluks kept a constant supply of slaves coming in from outside Egypt as well as maintaining large female courts (harems). These were the households in which the upper class women were kept. Most of these wives and concubines were Turco-Circassian, although Ethiopian and African slaves were also part of these princely courts. The particular form of sexual relations these women had with the princes determined their class standing, and women's sexuality became highly politicized within the harem (Hatem 1986: 257). Wives, of which four were permitted by Islam at any one time, had a status higher than a concubine (slave). However the concubine's position changed once she had children. She would ordinarily become free as soon as she bore a son for the master, and often she also was taken as a wife.

## Purity and Virginity: Honour and Shame

By the eighteenth century, women's position in this patriarchal system began to change and veiling became more than an indicator of economic and political status; it was also used to represent purity and virginity. By this time prosperous middle-class households were not very different from those of the ruling Mamluk upper classes, in that they contained both wives and concubines. Middle class women were also veiled and secluded like the upper class women in the elite group. For the Turco-Circassian and Ethiopian slaves seclusion and veiling previously had been a statement only of their status as the valuable property of men. But when veiling was extended to free middle-class women it assumed an entirely different rationale. Whereas virginity had not been particularly important in the decision to marry or purchase a slave, it became a central concern in marriages of free, middle class women. Veiling, seclusion, and restricted physical movement were the expressions of male fears that women's chastity might be endangered and, with it, family honour. The association of the veil with a woman's chastity was such that men came to fear contact with an unveiled woman. Ahmed (1992 113) repeats the story of Hajar (b. 1388), which was recorded by Al-Sakhawi. Hajar had been educated at home by her father and was among the foremost Hadith scholars of her time. But she did not wear the veil when she taught, a practice common among many old women. Al-Sakhawi disapproved of this and refused to study with her.

A great deal of scholarship has been devoted to studying the interrelated concepts of honour, shame, and female virginity (e.g. Peristiany 1966; Antoun 1968; Schneider 1972). It is not possible here to do justice to this field of debate; what is important to this study is how such notions were used to demand modest dress and head covering for women. In some

Islamic interpretations, men and women are regarded as sexual beings and sexuality is highly desirable (Mernissi 1977) as long as it is enjoyed in a socially approved marriage (El Guindi 1981). Over time these ideas became distorted, and women came to be viewed as highly sexed and lacking in control, while men's sexual transgressions were seen as due to the *fitna* (temptation; enticement) a woman possessed and displayed. Conservative Islamic literature regarded the woman outside her home as *fitna*, and a source of social anarchy. When a woman failed to wear the veil she became guilty of corrupting all the males who came into contact with her, and whose unbridled lust she incited (Al Sha'rawi quoted in Stowasser 1993: 17). Only modest deportment, and clothing which covered and blanketed the female shape, could bridle and control this male lust. Seclusion and veiling, sometimes together with the practice of cliterodectomy, came to be used as defensive measures to ensure the virginity of the female and thus protect the honour of the family group. As Jowkar (1986: 61) points out, the fear of loss of female virtue in the Middle East has led to the unidimensional presentation of women as sex objects, and the eroticisation of their total identity.

## Rising Feminist Consciousness and Development of a World Market System

By the beginning of the nineteenth century the veil and seclusion had taken on a new political dimension of global scale. The century opened with the French colonial encounter in the Middle East. It lasted for only three years, but set into motion, first, a relaxation of the restrictions on women, their dress and their movement, and, second, a local backlash after the French departed. During this brief period of time,

> many French officers converted to Islam to marry middle-class women and did so with the consent of the Egyptian patriarchs, who used this traffic in women to cement their social and political ties with the new French ruling authorities (Hatem 1986: 265).

These French husbands asked their wives to unveil in public. This act in itself was not an act of women's independence or defiance, but simply a response to the wishes of husbands. Egyptian men, however, regarded it as further evidence of the loosening of male control over women. When the colonial encounter with the French came to an end, under the pressure of a British naval blockade, there was a strong patriarchal backlash against those Egyptian women who had consorted with the colonists. Some European travellers reported massacres of women who were associated with the French in different parts of the country (Gran, as quoted in Hatem 1986: 267). Zaynab al-Bakri, who was rumoured to have had an affair with

Napoleon, was executed as an adulteress despite the fact that there were no witnesses and thus contrary to the requirement in Islamic law for four witnesses to an adulterous act. The execution of al-Bakri, as well as the massacres of other women, was, according to Hatem's interpretation, a warning and a disciplinary measure. Egyptian women were being reminded that they could not lightly challenge the rules of veiling and seclusion.

## The Colonial Experience and the Symbolism of the Veil

By 1892 a new colonial experience commenced – the British occupation of Egypt. British interests lay in promoting and developing the country's potential as a supplier of raw materials for British factories. The reaction in Egypt was complex, and in many ways reflected the Egyptian class structure. A new upper class, educated in Western-type schools, became civil servants and an intellectual elite. These modern men displaced the traditionally and religiously trained *'ulama* as administrators and civil servants. It was in this setting that the work of Qassim Amin was first published in 1899. Amin advocated primary school education for women, reform of the laws on polygamy and divorce, and, as the ultimate reform, the abolition of the veil. The ensuing debate constituted an important moment in Middle Eastern history. A new interpretation, in which the veil came to represent far broader issues than merely the position of women, was gaining ground. The veil was now the focus of the widening cultural gulf between the different classes of Egyptian society, and, as the result of the colonial experience, the conflict between the colonized and colonizer. Thus, two key issues concerning women and culture became fused in Arabic debate, discussion, and writing (Ahmed 1992: 145).

In order to understand why the contest over culture in Egypt should have centred on women and the veil, one needs to look at the ideas that were imported into the local situation from Great Britain. The centrality that the issue of women occupied in the Western and colonial narrative of Islam was the result of the mingling of several strands of thought. There was the largely negative medieval interpretation of Islam based on tales of crusaders and travellers. And there was an all-purpose narrative of colonial domination regarding the inferiority of all other cultures and societies. Appended to this discourse was the language of feminism which had developed its own vigour in Europe at that time, in opposition to the Victorian theory of the biological inferiority of women and the Victorian ideal of their domestic role. At home the Victorian male establishment derided and rejected the ideas of feminism, and dismissed the notion that men oppressed women. But overseas, in the colonies, the idea that other men – men in colonized societies – oppressed women was used by the colonists rhetorically to justify morally their obliteration of the cultures of colonized people. Their position regarding the Middle East was that Islam innately oppressed women, that the veil and segregation epitomized this oppression, and that these customs were the fundamental reasons for the backwardness of Islamic societies (Ahmed 1992: 152).

These views are particularly transparent when the statements of Lord Cromer are examined. Cromer believed that Islamic religion and society were inferior to the European ones. He reasoned that Islam as a social system has been a complete failure because it degraded women. He felt it was important that Egyptians be persuaded or forced to imbibe the true sprit of western civilization, essentially by changing the position of women in Islam, for it was Islam's degradation of women as expressed in the practices of veiling and seclusion, that set a fatal obstacle to elevating native thought and character (Ahmed 1992: 153). Even as he expressed such views, he pursued policies that were detrimental to Egyptian women. He held back girl's education by placing restrictions on government schools and raising fees. He discouraged the training of women doctors, and downgraded the existing women's medical school to a school of midwifery. His paternalistic views about the subordination of women were most clearly expressed back in England. The great advocate for the unveiling of women in Egypt was, back home in England, the founding member of the Men's League for Opposing Women's Suffrage (see Rover 1967: 171–73).

Qassim Amin's campaign to westernize Egypt and to liberate women by removing their veils was adopted by Egyptian feminists as a first step in their quest for true liberation. Led by Huda Al-Sha'rawi, in 1923, Egyptian women began to unveil in public. But this action reflected little more than the substitution of a Western-style convention for an Islamic-style patriarchy. The way in which the colonial narrative of women and Islam (the veil and seclusion) became the focus of the nation was more profound. In reaction to Amin and his supporters' modern intellectual movement, a nationalist conservative response arose to defend and uphold Islamic practices. Both sides affirmed that the wife's essential duty was to attend to the physical, mental, and moral needs of her husband and children. Indeed their recommendations for women differed only in the matter of clothing. The nationalist conservative intellectual tradition argued that women must veil, and the modernists' that they should unveil. The veil quickly came to symbolize the colonial resistance movement, rather than the inferiority of the local culture and the need to cast aside its customs in favour of those of the West. Particularly those customs that had come under fiercest colonial attack, customs relating to women, were tenaciously affirmed by the nationalists as a means of resisting Western domination. It was the Western discourse, ironically, that determined the new meanings of the veil and gave rise to its emergence as a symbol of resistance.

## Sexual Feminism and Islamicist Movements

By the second half of the twentieth century, three main ideological orientations could be seen in the Arab world regarding 'women in Islam': the modernist, the conservative and the Islamist (or, perjoratively, the fundamentalist). The modernists regard Islam as a dynamic, open religion. They perceive original Islam, as legislated in the Quran and Hadith, as a flexible blueprint for contemporary life. They see reform on women's issues as central to reform of society as a whole, particularly in terms of women's participation in the public sector. The conservatives view Islam as an inherited, balanced system of faith and action based on the Quran and Hadith, interpreted by the verifying authority of community consensus. For the conservatives, women's work is in the home. They unconditionally and categorically reject demands for women to work in the public sector, and consider female domesticity as a God given duty. The Islamists insist on a static and immutable Islam as legislated in the Quran and Hadith. Everyday realities can be judged as either right or wrong. Social reality and social development have no influence on religion. Religion unilaterally shapes and guides Islamists from above. Like the conservatives, they emphasize woman's natural domesticity, glorify the status awarded her in Islam, and predict certain doom if she deserts or is lured away from her traditional place in society (Stowasser 1993: 1–28).

Towards the end of the twentieth century the modernists became the minority voice, and both conservatives and Islamists dominated political and philosophical activity. During the 1970s feminism reappeared in the public arena. It coincided with the renewed open door capitalism of President Sadat. It also coincided with a second wave of the Islamic revival after the 1967 war especially among university students. This religious revival was directly related to the surprising and sudden defeat of Egypt in the Arab-Israeli war. Egyptians at all levels felt humiliated, cheated, and threatened. Disbelief gradually turned to disillusion, anger to depression, and discontent to resignation. One local interpretation for the defeat was put to the general decline of religious faith among Egyptians in recent years (El Guindi 1981: 469). Among the Islamists, a return to the veil and the home was a symbolic reassertion of the traditional notion of women's exclusive sexual and family roles. It is important to keep in mind, however, that the veiling styles of this contemporary Islamic movement was not a return by urban women to the elite veiling styles of the past. The latter were discarded by Egyptian feminists after 1923 as a symbol of their liberation and emancipation. From that time up to the present, elite women who previously veiled did not return to the veil again. The recent veiling by Islamist females is occurring among different strata and classes, mainly among lower and lower middle class women who are nearly always of rural origins (El Guindi 1981: 475; Hatem 1986: 34; Macleod 1991: 125–127).

## Oman and southeastern Arabia

Before 1970, Oman, occupying the southeastern corner of Arabia, was as geographically and psychologically isolated from the rest of the Middle East as Tibet had been from the rest of the world. Its ruler was intent on drawing the country up from abject poverty, but also on protecting his people from too rapid change or modernization. It was a society isolated from the changes taking place in the twentieth century. The Sultan himself decided which individual foreigners could travel into the country, he personally granted permission for the import of a very limited number of private vehicles, and he alone determined the few dozen pupils who were admitted into schools, while the unselected others had to be smuggled out of the country for education abroad. Oman has a land mass of nearly 275,000 sq. kilometres, at least 80 per cent of which is harsh desert, and another 14 per cent bare and rugged mountains. Its population was estimated in the 1970s to be between 500,000 and 1,000,000 people (Townsend, 1977: 15–23). Raw figures from the first national census in 1993 indicate an Omani population now of about 1,500,000 and a further 5,000,000 foreign guest workers.

Geography conspired to turn Oman's public face to the east. The western boundary of the country, the Empty Quarter, or Rub' al Khali, formed a nearly insurmountable barrier to the exchange of ideas or people overland. Earliest historical records show that Oman long ago turned to the sea for most trade and cultural exchange. The people of the northern part of the country, particularly the Batinah coast, have traditionally looked to the Indian sub-continent for trade in material culture and labour. Over the centuries communities of Persians, Baluchistanis, and Hyderabadis have settled in Oman and become part of the cultural mix of the country. The East African coast and the island of Zanzibar were originally important settlements for Omani merchants and sailors, and subsequently became integral territories of the Sultanate. The African immigrant element is now especially well pronounced in Salalah, the capital of the southern region, Dhofar. Large numbers of African slaves were imported there to serve in the palace compounds throughout the country. During the 1950s slaves were officially manumitted. Some remained attached to their former masters while others left and created their own distinctive culture and society in a number of urban and agrarian settlements.

The population of Oman was converted to Islam in the seventh century A.D. during the lifetime of Mohammed. By the eighth century Oman had adopted Ibadism, a sect which developed in Basra as a faction of Kharijite extremists. Although there are significant differences in terms of the election of an Imam and community consultation, in general, the dogma and politico-religious theories of Ibadism closely resemble those of Sunni Islam (Wilkinson 1976; Peterson 1978; D. Eickelman 1981). As early as the ninth century Omani merchants were preaching Ibadism in East Africa and elsewhere. By the twentieth century, the population was nearly 50 per cent Ibadi, 40 per cent Sunni and 10 per cent various Shiite sects.

### Women, Dress and Community

Mountain ranges separate Oman's coastal plains from the interior of the country in both the north and the south of the country. Many communities therefore are isolated with little external exchange of people or ideas. Furthermore, encapsulated ethnic and religious minorities often live side by side in single villages, where female dress is the most obvious, immediate visual badge of identity, status and class (cf. C. Eickelman 1984). In part of the interior, for example, Sunni Baluchi communities share villages with Ibadi Omani tribes. Dress identifies women as belonging to one community or another. The distinctive signs are sometimes as simple as length of dress, colour of head covering, or type of embroidery on trouser cuffs, but they are sufficient for local inhabitants to 'read' in order to place an unknown person into her ethnic, or community context.

In the Ibadi mountain communities of northern Oman women wear full-length, loose baggy trousers (*sirwāl*) under long sleeved shifts which often extend to the mid-calf or are knee length. The head and neck are covered with a long rectangular scarf (*laysu*) which is wrapped around the head and neck, leaving the face fully exposed (see Fig. 33). This reveals the hair of the crown of the head, which is ideally parted in the middle and slicked down

**Figure 33** Oman *laysu* head cover
Drawing by Imshi Burell

with perfumed oil. The fabric of the dress and trousers is bright and multicoloured, contrasting colours being favoured (e.g. orange or yellow trousers with green or purple shifts). The wealth or status of the family is revealed in the additional decoration – usually in gold or silver thread – on borders of the shift, the scarf, the *sirwāl*. Women's dress is similar to this among the Sunni communities along most of the Batinah coast, but with a tendency to match the fabric of the shift with the head scarf. Again the face is fully open, but along the coast women's hair and neck are fully covered.

Along the northern parts of the Batinah, however, among communities of settled nomadic pastoralists, Baluch farmers, and others with close ties to the Trucial coast (United Arab Emirates and Qatar) and to the Baluchistan coast of Makram (which stretches across from Persia to Pakistan), dress is similar to that described above, but with the very noticeable addition of a short face mask called *burqa* (more strictly *burqu'* or *burgu'*) (see Fig. 34). Wikan (1982:88–9) writes that the

> *burqa* dominates the woman's face, though it covers only minor portions of it. Hidden are, as a minimum, the upper lip, the central part of the cheeks above a line extending from the corner of the mouth, the front part of the nose and the lower third or fourth of the forehead, including the eyebrows. Left uncovered are the eyes, the upper and lower parts of the cheeks, the sides of the nose, the upper part of the forehead, and all of the chin. Thus enough of the face is left open to give the Western observer the impression that the Sohari *burqa* resembles most of all a bikini version of a one-piece bathing suit, the ... latter being the Bedouin *burqa*: a full mask covering all of the face, with the exception of the eyes, which peer through small slits in the mask (1982: 88–9).

**Figure 34** Sohari *burqa*
Drawing by Imshi Burell

Women in this northern Batinah area are very conscious that their face masks are different from those which the Bedouin women wear, but I would suggest that both styles of masks derive from the same tradition, probably introduced into Oman and the Gulf states from the Makram coast several centuries earlier during a period of Baluch emigration into the Gulf.

Among the Shiite communities, concentrated mostly in the trading towns of Matrah, Muscat and Ruwi, women are completely covered, but the style of dress is more Western in design. The gown is long sleeved, often fitted and with a floor-length, full skirt. The head cover frequently being a thin chiffon rectangular scarf of the same colour as the dress. The head is totally uncovered and the head scarf may be tightly wrapped around the face or left lying loosely over the head and shoulders (see Fig. 35). When leaving their homes, these women don the black shapeless cloak, called ʿabāya which elsewhere too in the Middle East is closely associated with women's proper public presentation of their bodies. Until recently in Oman, the ʿabāya was the item of clothing which identified and separated a Shiite woman (e.g. Khoja, Persian, Bahrani) from the rest of the female population.

Among the pastoral tribes of the interior deserts of Oman (e.g. Duru, Wahiba, Harasiis, Mahra, Beit Kathir) dress is more homogeneous. Women wear long-sleeved shaped dresses that are generally ankle length (*thawb*). These dresses are shaped, often with waists or constructed in what is called a princess line in the West. *Sirwāl* accompany the dress and black muslin lengths of cloth generally two to three metres long, are wrapped around the

**Figure 35** Muscat loose headscarf
Drawing by Imshi Burell

head over the *burqa* – a full face, black or deep blue fabric mask dyed in natural indigo or a chemical equivalent (see Fig. 36). For special occasions a sheer, black *tulle* overdress is put on giving the *thawb* a black sheen. Dress fabrics are generally black or sombre in colour. The total image is of a black apparition, its head and face totally covered except for two small eye holes or slits. Occasionally a hint of jewellery is glimpsed under the *burqa* of younger women. In young adulthood women are known to choose vibrant, strong colours for their clothes. So, too, the *burqa* tends to show some of the chin of young adults, progressively lengthening as the woman ages, until it completely covers the face and reveals nothing whatsoever.

The style of dress in Dhofar differs significantly from that of the north of the country. The dress is cut in a long, rectangular shape, and just the hands extend from the two ends of the top of the rectangle. A square cut neckline and a hem as much as twelve inches from the ground in the front, but touching or sweeping the floor from the back, make this a most distinctive tent dress. It is worn with *sirwaal*. The head is covered in multi-coloured cotton prints which are drawn up to cover the lower part of the face, or sometimes more when a woman feels uncomfortable in the presence of men or strangers. Women of formerly slave stock now also wear a full face *burqa*. Female slaves were not permitted to wear the mask in Oman prior to their liberation in the 1950s, only free women could do so.

## The significance of facial covering in the deserts of Oman

In order to explore the significance of facial covering I will focus on the Harasiis tribe and other pastoral communities of Oman's deserts. For although the *burqa* is also found in other parts of Oman, its use among the remote, isolated pastoral communities presents a less complicated picture.

**Figure 36** Bedouin *burqa*
Drawing by Imshi Burell

The pastoral tribes of Oman make up between 6 to 7 per cent of the total population. These communities are very thinly spread over the desert regions, yet have much in common. All are camel and goat-raising subsistence pastoralists, with men responsible for the management of camels, and women responsible for the care of goats. Their households are based on the extended family group – generally a three-generational family, but other kin-related households are also common. Descent is patrilineal, children generally belonging to the father's line. This pastoral society is basically egalitarian, social classes do not exist, and most statuses are achieved rather than acquired by birth. Women and their labour are extremely important for the group's survival, and relations between men and women reflect this mutual dependence. If Arab society is defined as patriarchal in general, then its pastoral communities have modified relations so as to give women a large voice and appearance of near equality (Chatty 1995; Lancaster 1981). Marriage for the most part is monogamous, and serial monogamy is common. The celibate state is very rare. Divorcees, widows, and widowers nearly always remarry. The demands of life in the desert are such that the single person cannot survive on his or her own; thus close cooperation and positive and effective social relations, are extremely important for the well-being of the community.

Among the Harasiis tribe, who are perhaps the most remote and most isolated of all the pastoral groups in Oman, residence after marriage is often matrilocal, becoming virilocal once the nuclear family is strong enough to split off and set up on its own. When serial monogamy characterizes an individual's marriage history, and when the woman's character is strong and self-sufficient (the Harasiis would use the terms honourable and admirable) the offspring are often known by both the father's and mother's name. Therefore, a son, Salim, would be known both as Salim bin Hamad – Salim son of Hamad (the father) – and, significantly, also as Salim bin Huweila – Salim son of Huweila (the mother).

As with all the pastoral tribes of Oman, the Harasiis consider themselves Muslim and try to follow the pillars of their faith. Men and women pray regularly, they fast, and undertake the pilgrimage to Mecca often more than once in their lifetimes. They also follow the social rules laid down in the Quran and the Hadith as well as they can. They see their lives as structured entirely by their understanding of Islam. This is particularly obvious in regard to the female life course. Like her brother, a young female girl is not considered to reach the age of reason until near the age of nine. By that age she will be expected to pray with her mother and sisters, and be careful to keep her hair covered. She will already have had long experience wearing a black scarf around her head, as would a boy have been taught to wrap a large square cotton cloth (*'amāma*) around his head. The Harasiis, like many pious Muslims everywhere, regard the uncovered head as improper and mildly irreligious. The same applies to exposure of a woman's ankles and face.

There are three important stages in a woman's life. The first is marked by ceremonial behaviour and a dramatic change in dress. The latter two are socially rather than physically obvious. The first ritual is a combined rite of passage marking puberty and marriage. This, the Harasiis say, occurs around the age of twelve, but my own material suggests that late onset of puberty (fourteen or fifteen years of age) is more common. Occasionally puberty will precede marriage, but this is probably due to an earlier menarche rather than actual planning. In late childhood and early adolescence a girl will start to make face masks for herself. She will have a free hand in deciding the length of the mask and the size of the eye holes. She will try on her masks for months, in preparation for the day she will be permitted to wear one. That day can occur with little ritual if her first menarche precedes her marriage. Generally though, her taking on the *burqa* will occur during her marriage ritual, a celebration of three or four days duration held at her parents household. The entire community is invited to participate in this event, which is marked by men dancing, women singing, and the ritual slaughter and preparation of meat for all guests.

The second important ritual occurs when a woman adds to her wifely status that of mother as well. It is marked by a lying-in period of forty days during which time she is set up in her own shelter within the compound and is meant to take absolute rest. She purifies herself and her infant during this time. This is repeated after the birth of every child. The third major transition in the life of a Harasiis women occurs more gradually. It starts at about the time she becomes a grandmother and stops bearing children herself, when gradually she grows into the role of the household matriarch and takes on the status attached to that role.

The Harasiis explain the importance of donning the head scarf and *burqa* in terms of female modesty, a virtue that requires women to cover their hair (they also cover their heads at puberty). That women should also cover their faces is explained in terms of the changed status of the female from girl to married woman. It is believed that women should remove their masks in only two situations: when they pray, and when they are in the presence of their husbands and other male kinsmen who they are prohibited to marry by Islamic rules (e.g. her sons, father, brother, father-in-law, father's brother, mother's brother, husband's brother and husband's son from a previous marriage). Like the women of Sohar described by Wikan, pastoral women in Oman keep their masks on far more often than their explicit rules suggest. One Harasiis woman brought to live in Manchester for two years, while her husband was being trained as an engineer, resolved a cultural conflict about veiling in her own way by wearing her mask at home (her husband often arrived home with male friends), but removing it when out shopping on the high street or elsewhere so as to avoid people noticing her and staring.

The *burqa* mask among the Harasiis connotes womanhood. Like the red belt among the Awlad Ali (Abu Lughod 1986: 136–137), it is associated with the fertility of the woman. Yet it is worn from the onset of puberty, even when that precedes marriage, and worn after menopause has occurred, women wearing the *burqa* long into their old age. I only came across two very old Harasiis women who did not wear the veil. One was so crippled with arthritis she could hardly move her arms. Her children simply draped a cloth over her head. The other woman, also very old, wore thick prescription glasses and could not manage to wear a burqa over her glasses. She covered as much of her face as she could with a scarf.

When young girls first start wearing the mask they occasionally display some awkwardness. On a number of occasions I have been pulled aside by a recently masked girl so that she could lift her veil to be better able to speak to me. Their initial awkwardness strikes me a bit like the excitement and mixed emotions that a Western girl feels when she is given or insists on being bought her first bra. She loves wearing it because it means to her that she is 'grown up', and by wearing it she feels she is announcing to the world that she is a mature female. At the same time she doesn't like the binding nature of the garment, and often moves her shoulders awkwardly trying to adjust herself to the binding contraption that she so eagerly had taken on. Among the Harasiis the obvious difference is that the girl has no choice but to wear the mask once puberty has occurred. And after maturity has been achieved, there is only one path to follow: marriage. But marriages are arranged with her consent, and as she is generally still part of her father's household, unhappy arrangements are easily broken in the early years. Even when the young wife has separated from her father's household and is established elsewhere, she can initiate a divorce or separation simply by leaving her husband's household and returning with her herd of goats to her father.

This freedom to act, however, presupposes that a woman has adopted the behaviour which her mask requires. I was told that the mask along with the black hair covering is a statement of the sexual modesty of the woman. Also tied up in this interpretation is the matter of personal dignity and the honour which decorous, generous, and stoic behaviour bestows on the family. An unmasked woman is unthinkable. Even in situations of serious illness, I have observed women and their kin struggle to keep their faces and hair covered. One serious asthmatic labouring for breath in a hospital bed insisted on keeping her mask on, even though this seemed to seriously impede her ability to get oxygen to her lungs. After long minutes of discussion, she was finally convinced to draw her black gauze head scarf across her face and remove her mask. To be maskless was to be not fully dressed, and thus to be socially and sexually compromised.

In this discussion of the Harasiis it is also important to raise the subject of seclusion. In many parts of the Arab world, the veil is associated with the seclusion of women and their segregation from men. The veil sets women apart and creates a barrier around their person as though they were in seclusion. Among the pastoral communities in Oman this element does not enter significantly into the analysis. Men and women simply cannot live their lives segregated from each other. The basic requirements of life do not permit such a luxury, nor is it sought. Their communal lives could not continue without the full labour of all members of the household. The onus of modest behaviour, sexual decorum, and honourable decorum falls upon both men and women without the crutch of physical sex segregation or actual barriers apart from dress.

## Significance of Head Covering in Urban and Agrarian Oman

Though some families are more equal than others (e.g. lineages from which leaders tend to be chosen), the prevailing ideology is that the tribes are made up of free and equal men and women, who are distinct only from the hired male foreign labourers. To this extent then, female dress as such cannot be used to distinguish one lineage from another. With the exception of hired male foreign labourers, pastoralists are all the same.

The situation in the urban and agrarian centers of Oman is very different. Class distinctions abound, as does stratification and hierarchy. Women's headcovers in urban settings do indicate the rank and status of their wearers as well as their families. The example of Sohar is particularly appropriate. Until recently the wearing of a *burqa* in Sohar was a statement of belonging to the 'middle class' of successful merchants and traders. Upper class women and the families related to the Sultan (e.g. Omani royalty) did not veil, but they did maintain a careful distance, if not actual seclusion, from men unrelated to them. Slaves (according to Wikan (1982: 96) once 15 per cent of the female population of Sohar) were prohibited from veiling, that being the uncontested prerogative of free women. Peasant or farming women did not wear any face covering; it was said to interfere with their work.

With the abolition of slavery in the 1950s, many ex-slave women adopted the *burqa*. Initially a statement of their newly experienced liberation, it rapidly became a marker of their having moved upward socially and the new found leisure that only those of some wealth could afford. The *burqa* not only indicated a free woman, but one whose husband's, or family patriarch's, wealth allowed her some leisure instead of keeping her fully occupied working in agriculture. This phenomenon is strikingly similar to that described by El Guindi (1981: 475) during the first half of the twentieth century in Egypt. There, 'when unveiled peasant women ventured to the city . . . they were eager to wear a veil as a symbol of urbanizing and 'moving up'.'

The political climate in the country changed dramatically with the accession of Sultan Qaboos bin Saiid to power in 1970. The tight-fisted, ultra conservative patriarchical rule of the previous Sultan was swept aside by the new ruler. Sultan Qaboos declared amnesties, emptied prisons and abrogated decades of repressive legislation. Omanis abroad were encouraged to return to Oman, many from lives in exile in Western countries. During the first few years of Sultan Qaboos' reign, there was an atmosphere of rejuvenation, growth, and freedom. Omani women who had been educated abroad returned eager to share in building up the nation. Their positive welcome during the crucial early years was not unlike the situation described by Dodd (1973: 40–54), Hale (1993: 167) and others when analysing the roles assigned to women in periods of crises (e.g. nationalist struggles or revolutions). Women as well as men were being mobilized rapidly to build up the nation to join the twentieth century. Women were allowed to join the police force, the armed forces, and a range of government ministries as well as private industry. Women were heard on radio and seen on television. They appeared to be, if not equal, at least partners in the building up of the country.

By the end of the decade, however, women's contribution was not as urgently required and returning male university graduates and exiles began to compete with women for jobs. Women began to face barriers. They started to be excluded from certain professions that they had won entry into earlier, and their dress style came under silent scrutiny. Most of these women had returned to Oman after years (sometimes nearly lifetimes) in exile. Their dress was western, and did not include head or face covering. During the 1970s these modern, educated, middle and upper middle class women gradually began to use the black outer cloak, the *'abāya* (originally only worn by Shiite women) and a loose head scarf when out in public. At first only a few women regularly dressed in this fashion, but over the following decade it became nearly universal. This unspoken pressure to conform, to adopt a more modest and conservative dress, was part of the general feeling in the country that women should not abandon their traditional Islamic role in life.

It was as though the 1970s had been regarded as a special period of nation building, when traditional sex roles and gender segregation had to be abandoned for a higher good. Having attained many national goals, women were figuratively and literally pushed back into what was assumed to be more correct traditional roles (for the analysis of similar phenomena in Algeria and Iran, see Moghadam 1994). For example, the national university which was set up in 1986, initially made all colleges open to all qualified Omani high school graduates. Selection into a college rested upon examination results. The colleges of Medicine and Engineering required the highest scores, followed by Science. During the first few years it became obvious that women, who almost always had the highest high school examination results, were dominating these colleges. Education administrators feared that the preponderance of women would reduce the academic status of the University and that it might gain a reputation for being only a woman's university. They therefore decided to create more favourable admission requirements for male students. Thus by the mid 1990s men outnumbered women at the University, and female entrance into the College of Medicine required a score in the top 5 percentile, while for male applicants a score within the top 10 percentile was admissible. For the College of Engineering the measures were even more extreme and women were no longer permitted to apply. A decision had been taken within the government to ban female students, as it was no longer thought appropriate for women to work in fields out of doors in mixed company. In dress, this conservativism was made manifest in the pressure women felt to cover themselves with *'abāyas* and to adopt the *ḥijāb* (headscarf). Interestingly, a number of the early female medical students (in the classes of 1986, 1987 and 1989) wore only western dress. Over the following few years they gradually began to wear the *'abāya* and the *ḥijāb,* first erratically, and then with regularity, until by the mid- 1990s all the female medical students wore the accepted dress advocated by conservative Islamists.

Not unlike the situation described in Egypt by El-Guindi (1981: 465–485), another garment associated with Islamism made its appearance at the university several years later. The full face covering with a black veil – the *niqāb* – marked the female students acceptance of the principle of her dangerous sexuality and domesticity (see Fig. 37). Those adopting this dress and ideology were originally few, and mainly from poor families or of former slave stock. Within two years of its appearance, the administration had prohibited female students from wearing the *niqāb* on campus in an effort to prevent this extreme form of cover and the related Islamist philosophy from taking root within the precincts of the university. The veil had to be lifted upon entering the campus and remain up until they left. Women disobeying this ban were given three warnings after which they would be expelled from the university. Women expelled themselves, as did the granddaughter of the exiled, and now deceased, claimant to the Ibadi Imamate, who decided to withdraw from the medical school rather than give up wearing the *niqāb*.

## Conclusion

Dress is many things to many people. It is a badge identifying a person as belonging to a certain community, class, and economic strata. Its meaning can change over time and it can convey a multitude of messages. The present association of the face and head covering, however, cannot be simply associated with the Islamist movement as appears to be the case in the popular press. In Oman, face veiling does not have that connotation, at least not yet. In the urban and agrarian regions of the northern Omani

**Figure 37** Dhofari *niqāb*
Drawing by Imshi Burell

coast, it identifies a conservative, middle-class population. In the south, it is a statement of upward mobility by former slaves or of the new wealth and leisure of the wealthy classes. Certainly in the desert communities where face veiling is considered part of the appropriate dress of a respectable women, a woman who refuses to comply courts social death. The one example in my notes of a young Harasiis woman who refused to don the *burqa* is accompanied by quotes from others about her mental state. Many people thought she was crazy: she had refused to accept that she had physically matured and was knowingly allowing herself to become a burden upon her family. Upon interviewing her myself, I had the distinct feeling that she was merely subnormal in intelligence. She didn't want to wear the *burqa*. She couldn't say why except that she didn't like it and she wouldn't keep it on her face. Her elderly parents knew that by this stance she had become unmarriageable and they requested government welfare assistance for her upkeep on the grounds that she was handicapped and would never marry or leave the family household. Government assistance was granted. Her action was regarded as no different from that of the severely retarded young man who refused to keep his clothes on. In despair his parents took him to the regional hospital where he was admitted as a long-term patient and kept in a padded room visible only to his male nurses.

Among some of the other pastoral tribes in Oman, I have heard of a few divorced women who have removed their *burqa's*. I was told that they were refusing to remarry and the removal of the veil was their public announcement of that fact. One to whom I did speak informally confirmed this: she was married once and did not wish to marry again, preferring to remain part of her father's household. Unfortunately, both men and women regard these 'rebels' as loose women, suggesting that they may even be engaged in some prostitution among the fish traders that regularly crossed their territory from Saudi Arabia to the Indian Ocean. Such a belief, whether true or not, reinforced the association of the *burqa* with the sexual modesty, moral excellence and general honour of a good woman. As elsewhere in the rapidly changing and confused social world of the Middle East, the significance of face covering can only be understood in the context of the totality of the society. Certainly to view face covering only as a modern political phenomenon is to fail to understand the way in which the parts of the total structure of personal appearance is consciously manipulated to assert and demarcate differences in status, identity and commitment as part of a much wider social reality.

# References

Abu-Lughod, L. 1986. *Veiled Sentiments: Honour and Poetry in a Bedouin Society.* Berkeley and Los Angeles: University of California Press.

Abdel Kader, S. 1984. 'A Survey of Trends in Social Science Research on Women in the Arab Region, 1960–1980'. In Amal Rassam, ed., *Social Science Research and Women in the Arab World.* Paris: UNESCO, 139–175.

Antoun, R. 1968. ' On the modesty of women in Arab Muslim villages: a study in the accommodation of traditions'. *American Anthropologist* 70, 671–694.

Ahmed, L. 1982. 'Western Ethnocentrism and Perceptions of the Harem'. *Feminist Studies,* 8, 3, 521–534.

—1992. *Women and Gender in Islam: Historical Roots of a Modern Debate.* New Haven: Yale University Press.

Chatty, D. 1996. *Mobile Pastoralists: Development Planning and Change among the Harasiis tribe in Oman.* New York: Columbia University Press.

Dodd, P. 1973. 'Family Honour and the Forces of Change in Arab Society'. *International Journal of Middle East Studies* 4, 40–54.

Eickelman, C. 1984. *Women and Community in Oman.* New York and London: New York University Press.

Eickelman, D. 1981. *The Middle East: An Anthropological Approach.* Second edition, 1989. Englewood Cliffs, N. J.: Prentice Hall.

El-Guindi, F. 1981 'Veiling Infitah with Muslim Ethic: Egypt's Contemporary Islamic Movement'. *Social Problems,* vol. 28, 4: 465–485.

Hale, S. 1993. 'Transforming Culture or Fostering Second-hand Consciousness'. Tucker, J. ed., *Arab Women: Old Boundaries New Frontiers.* Bloomington and Indianapolis: Indiana University Press.

Hatem, M. 1986. 'The Politics of Sexuality and Gender in Segregated Patriarchal Systems: The Case of Eighteenth and Nineteenth-Century Egypt'. *Feminist Studies* 12, 2, 251–274.

Jowkar, F. 1986 'Honor and Shame: a Feminist View from Within'. *Feminist Issues,* 45–65.

Kroeber, A. 1919. 'On the Principle of Order in Civilization as Exemplified by Changes in Fashion'. In *American Anthropologist,* 21: 235–263.

Kroeber, A. and Richardson, J. 1940 'Three Centuries of Women's Dress Fashions: a Quantitative Analysis'. *Anthropological Records,* V, 111–153.

Kuper, H. 1973. 'Costume and Identity'. *Comparative Studies in Society and History,* 15, 3: 348–367.

Lancaster, W. 1981. *The Rwala Bedouin Today* Cambridge: Cambridge University Press.

Levy, R. 1965. 'The Status of Women in Islam'. *The Social structure of Islam.* New York: Cambridge University Press.

Macleod, A. 1991. *Accommodating Protest: Working Women, the New Veiling, and Change in Cairo.* New York: Columbia University Press.

Mernissi, F. 1987 (orig. 1975). *Beyond the Veil: Male-Female Dynamics in a Modern Muslim Society.* Bloomington: Indiana University Press.

Moghadam, V. (ed.) 1994. *Gender and National Identity.* London and New Jersey: Zed Books.

Nelson, C. 1973. 'Women and Power in Nomadic Societies in the Middle East'. In Nelson, C., ed., *The Desert and the Sown: Nomads in the Greater Society.* Berkeley: University of California, Institute of International Studies, 43–59.

Peristiany, J. (ed.) 1966. *Honour and Shame: The Values of Mediterranean Society.* Chicago: University of Chicago Press.

Peterson, J. 1978. *Oman in the Twentieth Century.* London: Croom Helm.

Rover, C. 1967. *Party Politics in Britain 1966–1914.* London: Routledge and Kegan Paul.

Schneider, J. 1972. 'Of Vigilance and Virgins: Honor, Shame and Access to Resources in Mediterranean Societies'. *Ethnology* 10, 1–24.

Stowasser, B. 1993. 'Women's Issues in Modern Islamic Thought'. In Tucker, J., ed., *Arab Women: Old Boundaries New Frontiers.* Washington, D. C.: Georgetown University, 1–28.

Townsend, J. 1977. *Oman: The Making of the Modern State.* London: Croom Helm.

Wilkinson, J. 1987. *The Imamate Tradition of Oman.* Cambridge: Cambridge University Press.

Wikan, U. 1982. *Behind the Veil in Arabia: Women in Oman.* Baltimore and London: Johns Hopkins Press.

# Chapter Nine

# Faith and Fashion in Turkey

*John Norton*

Turks can judge by appearances. They are acutely aware that dress[1] denotes difference, devotion and defiance. A glance at what a stranger is wearing is often enough to tell them that person's religious and political stance. Clothes can tell them the wearer's defiance of or devotion to the principles of Kemal Atatürk, the reformer who founded the Turkish Republic and banned the fez. In the late 1970s, at the height of the disorder preceding the 1980 military coup, gunmen mowed down unknown victims simply because their appearance proclaimed them to be political opponents. Nowadays women's head-dress sends signals that announce the wearer's attitude to Islam, thereby antagonising some compatriots while attracting support from others.

The Turks' ability to read the language of dress is centuries old. So, this article begins with a brief survey of what the Ottoman Turks wore. It then reviews Atatrk's attempts to change the appearance of his compatriots. Finally, it traces developments since his day and comments on the present situation in which dress marks the front line in the battle between Islamic radicals[2] and ardent secularists.

## The Ottoman Heritage

Numerous accounts by visitors to Ottoman lands confirm the impact made upon them by the varied and colourful dress they saw. Much of that dress was strictly regulated by law. Frequently it indicated rank and position in the service of the sultan or membership of a particular religion or dervish order. Different ethnic or regional dress distinctions added to the variety. For some centuries changes in fashion were mostly minor and sprang from the Sultan's preference for, say, a new style of towering headers for leading officials. Sometimes the rulers felt the need to curb extravagance through sumptuary laws that limited the privilege of wearing certain luxury materials, but the general impression remained striking. Raphaela Lewis describes the city dwellers' appearance thus:

> Their dress and turbans were of the widest variety. Shortly after the capture of Constantinople, Sultan Mehmed the Conqueror laid down the regulations by which the clothes of the civil and military hierarchy were to be distinguished, and the shapes and colours of the outer garments of all ranks were specified and adhered to with only slight variations until 1826. Thus, the upper ranks had turbans of various colours wound round tall felt caps; members of the ulema had lengths of dazzling white muslin bound round gold-embroidered skull-caps, which gave the completed turban a much flatter shape. These snowy turbans and the sombre black gowns of the religious dignitaries and medrese students, the rich caftans and head-dresses of the aghas, the naval officers and Arsenal guards with knives in their belts, the dervishes in homespun, the street scavengers in red leather smocks, with brooms and wooden shovels, the gypsies with their dancing bears, all contributed to the vivid scene (Lewis 1971: 88).

The head-dress worn by officers and officials presented the most imposing feature of Ottoman dress up to the early nineteenth century. Over a hundred different types of headgear were in official use. One writer has likened these to exotic plumage: '...like so many parrots of Nepal, Bengalees, the blue magpies of the Himalayas, birds of paradise, blueheaded parakeets, pennant parakeets of Australia. The whole of Turkey seemed an ornithological department spread over this immense zoological garden of the world (Olivero 1952: 111–2).

As Dr. Sedat Kumbaracilar claims, 'There was no other imperial power or state in the world like the Ottoman empire insofar as it had distinctive head-dress for every profession and for different classes and ranks of officials and military personnel' (n.d.: 3 and see Fig. 38).

The *kavuk* - a padded or quilted cap around which the sash of a turban could be wound – and other items of official dress provided instant identification that frequently led to instant clashes between rival groups, particularly rival religious groups. Military dress, particularly that of the Janissaries, had the power to strike instant terror, not only among enemies of the state but also among its citizens who feared their arbitrary powers. But even janissary uniforms could not compete in magnificence with those of the *sipahis* (cavalrymen). The *sipahis* concern for their appearance, however, led to their demise. Because they scorned the use of firearms whose gunpowder would soil their uniforms, they had to be replaced by troops willing to fight with modern weapons (Goodwin 1995: 66–7).

Various sartorial distinctions marked ethnic identity. Wittman, the doctor accompanying a British military mission to Turkey in 1799, noted,

**Figure 38** Ottoman official headgear
Drawing by Howard Tangye from the cover of Izzet Kumbaracılar's *Serpuslar*

The dress of the [Greek] men nearly resembles that of the Turks; but they are not allowed to wear the kowouk [kavuk], or turban of white muslin, for which they are obliged to substitute the calpac [kalpak], or blue turban, and none of the Greeks can wear yellow boots or slippers, except those who are in the service of the foreign ministers, etc (1971: 24; orig. 1803).[3]

So far we have been concerned with male attire. Many women in rural areas wore the distinctive costume of their region or tribe. This could be very colourful. Since these women were usually engaged in hard toil on the land, veiling was impractical. In the 14th century the famous Arab traveller Ibn Battuta recorded that in Anatolia Turkish women were unveiled. He could see the tears in their eyes when they said goodbye. Their normal head-covering was the patterned headkerchief called *yemeni*, which, though protecting the head from dust did not conceal all the hair. It was usual for *yemeni* to be fringed with *oya*, decorative lace or beads. A plain square of white muslin covered their heads when they performed their *namaz*, the ritual act of prayer.

Turkish townswomen in the Ottoman Empire wore the outdoor dress that was common to Muslim women of the region: a knee-length chemise *(gömlek)*, full trousers *(şalvar)*, a waist-sash *(kuşak)*, a waistcoat *(yelek)* and a long gown *(entari)*, all enveloped in either a *çarşaf* – a shapeless ankle-length outer garment, or a more fashionable *ferace* – which also concealed the whole body and had straight sleeves extending to the finger-ends. On their feet the women might wear boots or totter on raised decorative clogs to keep their clothing from contact with unclean pavements. Indoors, backless slippers would be worn, and in wealthy families women might adorn themselves in the flimsy and seductive wear so brilliantly depicted by the miniaturist Levni. And, as Lady Mary Wortley Montagu noted, they might spare no expense on, for example, 'the girdle, of about four fingers broad, which all that can afford have entirely of diamonds or other precious stones'. She said that as these ladies sat upon sofas their slaves were behind them but without any distinction of rank by their dress, all being in the state of nature, that is, in plain English, stark naked, without any beauty or defect concealed' (Melville 1925: 128–132).[4] Wittman was not privy to such domestic scenes but reported what he saw on the streets of Istanbul as follows:

> The dresses of the inhabitants are as varied as the languages. The Turkish women are fair; they cover the face, the eyes and part of the nose excepted, with a piece of white muslin: another piece of muslin envelops the head. This part of their dress is styled *mahramàh*. In stature they are rather low, and corpulent, the latter condition being much admired among themselves: they are usually clad in a long green garment, which hangs very low behind, with a square cape, resembling on the whole a riding dress, and it is called *feredgè [ferace]*. They wear yellow boots with slippers over them, but the latter they take off on entering a house. They stain their finger–nails of a red colour, or, more properly speaking, of a very deep orange, with the dried leaves, diluted with water, of the henna, or Egyptian privet ... (1971: 23–24).

## Ottoman dress reforms

Eight years after Wittman first saw these sights, a dress decree led directly to the downfall of the Sultan when Selim III's attempt to put his auxiliary troops into 'Frankish' dress provoked a mutiny that brought about his deposition.

In 1826, Mahmud II was more successful. After annihilating the Janissaries, he established a new army to replace them, the *Asakir-i Mansur-i Muhammediye* (the victorious Muhammedan soldiers). At first they retained the *kavuk* and *şalvar*. Later they were issued with *setre* (an old-fashioned form of European frock coat) and trousers, to resemble their European contemporaries (Lewis 1969: 98).[5]

Confident that he had achieved unassailable strength, Mahmud II then went further. He took a liking to the fez and ordered that it should be worn by the army. This met with resistance. There was an initial reluctance to abandon the turban, which, according to Hadith, conferred blessings upon the wearer: for, example, 'Two prostrastions with the turban *outweigh seventy without the turban*', and 'The turban *is the barrier separating belief and unbelief*'. In the protests that ensued ten people were reportedly killed and forty injured (Ellison 1928: 92). But since both the Chief Mufti and the Grand Vezir had approved the sultan's choice, this resistance was brushed aside (Lewis 1969: 99–100).[6] Indeed, on 3 March 1829 the Sultan issued a further decree extending the clothing reform to civilians. Only members of the ulema were permitted to retain the robe and turban; other people were obliged to abandon different forms of headgear in favour of the fez, while frock-coats, capes and trousers replaced robes, and slippers gave way to black leather boots (*ibid.*: 100; see also Kumbaracilar n.d.). The order was swiftly obeyed. An American in Turkey in 1831 and 1832 wrote:

> From the more recent gravestones even the turban, that hitherto invariable emblem of the Turk, has disappeared and its place is occupied by the representation of a fez or red cap which is now universally worn I am aware that I am about to utter what may be considered as a heresy by the lovers of the picturesque; but to my mind the fez is a more beautiful and becoming article than even the gorgeous and imposing turban. It is connected, too, with visions of the future prosperity of Turkey, while the turban carries us back to the savage times of the cut-throat crusaders (Dekay 1833: 159).

A more typical Western reaction to the changed appearance of Turkish men came from a contributor to the Asiatic Journal of 1838, the year before the Imperial Rescript that launched the Tanzimat Reforms:

> What a change Turkey is undergoing! The old regime of the Mustafas and Mahomeds is gone, and with it all those fierce characters that surrounded an Eastern despot; and our Arabian Nights fancies of fine shawl dresses, and handsome bearded Turks, are now only to be found in the far East. The modern Turk, in his tight small clothes, looks a miserable creature; and when brought in close contact with the remains of the haughty race, who still wear their fine becoming robes of gay colours, certainly sinks very much in the appearance of the outer man (Asiatic Journal 1838: 39).

Warington W. Smyth, another observer who travelled extensively in Turkey in the mid-nineteenth century, noted:

> In the remoter districts, the sweeping reforms of Sultan Mahmoud produced for some years but a small impulse; and the very rapidity with which he introduced them in his own immediate neighbourhood was the means of retarding them in the provinces. He is entitled to admiration for the intelligence and freedom from prejudice which he displayed; but there may have been some lack of judgement and ignorance of his own people, in commencing by a change in externals, which, with uneducated men, taught by their religion to hold themselves above all other nations, was precisely the point to awaken most distrust and opposition. The European dress, for its scanty and thriftily-measured proportions, has long been a subject of ridicule to the flowing-draperied Oriental, who, besides having a natural appreciation of the beautiful, considers a display of the person in a tight garb ungainly and indecent. Yet the Sultan suddenly ordered his subjects to adopt these hated vestments, unsuited not only to their climate, but to their customs and habits of life. Here were men who never entered a room without taking *off* their shoes at the entrance, at once expected to force their feet into close-fitting boots; and a whole nation which had never known of the existence of a chair, ordered to don the tight continuations of Europe, in which should they attempt to sit down in their familiar attitude, bursts of seams and rents and pains in the joints must ensue. These and many similar difficulties are being gradually overcome, but it will require years to accustom the country at large to any part of the Nizam dress except the fez; and there is little reason to doubt that other and more important parts of the reform movement are in the meanwhile making more decided progress (Smyth 1854: 244–5).

## The fez finds favour

The new headgear created new employment. Fez makers were brought from Tunisia and a fez factory was established in the Eyup area of Istanbul. In course of time many different styles of fez came off the production lines. Kumbaracilar's book contains illustrations of over thirty distinct varieties. Their tassels also varied in length and material. Early ones of silk were prone to become entangled during wet and windy weather so opportunistic Jewish children – forerunners of today's 'squeegee merchants'! – would roam the streets eager to comb tassels in return for small change. Making moulds for fezzes soon constituted a recognised craft. The cleansing, reshaping and pressing *of* fezzes gave work to yet more people, many of whom were skilled in spraying mouthfuls of water over the objects of their care before special equipment was devised to perform the dampening process (Kumbaracilar n.d.: 35). By 1868 there were ten groups of fez-makers in Istanbul compared with five of hatmakers (many producing for export) and seven of bookbinders (Yurt Ansiklopedisi: 3843).

Fezzes were at the centre of an important political gesture soon after the Young Turk Revolution of July 1908. In October that year the Committee of Union and Progress organised a boycott of Austrian goods in protest against the Austro-Hungarian annexation of Bosnia-Herzogovina. By this time the Austrians had become the main suppliers of fezzes to Turkish gentlemen of fashion. From 11 October, in what was dubbed the 'fez boycott', those gentlemen took to wearing either an *arakîye* (a form of skull-cap) or a *kalpak* a brimless sheepskin or astrakhan cap instead. The boycott lasted two months and by the end of it the *kalpak* had become an accepted item of dress (*Yurt Ansiklopedisi* 1982: 3851).

## Female fashions

Women's dress did not undergo as great a transformation as men's but changes did occur from time to time. Although women wore the yashmak in the reign of Sultan Abdülaziz (1861–76), a thick black veil replaced this flimsy white article in Abdlhamit II's time (1876–1909) and gloves were always worn (Zayneb Hanoum 1913: 135; see Fig. 39).

At least temporarily, the Empress Eugenie's visit to Abdülaziz in Turkey had a profound impression on the fashion, especially the indoor fashion, of Turkish society women. Zeyneb Hanim records:

> It was after the visit of the empress Eugenie that the women of the palace and the wives of the high functionaries copied as nearly as they could the appearance of the beautiful Empress. They divided their hair in the middle, and spent hours in making little bunches of curls. High-heeled shoes replaced the coloured *babouches* (Turkish slippers without heels); they even adopted the hideous crinolines, and abandoned forever those charming Oriental garments, the *chalvar [salvar]* and *enturi [entari]*, which they considered symbols of servitude, but which no other fashion has been able to equal in beauty.
>
> As might be supposed, the middle class soon followed the example of the palace ladies and adopted Western costume. Then there was the craze for *everything* French. The most eccentric head-dresses and daring costumes were copied. To these Oriental women were given more jewels than liberty, more sensual love than pure affection (*ibid.*, 97–8).

## The Veil

This deviation from Muslim norms was limited and brief. For almost all Turkish townswomen the veil was the inevitable lot. Girls were veiled as

**Figure 39** An Ottoman woman dressed à la Franka in the early 20th century

Drawing by Howard Tangye from photograph reproduced in Zeyneb Hanoum's *A Turkish Woman's European Experiences* (1913, facing page 134)

soon as they were of marriageable age, usually at about 12. Numerous accounts record the dread with which they approached this sudden end to the freedom of childhood and the dreariness of life thereafter. Typical was Selma Ekrem, who after seeing her elder sister undergo the veiling process, lamented:

> The tcharshaf had entered my life brutally and from now on would hang over my childhood. I could not wrench the idea from my head, and the dread of it was worse than any other fear I had known. One escaped sultans and cyclones, but not the tscharshaf. Millions of women had worn it before me. And to my eyes came these women in thick clusters, wrapped in blackness, their faces covered. These millions of black bundles of resignation smothered me (1931: 155).

In similar vein, in 1907 another woman recorded:

> An awful agony had seized and numbed my soul; the words which he [the imam] had uttered resounded in my brain, and little by little sank into my understanding – 'Neyr, you must be veiled' that is to say, to be forever cloistered like those who live around you; to be a slave like your mother, and your cousins, and your elder sister; to belong henceforth to the harem; no longer to play in the garden unveiled; nor ride Arabian ponies in the country; to have a veil over your eyes, and your soul; to be always silent, always forgotten, to be always and always a thing' (Melek, N. Neyrel-Nurs in Zeynab Hanoun 1913: 89).

Both these writers went on to note the spirit of rebellion this veiling provoked within them. (Women rebelling against today's established order are doing so for the opposite reason: the right to *don* the veil.)

By the early years of the present century, some of the wealthier women had taken tentative steps wearing western dress in public. When they went out, this was, as Jennifer Scarce notes, 'concealed beneath an elegant cloak while the face veil had dwindled to a becomingly transparent wisp of material which in time was abandoned altogether' (1981: 21). Not surprisingly, they were rebuked for this by the religious authorities. In 1911, for example, the Şeyh-ul Islâm warned Muslim women not to wear European dress. Despite such warnings the trend continued. As Shaw notes, 'City women ... began to discard the veil in public and appear in European-style clothing long before such matters were decreed by the Republic'(1985: 307), though the traumas of the First World War and the Turkish War of Independence leading up to the proclamation of the Republic on 29 October 1923 left Turks with more urgent concerns than fashion. Many Turkish women in the towns, especially in the small towns, still remained veiled in public. ('Veiled' here means that in public their heads were covered so as to conceal at least all their hair, their necks and their shoulders. Their faces were usually covered with a *peçe* (veil) while their bodies were concealed by a *çarşaf* (also known as a *car*). These were usually black, though sometimes coloured, and made of silk, wool or cloth. Below the waist, some were in two pieces, others, particularly those worn in Anatolia, were made of a single piece, and known as *torba çarşaf*, the bag charshaf) (Could that be what inspired the later Western fashion called 'the sack'?!).

## Republican Attire

While the Republic was still in its infancy the issue of dress was again forced to the top of the agenda. Mustafa Kemal's burning ambition was to modernise and westernise Turkey, to bring Turks up to the level of 'contemporary civilization'. But the outward appearance of most of his compatriots still clearly marked them out from western Europeans. It proclaimed their allegiance to Islam and in some cases their position within the faith.

Prominent men of religion, mullahs, many members of dervish orders and the like wore *şalvar,* or *çakşir* (trousers secured round the waist in folds and sewn to light leather boots at the ankles, *cübbe* (robes) and *kuşak* (cummerbands) and distinctive and varied *külah* (conical hats) on their heads. Functionaries of other religions added to the variety by following their own dress traditions.

Educated men with leanings towards the West wore shoes, trousers, jackets, ties or bow-ties, but above all that was usually a tasselled red fez, though many men who had wished to indicate their devotion to the nationalist as opposed to the Sultan's cause during the War of Independence still preferred the *kalpak,* which had earlier been the politically correct wear during the 1908 fez boycott.

This un-European appearance did not accord with Mustafa Kemal's vision for the new Turkey. Nor did the strong influence of Islam in the affairs of the state. He therefore set about eliminating much of the formal structure of Islam. In March 1924 he abolished the Caliphate and then the office of Şeyh-ul Islâm. He closed religious schools and medreses. He abolished religious courts. But the dress of most Turks remained Islamic and Mustafa Kemal determined to change it.

## Off with the fez and on with the hat

Mustafa Kemal first focused his attention on male headwear (see Fig. 40). Since they lacked brims, both the fez and the *kalpak* allowed the Muslim worshipper's forehead to contact the ground in the ritual act of prayer and thus were often taken as a symbol of Islamic allegiance. They were not, however, exclusively Muslim wear; some Greeks, Armenians and other Christians also wore fezzes or *kalpaks*. But, as *hats* had brims that prevented contact between the forehead and the ground, they proclaimed to all Turks that the wearer was not a Muslim and was, in fact, a *gâvur*, infidel. The devout therefore felt that to don a hat was to deny one's faith. Indeed, at that time the expression *şapka giymek* 'literally: to wear a hat' meant to apostasize and become a Christian (Lewis 1974: 102) and the mere sight of a hat could provoke hostility. In the late nineteenth century Muslim children in Maraş would hurl pebbles at Christian children to cries of 'Here come the Hatwearers!' (Padwick 1958).

Any attempt to remove the fez from Turkish heads and replace it with a hat was therefore fraught with danger and required caution as well as boldness. Mindful of the problems faced by Selim III and Mahmud II in their dress reform attempts, Mustafa Kemal proceeded with both caution

**Figure 40** Drawing by Howard Tangye of a well-known and widely displayed photograph taken in the mid-1920s of the hatless and formally dressed Ghazi Mustapha Kemal Pasha, President of the Turkish Republic

and determination. He prepared the ground carefully before each step. Like Sultan Mahmud II a century before, Mustafa Kemal introduced changes to military headgear before turning his attention to the population at large. He made his bodyguards wear peaked hats, then, pointing out the protection a peak provided against dazzling sunshine, he made this part of the normal Turkish military uniform, which was by then in other respects similar to Western European uniforms. Next, he wore a Panama hat on his model farm. Then, in the same headgear, he went to the conservative province of Kastamonu in north-central Anatolia and on 24 August 1925 made a speech attacking the fez. He later explained that he chose Kastamonu as the place to start this campaign because he had never been there before, so the people would not notice that he himself had adopted a new form of headgear, and would accept it as his norm, whereas if he had first appeared in a hat in Izmir, where he was well known, his changed appearance would immediately have caused an adverse reaction (Mumcu 1979: 167–8).

Four days later, in the same province, at the Black Sea port of Inebolu he continued his 'civilising mission' with a speech in which he declared:

A civilized, international dress is worthy and appropriate for our nation, and we will wear it. Boots or shoes on our feet, trousers on our legs, shirt and tie, jacket and waistcoat – and, of course, to complete these, a cover with a brim on our heads. I want to make this clear. This headcovering is called 'hat' (Lewis 1969: 263).[7]

Encouraged by the first reception of his own hat, Mustafa Kemal became bolder and decided to make hats compulsory for men. So, on 25 November a law was passed banning the fez and requiring all men to wear hats. The enforcement of this law was made easier because the Law for the Maintenance of Order was still in effect following Şeyh Said's rebellion. Some Turkish writers, allowing their devotion to Atatürk to dull their critical faculties, have portrayed the change as a measure that simply had to be desired by him in order to be enthusiastically welcomed by his compatriots. Ahmet Mumcu, for example, claims,

> The immediate acceptance of the hat by the people of Kastamonu spread to every part of the country. Everyone immediately cast off the fez. This event shows that the Turkish nation had never adopted the fez. When Atatürk's experiment ended in success, the 'Law concerning the wearing of hats' was promulgated on 25 November 1925. From that date onwards the hat and the cap became the genuine attribute of the Turkish nation and society became westernized in appearance. With the hat the West's symbol of civilization was adopted by the Turkish nation (1979: 168).

But in fact this seeming assault on their faith so upset some believers that there were demonstrations in favour of the fez – the very item that less than a century before believers had taken exception to. A more accurate account of what took place in 1925 was given by Lyman MacCallum, who had lived in Turkey before and returned at this time:

> The outlawing of the fez and of the brimless sheepskin cap *(kalpak)* occurred shortly after my arrival in 1925 and I would have difficulty in making you feel the excitement of those days. To you it seems a thrilling change, but to those who underwent it nothing could have been more shocking.
>
> The reformers saw that this distinction of headgear was the most obvious of the outward differences separating Turkey from the West. It made the Turk picturesque, an object of gaping pleasure to tourists. Therefore it had to go. But for millions of Turks the hat or visored cap was the badge of the loathsome unbeliever, and the wearing of it a sin for the Muslim, who could not then touch his forehead to the ground in the course of his daily prayers. Divorce had been obtained by women who had satisfied the court that while in Europe their husbands had donned hats.
>
> Kemal Pasha proceeded with great caution. While working in the sun on his farm he wore a panama once or twice, and the photograph appeared in every paper. There was a quiet but steady press campaign. Then he went to one of the most conservative districts of the country, held a mass meeting of villagers,

enthused them with his oratory to the point where they threw their fezzes, turbans and *kalpaks* on the ground and leapt upon them with cries of 'Cursed be our fezzes, our *kalpaks!*' Then Kemal could do nothing but bow to the expressed wish of the people and abolish the fez.

In Marash, the town of my boyhood, there was some public disturbance over the reform, resulting in shouting and public executions. With this slight show of force the great reform was effected. Kemal Pasha's aide told some of us this year that this was the most difficult and most fundamental of all Kemal's reforms. After the Turks had crossed that ditch there was no reform that he could not have forced on them (Padwick 1958: 49–50).

Even that extract does not convey the full extent of the government's anxiety over the Hat Law. As Geoffrey Lewis records, 'So grave were the disorders that a cruiser was ordered to Rize, on the Black Sea, and Independence Tribunals went into action. Not a few *hocas* were hanged for preaching against the new law' (1974: 104) .

Some sources claim that about ten men suffered martyrdom rather than adopt 'infidel headgear' – the same number as those who reportedly died a century before resisting the introduction of the fez rather than abandon the previous symbol of Muslim identity, the turban (Ellison 1928: 92). This may well be an underestimate considering the number of places where executions to quell resistance were reported. Certainly the implementation of the reform was made easier because the draconian independence tribunals executing the Law for the Maintenance of Order, passed after the Şeyh Sait rebellion of February and March 1925, were still operating.

The introduction of hats on a countrywide scale was not without its comic as well as its grim side. Unsurprisingly, supplies of brimmed or peaked male headgear were insufficient for the sudden new demand. The foreign press had fun describing senior civil servants so desperate to obey the latest dictate that they appeared in women's hats. They were not alone. Armstrong notes, 'In one village behind Smyrna the villagers discovered, in the closed shop of a deported Armenian, a pile of women's summer hats. They wore them feathers, ribbons and all'. (See Armstrong for a fuller account of the implementation of this reform (19 : 287–290).

When, on 25 October, 1925, the Grand National Assembly debated the proposal to make all men wear hats, there was only one objection. Nurettin Pasha, the deputy for Bursa, who had a reputation for fanaticism and was regarded by some people as guilty of the torching of Izmir in 1922, claimed that such a rule would be contrary to Article 103 of the Constitution that guaranteed personal liberty.[8]

Two years after he forced the hat on Turkish heads, Kemal explained his reasons in his marathon speech of 15–20 October, 1927: 'Gentlemen, it was necessary to abolish the fez which sat on the heads of our nation as an emblem of ignorance, negligence, fanaticism and hatred of progress and civilization, to accept in its place the hat, the headgear used by the whole civilized world, and in this way to demonstrate that the Turkish nation, in its mentality as in other respects, in no way diverges from civilized life' (Lewis 1969: 263).[9] In the same speech he said that he had not revealed all his reforming intentions in his Manifesto of 8 April 1923 because that would have 'given reactionaries the chance to poison the whole nation.' His step by step approach to revealing his plans is well known. It is therefore interesting to note that back in 1922 he had said to Grace Ellison, an Englishwoman in Ankara, 'In two years from now, every woman must be freed from this useless tyranny [the veil]. Every man will wear a hat instead of a fez and every woman have her face uncovered.' Grace Ellison published this prediction but it was ignored in Europe because no-one believed it could be achieved (1923: 185).

As if to emphasise that both faith and fashion were his to command, Mustafa Kemal ordered Istanbul MP Edip Servet and former governor of Yemen Mahmut Nedim to wear hats in Mecca while attending an Islamic conference in July 1926 as representatives of the Republic (*2000'e doğru*, 17–23 May 1987: 9).

A few years later the Hat Reform had interesting repercussions in the Hatay when the future of that province was in dispute before it was eventually united with the Turkish Republic in 1939. When Turkish inhabitants *of* the region started agitating in the 1930s for the province to become part of Turkey, they donned hats like their future compatriots across the border. Thereupon Greek and Armenian residents, who were accustomed to wearing hats, abandoned them in favour of the fez so as to prevent hat-wearers forming a majority and thereby strengthening Turkey's claims. Thus, in the Hatay, the hat became the symbol of those who wanted Turkish rule and the fez the symbol of those who wanted to be citizens of Syria (*Yurt Ansiklopedisi* 1982: 3408).

## The veil discouraged

Unlike the fez, the veil was not the subject of state legislation, though its use was discouraged with varying degrees of enthusiasm and some local authorities prohibited it (Lewis 1969: 338, n.62).[10] It was wisely considered that an outright ban on the veil would provoke a catastrophic storm. For devout Muslims such an affront to their modesty would be intolerable. Arthur Goldschmidt, commenting on the forced unveiling of women in Iran under Reza Shah, aptly compared the shock to the feelings Westerners would experience if women of all ages were forced to go topless in public (1983: 210).

The message was nevertheless clear: un-Western dress was uncivilized dress. In his speech at Kastamonu where he derided the fez, Mustafa Kemal also touched on women's dress and their practice of hiding their features from men. He said it was a spectacle that makes the nation an object of ridicule and it must be remedied at once (Lewis 1969: 265).

Some devoted Kemalists promote the myth that thereafter Turkish women in general *joyfully* cast off their veils and appeared in western fashions. Ahmet Mumcu depicts the development as follows:

> Atatürk regarded it as the greatest reproach to Turkishness that Turkish women were going around in medieval garb. It was a fact that in pre-Islamic times Turkish women had not gone around like ogres, instead they had taken their place beside men in every sphere. When our women gained their rights they cast off their medieval dress. Clad in modern mode, they took their places beside men. That strange costume, the *çarşaf* and the *peçe*, in which our womenfolk had been unwillingly wrapped, soon disappeared in the course of natural development. The Turkish reforms used no compulsion in this matter. Claiming their own rights, our womenfolk put an end to this *affront* to their self-respect. This is another concrete example of the sensible and modern direction of the Turkish reforms (1979: 169).

In reality the process was by no means so swift or so universally popular. Nevertheless, many women embraced the new freedom of dress eagerly. Soon after it was introduced a Turkish mother talked enthusiastically of the advantages her daughter would enjoy:

> When I compare her freedom with all the unnecessary restrictions placed upon us by religion and custom; when I feel that she will never know what a veil means; can you wonder at the veneration we women have for our great Ruler, who has made this change possible and given us the right to take our part in the life going on around us? Loyalty and affection can never repay him for what he has done for us. It would be a poor specimen of a Turkish woman who did not thank Allah for the Ghazi (Ellison 1928: 179).

As Westernisation proceeded apace new forms of dress occupied the thoughts of privileged Turkish women. In Istanbul, Grace Ellison reported:

> Going into mixed society has made women very vain; they have morning, afternoon and evening dresses. The arrival of *Femina* with new models is awaited with feverish excitement. My friend, with her pencil, like a schoolmistress, marks her copy: the new Drecoll for A; Lanvin for B; Vionnet for C. By the time that the friends arrive their dresses are all chosen for them. They hunt the bazaar for stuffs, one cuts, another fits, another machines, another does the skirts, another the sleeves .... Who ever would have supposed in the old days that my friend could have turned out such excellent dresses! (1928: 176–7).

In the mid-1920s she was in Konya and witnessed the first public ball there, an event organized to raise funds for the Red Crescent.

... the army supplied the band; *Femina* suggested many of the dresses which the ladies made themselves, and those who were skilful enough offered their services as hair cutters.

The question of all questions, however, and one which needed the most careful handling, lest it should ruin the whole ball, was the question of sleeves. 'Sleeves or no sleeves?' asked the dancers; it was a question for my friend's husband to decide, and he at first set his teeth firmly against his wife's wearing a sleeveless dress. To unveiled hair and low necks he had grown accustomed, but sleeveless or short-sleeved dresses he disliked, and so his final decision of 'No sleeves' was something of a triumph. What my friend did the other ladies would do.

Yet on the day of the ball, many had not the courage to show themselves except with high necks, sleeves, and turbans. Others dared not separate themselves from their fur coats (Ellison 1928: 262–3).

As the general secularising reforms began to take effect in Turkey and young people left schools and colleges imbued with the spirit of Kemalists, the outward appearance of Turkish urban women increasingly followed western fashions and veiled women became an oddity. Some women went so far as enter beauty competitions clad in bathing costumes, and great was the rejoicing among Kemalists whenever a Miss Turkey won an international competition.[11]

## Reforms consolidated

By the time of Attaturk's death in 1938 urban Turks of both sexes had become thoroughly accustomed to western costume. Four years earlier another dress law had forbidden the wearing of religious garb outside places of worship though eight chiefs of various religions were granted exemption (Lewis 1969: 264, n.57). This law not only placed further restraints on Islamic functionaries, it also deprived unscrupulous fraudsters of opportunities to deceive the gullible by posing as men of religion.

In rural areas the dress reform changes had less effect than in the towns. Peasants' dress was still chiefly determined by a mixture of practical considerations and tradition. The tradition was not exclusively Islamic. Where peasant men and women worked together in the fields, strict veiling had never been the norm. Moreover, regional or group identities were – and still are – often manifested in colourful traditional dress. The *Tahtacıs*, for example, who may be seen in hill villages above Edremit, Silifke and elsewhere, are easy to distinguish. Many items of their elaborate costumes represent aspects of their beliefs and important events in their history.

As townspeople's dress became more westernised, so the contrast between urban and rural dress became more marked. Thus, to the peasants a *kravatlı* (or in rural speech, a *gravatlı*) – a man in a tie – was seen as someone in authority, someone who more than likely would be making demands upon them. This one item of dress provided playwrights and novelists with a ready means of characterisation. A further distinction was in the headgear. Although hats were *de riguer* in the cities, it was the peaked cap that adorned the peasant head. This, as well as satisfying the law, bestowed a double benefit: its visor could keep the sun out of the eyes, but it could also be reversed when prayer time arrived and so permit the forehead to touch the ground. (It could not, however, protect its wearers from the haughty disdain of many townsmen, a disdain akin to that displayed nowadays in Britain to youths wearing reversed baseball caps!)

After Atatürk's death the cult of Kemalism continued. Young people were brought up to revere him to the point of worship. So the dress reforms became further consolidated. Even after the introduction of multi-party politics resulted in a change of government in 1950 and a softening of the anti-Islamic campaign, there were no moves to revert to Islamic forms of dress. There was no desire to bring back the fez. No veiled women were to be seen in universities or employed in government offices.

## The Islamic challenge to the reforms

Leaders of the 1960 military coup that ousted Menderes strove to reinforce the Kemalist tradition. But later in the decade, as party politics again became more bitter, challenges to that tradition appeared. In 1969 there was the first example of a problem that was to become a major headache for Turkish governments in the 1980s and 90s: a young woman was expelled from the Theology Faculty of Ankara University for insisting on covering her head. The long-stifled resentment of the devout at Atatürk's demotion of Islam in their country soon began to find expression.

In the 1970s the National Salvation Party, led by Necmettin Erbakan, tried to create 'indigenous dress styles for Muslim women', and to legitimize 'traditional Islamic dress'. As a consequence, Turkish women clad in long fawn raincoats and headscarves soon became a common sight on Turkish streets. This garb marked them out as followers of what was regarded as the Islamic Party.

As the 1970s drew to a close, serious violence spread throughout Turkey and dress became a matter of literally vital importance. In numerous incidents Leftists and Rightists shot each other on sight, because the outward appearance, such as the style of hair, beards and moustaches, proclaimed the inward political and/or religious conviction. Even factional differences were reflected: the droop of a moustache would serve to distinguish a Maoist from a Marxist.

The situation had grown so serious that there was a general sense of relief in Turkey when the armed forces, led by General Kenan Evren, stepped in on 12 September 1980 to oust the politicians and impose military rule yet again.

One of the first acts of the new military rulers was to introduce 'Dress and Appearance Regulations' prohibiting employees while on duty in public agencies, offices, and institutions from wearing, in the case of men, moustaches, beards, long hair, and in the case of women, mini-skirts, low-necked dresses, and headscarves *(başrütsü)*. This regulation was interpreted as applying to students as well as civil servants and was intended to prevent the instant identification of a person as a political or religious friend or foe and thus to halt the ruthless killings that had become so commonplace.

In an attempt to bring the nation together the military stressed their devotion to Kemalist principles, thinking that these would still serve as a generally accepted basis on which to rebuild Turkish democracy. It soon became apparent that allegiance to Atatürk no longer commanded the unquestioning respect of the whole population. Many religious Turks had reordered their priorities and now wished to emphasise Islamic rather than Kemalist teaching. With some official sanction a new doctrine, the Turkish-Islamic synthesis, emerged. It attempted to reconcile the demands of Islam with those of a modern Turkish state and reach a compromise that would be widely acceptable. Its overall effect was to boost the confidence of religious Turks and upset the secularists.

As the 1980s progressed, religious elements became more vociferous in Turkey and began to exert greater pressure, particularly after the restoration of civilian government. They forbade the exploitation of religion for political purposes but religion nevertheless became an increasingly important issue in the competition for votes. It was not surprising, therefore, that Prime Minister Turgut Özal, a moderate practising Muslim himself as well as a consummate politician, took the opportunity of an official visit to Saudi Arabia in February 1984 to become *Hacı* (Hajji) Turgut Özal. Pictures in the Turkish press showing him clad in the plain sheet-like garment of a humble pilgrim elicited a predictably divided response from the Turkish public: the devout were delighted, the secularists were disturbed. When President Evren later followed the same trail, secularists were further perturbed.

## The *Türban* Issue

The chief issue that brought the deep divisions between secularists and devout Muslims into the open was, however, the disputed right of women to cover their heads for religious reasons. Since this topic assumed such great importance it is appropriate to deal with it in some detail, first mentioning the key words used by protagonists, and then outlining the course of events before recording some reflections on them.

## Terminology

Three words appear frequently in reports of the head-covering issue in Turkey: *başörtüsü, tesettür* and *türban*. Since the topic has acquired a linguistic as well as a religious and political dimension, the actual meanings attached to these words tend to vary according to the attitude of the person using them. There have semantic shifts since the matter achieved prominence. Because the whole subject is very sensitive, anyone asking the vigorous campaigners involved to define these terms can expect to be met with suspicion or refusal. I am grateful to many friends for aiding my research by persisting in the face of difficulties to discover from a variety of sources how different groups were using these words.

Taking a starting point well before the current controversy arose, the definition of *başörtüsü* given in the 1955 edition of the Turkish Language Society's dictionary says it is 'a covering made of muslin or something such as silk that women wrap round their heads to cover their hair.' In those days it was a neutral term having no special religious connotations. *Başörtüsü* was the sort of headcovering favoured by maids and many peasant women and it usually left some hair exposed and made no attempt to conceal the face or neck. Since it was favoured by peasants and the first generation of migrants to the towns, people who were well established in society tended to perceive *başörtüsü* as an indication of lowly status (Ilyasoğlu 1994: 107). So, the general public found it socially as well as politically and religiously disconcerting when women at universities started to wear *başörtüsü* – albeit of a sort that concealed more of their features than the traditional variety. On 22 July 1984 the newspaper *Milliyet* attempted to clarify the definition of *başörtüsü* with pictures illustrating how headscarves needed to be arranged. When the dispute progressed inn the 1980s, the word *başörtüsü,* as used by many religious people, acquired symbolic Islamic significance, as they said that *başörtüsü* should conceal the head, neck and shoulders as well as part of the face. The most ardent argued that it should be almost synonymous with *tesettür.* The dictionary defined *tesettür* as 'a concealment from men; veiling of Muslim women.' The meaning of this word has not undergone much change. It denotes the covering not only of the head but also the body and legs down to the ankles. The word *türban* does not appear in either the 1955 or 1974 Turkish Language Society dictionaries. It was introduced into the dress controversy in the 1980s in an attempt to defuse the increasingly troublesome *başörtüsü* issue. The Higher Education Council ruled that 'a modern turban (*türban*) may be worn instead of a headscarf'. (The traditional Turkish word for a turban was *sarık*.) Keen Kemalists took the view that the permitted *türban* should mean a modern western woman's fashionable item of headwear with perhaps a dash of oriental glamour, since up to that tame it had been a little-used term to describe fashionable women's head-covering of a style associated with older members of well-to-do families. At the other extreme, when Islamic radicals adopted the word, they claimed that the right to wear a *türban* meant women could cover their head and shoulders completely as part of an Islamic costume that concealed the rest of the human form too (thus, for them, it too became virtually synonymous with *tesettür.*

The styles of women's head-covering vary. Some women wear coloured and patterned headscarves, and those who are not wearing it for religious reasons may leave some of their hair exposed. Some other women, perhaps vying with one another to display the intensity of their piety, don black, sometimes together with a black *çarşaf* (an all-concealing, shapeless garment that covers a woman from head to foot) and, as the final item in their *tesettür,* dark glasses to hide their eyes. It is claimed that some women who belong to particular religious groups or movements reveal their membership to those in the know by the way they secure their headscarves. But whatever colour or style of head-covering is worn, they all come under the dictionary definition of *başörtüsü.*

*Tesettür,* that full concealment of the body from male gaze, also takes a variety of forms in accordance with the wearer's brand of belief. Rather than wear a *çarşaf* many women opt for ankle-length outercoats resembling long raincoats, usually in plain colours (fawn and light lilac are popular). Special fashion shows for women who opt for Islamic dress confirm that clothes manufacturers are alert to the sales potential of this segment of the population and that many of the wearers are drawn from financially secure sectors of society. In the 1990s religious attire is not a sign of poverty.

## The course of events

The 1969 expulsion of the covered female student already mentioned was remembered in July 1984 when four female medical students were suspended from Uludağ University for going to their examinations wearing scarves wrapped round their heads. This time the matter did not end there. Four days later the newspaper *Milliyet* showed Dr. Koru, Assistant Professor of Chemical Engineering in Ege University, Izmir, in her headscarf. She claimed that any ban on this would violate her human rights, but the rector of her university took a different view. 'Off duty she can do as she likes, but on duty let her take off her headscarf.' He went on to say, 'I have found a solution to this problem. If she wishes she can tie on a turban, then no-one can see her head or her hair'. The matter later went to court and the court decided that Dr. Koru's constitutional rights had not been violated.[12]

The dress dispute dominated the headlines throughout the last days of that month. *Milliyet* published photographs of women in *çarşaf* and men ignoring the law against turbans and skull-caps. It also reported that two students had been turned away from the library of the Grand National Assembly because they were wearing head scarves. Another paper reported that the privilege of making the traditional speech at the Medical Faculty of Ankara University had been denied to the top student because she was wearing a 'turban'.

The head-covering issue gradually assumed larger and larger proportions. In October 1986 there were demonstrations in Ankara against the ban. In 1987 President Evren felt obliged to refer to the subject in his New Year message to the nation. Prime Minister Turgut Özal publicly took a much more accommodating line. In the universities some female students tried novel means to thwart staff who tried to make them remove their scarves. They immediately replaced the scarves with wigs! On 8 December 1988, YÖK, the Council for Higher Education in Turkey pronounced, 'In our opinion a modern *türban* is 'contemporary' [and therefore acceptable in Kemalist language] but the covering of the hair and neck for reasons of religious belief falls outside this ruling'. Prime Minister Minister Turgut Özal had by this time adopted the term *türban* as a convenient way of fudging the issue.

The dispute then rapidly escalated. In January 1989 President Evren took the matter to the Constitutional Court, and thirteen university teachers asked the Council of State to disallow a regulation permitting the *türban*. On 7 March the Constitutional Court ruled against allowing head-covering. Reaction was swift and stormy. 10 March 1989 was dubbed Black Friday on account of the mass demonstrations and clashes with police in major cities over this issue. Women clad in black laid symbolic wreaths. It was part of a more vociferous expression of Islamic identity on the part of those people who felt they were being denied rights taken for granted elsewhere. Amid allegations that the demonstrators were receiving help from outside the country, international tension rose with reports of eight Iranians being arrested in Istanbul for provocative acts. It was also alleged that Iranian broadcasts lauding the demonstrations in Turkey had declared, 'the Shari'a cannot be introduced without bloodshed.' Turkish secularists were enraged by the *türban* campaign, regarding it as a deliberate move in an overall plan to make Turkey an Islamic state. They feared that if ever these Islamists formed a government they would force everyone to observe Islamic dress rules and other regulations.

Further demonstrations to demand the right to wear *başörtüsü* followed in Istanbul and Ankara before the Higher Education Bill, published on 28 December 1989, allowed universities to make their own regulations on whether or not women should be allowed to cover their heads in class. In practice it was mostly left to departmental heads or individual lecturers to decide what they would permit. Some teachers maintained vehement objection to headcovering, others allowed it (see Fig. 41).

In March 1990, Turgut Özal, by now President of the Republic,

**Figure 41** Women students take advantage of the relaxation in university dress regulations

Drawing by Howard Tangye from the front page photograph in the secular daily newspaper, *Cumhuriyet*, 31 October 1990.

attempted to defuse the issue by saying, 'What does it matter if one or two girls march? It isn't going to overthrow the secular nature of the Turkish state' (Özal 1989). Sadly, the problem did not go away. Some of the heat had been taken out of it when universities were given greater freedom to regulate themselves, but on 6 October 1990 Professor Bahriye Üçok, a prominent secularist and opponent of the Islamic radicals, was assassinated.

The electoral victories of the Refah Party in some major cites, including Ankara and Istanbul, in the March 1994 municipal elections – albeit with under half of the total votes cast there – were followed by women employees of those municipalities being allowed, but not forced, to wear *başörtüsü* at work. But that has not stopped extremist violence. In July 1995, the lawyer Ali Günday, Chairman ot Gümüşhane Bar Association, was assassinated for his opposition to the campaign for the right to wear headscarves. In August 1995 a father from the Black Sea region killed his daughter because she refused to cover her head.

## Observations

The polarisation over the issue leaves extremists on each side claiming a monopoly of virtue. They are convinced that their opponents' motives are malign. Each side looks to its own sources of inspiration to justify its stance. Ardent Kemalists feel duty-bound to oppose any concession that they fear might weaken the secular basis of the state. Pious Muslims point to the authority of sacred texts. Fierce debate, impassioned pamphlets and countless press articles have therefore focused on the interpretation of Koranic references to dress and decorum. These (in Pickhall's translation) are the verses most often quoted:

> Surah XXIV, v. 31. 'And tell the believing women to lower their gaze and be modest, and to display of their adornment only that which is apparent, and to draw their veils over their bosoms, and not to reveal their adornment save to their own husbands or fathers or husbands' fathers, or their sons or their husbands' sons, or their brothers or their brothers' sons or sisters' sons, or their women, or their slaves, or male attendants who lack vigour, or children who know naught of women's nakedness. And let them not stamp their feet so as to reveal what they hide of their adornment. And turn unto Allah together, O believers, in order that ye may succeed.'

> Surah XXIV, v. 60. 'As for women past child-bearing, who have no hope of marriage, it is no sin for them if they discard their (outer) clothing in such a way as not to show adornment. But to refrain is better for them. Allah is Hearer, Knower.'

> Surah XXXIII, v. 59. 'O Prophet! Tell thy wives and thy daughters and the women of the believers to draw their cloaks close round them (when they go abroad). That will be better, that so they may be recognised and not annoyed. Allah is ever Forgiving, Merciful.' .

In addition to these verses, various Hadith are cited in support of minor differences between rival Muslim groups.

But the essential gulf lies between the devout and the secularists. And that gulf remains so wide that neither side can appreciate the other's attitude.

One hotly disputed question at the height of the dispute was whether Saudis and Iranians were paying Turkish students to cover their heads. Islamic radicals denied this, but many members of university staff had no doubt that it was so. Some students who had privately admitted receiving payment would put on the headscarves at university and remove them when nearing home. As the campaign intensified many people regarded the covered women as militants or even terrorists. Secularist lecturers in the universities feared these demonstrators were clamouring for a return to the dark ages.

The challenge seemed all the more alarming to Turkish leaders since it was not between a lofty educated elite and underprivileged illiterates ignorant of the modern world. This battle was being fought in the campuses of universities created to fulfil Atatürk's aim to bring Turkey up the level of contemporary civilization. Both sides were familiar with modern technology and both sides could manipulate the media. No longer could it be assumed that educated women would automatically adopt the smart suit and western hair-styles that had previously signalled their membership of the elite.

The youthfulness of the protesters prompted some commentators to conclude that this was an example of the challenges that younger generations the world over make to their elders in an effort to assert their own independence and build a brighter future.

The challenge also had feminist overtones. Although men joined in the demonstrations, the campaign for the right to be covered when in public places was chiefly fought by women for women. Their self-assertiveness brought some of these women into contact with political parties and policies. As a consequence, the face of politicised Islam in Turkey changed, becoming more distinctive and less closely associated with the political right in general (Ilyasoğlu 1994: 57).

In the growing mood of self-assertiveness it was official attempts to stop the headcovering that actually prompted some students to take an interest in the subject and to cover their own heads. The confrontational aspect of the dispute served to strengthen their resolve. Many became eager to use this means to make a public proclamation of their faith and their rejection of lax western moral standards.

One such student, clad completely in black, outlined her views to me with deep conviction, a conviction she had demonstrated by refusing to take her final examinations for her degree because she was not allowed to do so veiled. She was veiled, she assured me in an interview in 1992, because she was a Muslim.

> The law requiring men to wear hats is still in force, but no-one now does so and no action is taken. On the other hand, although the veil was never banned by law, there is discrimination against women who choose to wear it. There is propaganda and pressure to persuade Turkish women to dress in 'contemporary style' like western women. Veiled people are likened to tortoises in their shells and told to open up. Some women who would like to veil do not because they would be banned from their offices. I have not received payments from Iran, Saudi Arabia or elsewhere to wear the veil. My own family are not in favour of me wearing it.

It is alleged that the wearers were not on speaking terms with their husbands. Such practices continue. In 1979, for example, fans of the singer Zeki Müren could buy or make *oya* representing his famous eyelashes, while a woman wishing to support the leader of her political party could wear *oya* named 'Ecevit's nose!' But these minor dress distinctions are part of a private language usually unintelligible to outsiders.

## Men's dress

In recent years men's dress has caused far less controversy than women's. There has not been any campaign in favour of the fez. In 1984, members of still illegal *tarikats* (*sufi* orders) wore skull-caps and other headgear peculiar to their particular orders at the funeral of the Halveti-Cerrahi leader Sheikh Muzaffer Ozak. This action was still sufficiently unusual to provoke fierce condemnation from the strongly secular *Cumhuriyet* newspaper. (Skull-caps, along with the fez and berets had been banned by the 1925 Hat Law.) But now, visitors to areas such as the Fatih district of Istanbul are struck by the proliferation of skull-caps and other sorts of prayer-hats worn in public. They also encounter many men eager to show their devotion to the Prophet by wearing their beards trimmed to the exact shape that he is said to have preferred. (There is not, in fact, complete agreement about the proper shape, but the most favoured is the round trimmed beard known as *çember sakal.*) The fact that such Islamic male dress no longer excites much interest shows how the Islamic resurgence has gained ground in recent years, though recently young boys from particularly pious families have been dressed in skull-caps, causing some Turks to liken their appearance to that of orthodox Jewish boys.

But virtually no one wears the fez – a tacit acknowledgement perhaps that it would make them figures of fun. Yet the popular daily Milliyet (13.4. 1996) reported a threat to law and order in the Sorgun district of Yozgat when Islamic activists demonstrated their displeasure at the arrest of eight like-minded believers who had been arrested for going round in turbans and fezzes in contravention of the Dress Law.

Dress regulations continue to have their effect on public sector employees, and a necktie still confers status. It is observable that Turkish customs officials are more likely to wave through a passenger wearing a tie than one whose dress suggests he is of less account.

## School books

The Turkish school curriculum includes instruction on the subject of dress. The approved textbooks for the course on religion and social studies teach all children the virtues of clean, smart, and appropriate clothing but they ignore the question of headcovering (See, e.g. Fiğlali 1988: 113).

## Alevis

Up to the present time, Turkish school textbooks have also ignored Alevis and Bektashis, the non-Sunni devotees of Ali, the fourth Caliph, who constitute – according to some estimates – as much as twenty per cent of the country's population. There are periodic clashes between Sunni extremists and Alevis, who from the first have been staunch supporters of Mustafa Kemal, whom they hail as their liberator from Sunni oppression. Alevis side firmly with the secularists in efforts to prevent religious interference in state affairs. They have traditionally proclaimed the equality of women with men. Alevi women have never been veiled and although they often wear headscarves they feel no obligation to conceal all their hair or cover their faces.

## The Military

Turkish military uniforms are now completely westernised. The Turkish Armed Forces remain the strongest bastion against religious reaction as they are imbued with Kemalism and rigorously root out any officers or NCOs associated with groups wanting to make Islam dominant again in state affairs.

## Conclusion

While this article was being written the issue of dress continued to capture the headlines in Turkey. On 1 December 1995, with general elections imminent and Necmeddin Erbakan's pro-Islamic Refah Party tipped to win the greatest number of seats though not enough to form a government in the new parliament, *başörtüsü* items still claim front page space in national newspapers. The staunchly Islamic *Millî Gazete* reports that a professor in the medical faculty at Haccettepe University in Ankara is refusing to accept a veiled student. The popular daily, *Milliyet,* noting Refah's reason for not putting forward any women as candidates in the election ('Turkey is not ready for veiled MPs in the Assembly') reports the disillusion of some women who had worked hard for the party. Some who had taken part in the *türban* campaign in universities now think there should be campaign to force parliament to accept MPs in *tesettür.* Another report in the same paper notes that women in *tesettür* are enrolling in increasing numbers for karate and aerobics classes at a Women's Cultural Centre in Istanbul. The front page of *Hürriyet* shows a group of young women in headscarves enthusiastically singing the praises of Refah. The caption reads: 'Refah's turbaned pop singers'. Thus dress remains very much at the heart of religious and political concern in Turkey. The importance of dress is evident to all as rival party leaders bid for the allegiance of Turkish voters. Necmeddin Erbakan, who has 'his' women's heads securely wrapped, leads the Islamic challenge to the Kemalists. In her chic Chanel dresses, Tansu Çiller, Turkey's elegantly coiffured first woman prime minister, personified the realisation of Atatürk's ambition to make Turks part of the modern Western world. These contrasting styles convincingly demonstrate that the dress of its citizens conveys clear messages about the state of the Turkish nation. Similarly, the decision of Erbakan and Çiller to unite in a coalition government in the mid-1996 illustrates the unpredicatable nature of Turkish Politics.

## Acknowledgements

I should like to acknowledge my thanks to many Turkish academics who helped me with advice and information in the preparation of this article. I am particularly indebted to Dr. Akile Gürsoy of Marmara University for most generously making available to me her own collection of relevant press cuttings and other material. I must also record my special gratitude to Professor Engin Uzmen, Dr. Hamit Ersoy, Dr. Nurgün Oktik, Dr. Kunt and B. Uslu.

## Notes

1 A useful definition of dress is given by Joanne B. Eicher and Mary Ellen Roach-Higgins: 'an assemblage of body modifications and/or supplements displayed by a person in communicating with other human beings.' Thus it is 'a comprehensive term to identify both direct body changes and items added to the body' (1993: 15). Conveniently for our purposes, this definition allows the inclusion of beards and moustaches.
2 The term 'Islamic radicals' is adopted here since many Turkish Muslims object to the use of 'Islamists'. In Prime Minister Tansu Çiller's words (interview in *Time*): 'I'm a Muslim myself, so we should not say the Islamists. It is the radicals ... We have to fight the radicals.' She distinguished herself from the radicals by saying, 'I represent Westernization, secular government, liberalization, the link with Europe.'
3 Fatma Müge Göçek notes that 'the Ottoman minorities disturbed the Ottoman state by changing the attire they had traditionally been assigned. They started imitating Western styles of dress. An imperial decree of 1758 banned the minorities from 'wearing Western style clothing' as 'this abominable situation disturbed the order among the subjects' (1987: 124).
4 Göçek (1987: 46) confirms the great difference between outdoor and indoor dress for Ottoman women.
5 Illustrations of dress before and after the change are reproduced in Midhat Sertoğlu (1958: 18–19) from originals in Mahmud Şevket Paşsa, *Osmanli Teşkilât ve Kıyafetı Askeriyesi*.

6　For a more detailed account of the introduction of the fez for these troops, see Uzunçarşılı (1954: 223–230).
7　From *Soiled,* ii, 212–13. See also SAN. Özerdim, *Atatürk Devrimli Kronolojisi.*
8　Cf. Luigi Olivero (1952: 116), Turkish Ministry of Press Broadcasting and Tourism (1961); Kinross (19 : 314) notes that Nurettin 'had visiting cards printed with the title 'Conqueror of Smyrna'.'
9　Cf. *Nutuki,* 895; cf. *Speech,* 721–2.
10　See also Naval Intelligence Division (1942: 338): 'The veil was, however, prohibited at Trabzon by an ordinance of the local council on 5 December 1926.' Many books erroneously give the impression that the veil, like the fez, was banned throughout Turkey. See, for example, Wilcox (1992: 350): 'Turkish Moslem headdress banned 1928 – face veil or yashmak'.
11　Lewis (1969: 264n). See Plate VIIb showing Güneşli Başar, who was elected Miss Europe in 1951, and note the contrast to Plates VI and VIIa of Turkish women in earlier times.
12　See Olson (1985) for a valuable analysis and more detailed account of the early stages of the *türban* issue.

# Bibliography

Armstrong, Harold Courtney 1932. *Grey Wolf: Mustapha Kemal: an Intimate Study of a Dictator.* London: A. Barker.
Dekay, J. E. 1833. *Sketches of Turkey in 1831 and 1832 by an American.* New York: J. &Œ. Harper.
Eicher, J. B. and Roach-Higgins, M. E. 1993. 'Definition and Classification of Dress: Implications for Analysis of Gender Roles'. In Ruth Barnes and Joanne B. Eicher (eds), *Dress and Gender: Making and Meaning.* Providence and Oxford: Berg Publishers.
Ellison, G. 1923. *An Englishwoman in Angora.* London: Hutchinson.
—1928.*Turkey Today.* London: Hutchinson.
Fığlali, E. R. 1988. *Ortaokullar için Din Kültürü ve Ahlâk Bilgisi,* 3. Istanbul: Millî Eğitim Basımevi, p. 113.
Göçek, F. M. 1987. *East Encounters West: France and the Ottoman Empire in the Eighteenth Century.* Oxford: Oxford University Press.
Goldschmidt, A., Jr. 1983. A *Concise History of the Middle East* (2nd ed.). Boulder, Colorado: Westview Press.
Goodwin, G. 1995. *The Janissaries.* London: Saqi Books.
Hanoum, Z. 1913. *A Turkish Woman's European Impressions.* London: Seeley, Service & Co .
Ilyasoğlu, A. 1994. *Örtülü Kadin.* Istanbul: Metis Yayınıarı.
Kinross, J.P.D. 1964. *Atatürk: The Rebirth of a Nation.* London: Weidenfeld & Nicolson.
Kumbaracılar, I. n.d. *Serpuşlar.* Istanbul: Türkiye Turing ve Otomobil Kurumu Yayını.
Lewis, B. 1969. *The Emergence of Modern Turkey.* London: Oxford University Press.
Lewis, G. 1974. *Turkey* (4th ed.). London: Benn.
Lewis, R. 1971. *Everyday Life in Ottoman Turkey.* London: Batsford.
Melville, L. 1925. *Lady Mary Wortley Montagu: Her Life and Letters (1689–1762).* London: Hutchinson.
Mumcu, A. 1979. *Tarih Alçinidan Türk Devrimin Temelleri ve Gelişimi,* Istanbul: Inkılâp Aka.

Naval Intelligence Division, 1942. *Turkey,* Vol. I, London.

Olivero, L. 1952. *Turkey without Harems.* London: Macdonald.

Olson, E. A. 1985. 'Muslim Identity and Secularism in Contemporary Turkey: 'The Headscarf Dispute'.' *Anthropological Quarterly 58,* 4, 161–171.

Özal, T. 1989. Briefing, 13 March.

Padwick, C. E. 1958. *Call to Istanbul.* London: Longmans, Green.

Scarce, J. M. 1981. *Middle Eastern Costume from the Tribes and Cities of Iran and Turkey.* Edinburgh: The Royal Scottish Museum.

Sertoğlu, Midhat, 1958. *Resimli Osmanlı Tariki Ansiklopedisi.* Istanbul.

Shaw S.J. & Shaw, E.K. 1985. *History of the Ottoman Empire and Modern Turkey,* Vol II. Cambridge: Cambridge University Press.

Smyth, W.W. 1854. *A Year with the Turks. Sketches of Travel in the European and Asiatic Dominions of the Sultan.* New York: Redfield.

*The Asiatic Journal and Monthly Register for British and Foreign India, China, and Australasia.* Vol XXVI – New Series, May-August, 1838, London.

*Time,* Vol. 46, No. 21 (November 20, 1995).

Uzunçarşılı, I. H. 1954. 'Asâkir-i Mansüre'ye Fes Giydirilmesi Hakkinda.' *Belleten,* Vol. XVIII, No. 70 (April), 223–230.

Wilcox, R. T. 1992 *The Dictionary of Costume.* London: B.T. Batsford.

Wittman, W. 1971 (1803). *Travels in Turkey, Asia Minor, Syria and Egypt.* New York: Arno Press & The New York Times.

*Yurt Ansiklopedisi.* 1982. Istanbul: Anadoln Yayıncılık.

# Chapter Ten

# Politics of Dress: The Dress Reform Laws of 1920/30s Iran

*Patricia L. Baker*

The following extract from Foreign Office (Persian desk) minutes, dated 5th July 1935, relating to a confidential report from the British Embassy in Tehran serves to introduce this paper. The paper explores the dramatic changes in dress in Iran, as recorded primarily in contemporary British diplomatic correspondence. It also reveals the tenor of Whitehall evaluation of current socio-political happenings in Iran and Turkey (see also Baker 1986), which to the modern reader smacks more of post-prandial conversations in certain London club-rooms than a considered critique from the corridors of power. The Whitehall official is commenting on news of the abolition of a special cap, introduced by Reza Shah in 1928 and the establishment of a Tehran Academy on the lines of the Academie Française,

> I should be inclined to trace the close association of clothes with politics at any rate as far back as the red shirts of Garibaldi and the blue spectacles of the Nihilists – not to speak of the role played by the *lack* of a garment in the days of the sans-culottes. Nor is it only in Asia that the hat is a sign of regeneration, since the top hat is associated not only with the Industrial revolution in England, but also with the dawn of a new day for the enslaved peoples of Africa.
>
> The association of the new headgear with the foundation of the Academy is a particularly happy one, and there are plenty of fanciful precedents for the celebration of the hat in art – as for example the 'plaited hive of straw' which waked to ecstasy the living lyre of Shakespeare, or the elaborate headgear of a certain Lady Edward Bentinck which provoked an impromptu masterpiece from Romney.[1]

In fact the association of clothes with politics had a long history in the Islamic world. From Abbasid times (749–1258 CE) if not earlier, Islamic dynasties frequently favoured a particular colour or item of clothing:

> Black was used for the flags [and garments] of the Abbasids. Their flags were black as a sign of mourning for the martyrs of their family... and as a sign of reproach directed against the Umayyads who had killed them' (Ibn Khaldun 1967; 50–1).

It was required dress for Abbasid high officials at the twice-weekly audiences. Neglect or disinclination to don the dynastic colour or garment was perceived as a sign of disloyalty by the ruling regime (Salem 1977: 61). Similarly removal in public, voluntary or forced, of this distinguishing mark of allegiance signified to all observers the formal breaking with that grouping. Thus in more senses than one, the *kolah*, the tall black lamb-skin headdress of the 19th century Qajar regime worn by Iranian men, replaced the four-pointed cap of the former Afsharids (Otter 1748: 40; Algar 1969: 41) suggests that the four points represented Nadir Shah's political control over Iran, Afghanistan, India and Turkistan, but as Diba (1987: 96) argues it probably signified allegiance to Sunni Islam and the four caliphs of the Rashidun caliphate.

In Iran, as in Ottoman Turkey and then Afghanistan, official reform programmes of 'modernization' were accompanied by dress regulations; the 'New Order' yet again was to be manifested in new forms of dress. Unlike its territorial neighbours, the Qajar dynasty moved comparatively slowly in the direction of 'modernisation'. The country itself was less open to Western influence; in 1860–63 there were only some 25 British and 50 French residents in Iran, and some 42 Iranians studying abroad (Issawi 1971: 237; Neshat 1982: 155ff). It was in the spring of 1873, over forty-seven years later than in the Ottoman world, that the *sardari* and a fez-like head-dress were introduced as required dress for government officials. As with earlier attempts to 'modernize' military and court attire in the 1830s and 1840s, the Iranian *'ulama* viewed the innovation with dismay and anxiety, warning of Christian infiltration mindful that European and American evangelical missionaries were active in the Middle East at that time, and young Shi'i men wishing to be considered as *'adel* (honest, jurist material) were advised to avoid dressing like non-Muslims (see Algar 1969: 78, 181; Bakhash 1978: 112) He also had to avoid wearing gold and abstain from major sins (e.g. adultery, drinking alcohol).

There was also movement afoot in the Tehran *anderuns*. Several 19th century European writers considered the striking changes in the ladies' dress had resulted from the visit of the Qajar shah, Nasir al-Din (1848–96), to the Opera in Paris during his state visit of 1873,

> where the filmy skirts of the ballet-girls had produced a formidable effect...
> In consequence, he bought a quantity of ballet-girl costumes, and on his arrival [back] in Tehran had all his harem dressed like operatic fairies (Lorey & Sladen 1907: 107).[2]

One critic sourly commented that there were only two types of ladies who wore such 'European' affectations: 'those who can afford to lose their decency, and those who do not even know they have no decency to lose' (Sparroy 1902: 228). Such criticism did not dampen interest; by 1920 Parisian dressmakers were well established in Tehran.

The Qajar dynasty came to an end with the abdication of Shah Ahmad in the winter of 1925. Reza Khan, the Premier and Minister of War, took the crown and the dynastic name Pahlavi. His relations with the *'ulama* were cordial at this stage and although a debate regarding the abolition of veiling (wearing of the *chador* and *pecheh*) was already being aired in certain newspapers published in the capital (Paidar 1995: 92–5), he was presumably well aware of theological reservations. One established theologian, Hajji Shaykh Yusuf of Najaf and Gilan, prophetised that abolition would result directly in social disharmony and depravity; unattractive females would be scorned, and young men would turn to paedophilia (Pittman 1943: 209).

Observers in Tehran considered the impetus which spurred Reza Shah into dress reform was the short state visit of Amanullah and Soraya of Afghanistan returning from their European tour in the summer 1928, during which time Queen Soraya was seen in public unveiled. By this time a major re-drafting of Iranian legal codes relating to commercial, civil, family, and penal matters was well underway (Savory 1978: 92). The move away from *Shari'a* law in the direction of a European legal system was accompanied by an official requirement for judges, lawyers etc. to wear secular dress (i.e. not the long robes and turbans associated with the *'ulama* jurists). Among other projects, there was also a concerted drive to combat massive illiteracy and improve education, with schools, colleges and adult literacy programmes established. On a social level, word came from the palace that it was now acceptable behaviour that husbands and wives, brothers and sisters, should walk on the same pavement and visit cafes, theatres and cinemas together.[3]

Noting that for a number of months the Shah had been urging stylistic changes in dress, the British ambassador reported to London in early September 1928 that receiving a deputation of merchants wearing (as advised) European frock coats and a certain kind of headwear, later to be called the Pahlavi hat, Reza Shah was

> enormously pleased and made a little speech about uniformity of dress and manners which, he said, would lead to *'uniformity in life and politics and would finally weld Persia into one uniform whole'* (emphasis added).[3]

The ambassador recalled that the Shah was constantly 'advocating uniformity of dress', and recently had refused to receive Iranians wearing turbans. Something was clearly in the air.

On September 26, the cabinet announced the correct dress for men to be a Western coat, jacket, trousers with leather belt, and leather shoes in European styling. All government workers and school boys were to wear the so-called *kolah-i pahlavi*, as devised by the Shah.[4] The ambassador was unimpressed by the new head-gear:

> The Pahlavi cap is not prepossessing. It is nothing more than the round 'Kola' [*kulah*: a brim-less cap] with the addition of a straight peak and, worn with a short coat, it makes the wearer look like a railway porter.[5]

The stipulation to wear 'the uniform attire' (Wilber 1975: 138–9n) was extended on 25 December 1928 to all Iranian males, excepting Shi'i and Sunni *'ulama*, non-Muslim religious dignitaries and male children under the age of 6 years.[6] Members of the *'ulama* seeking exemption from the ruling had to present evidence of qualifications and training (this heralded a crackdown by the Ministry of Education on religious educational certification) (Akhavi 1980: 43–44). The law came into effect at Nauruz (March) 1929, but it was noted if circumstances required, its implementation in rural regions could be delayed for a year; originally, it had been mooted to make it compulsory only in the major towns. Non-compliance by townsmen was punishable by a fine of one to five tomans (later increased to thirty tomans),[7] and a jail sentence of one to seven days; villagers and tribesmen escaped the fine but not detention. The government ordered that the monies so exacted were to be used to purchase the new style of clothing for the poorer members of society.

The order came as no surprise to the British diplomats who were aware that for some months police in most towns had been

> busy in 'inviting' somewhat strenously the populace to change their old fashioned apparel for the new and when the 'invitations' have appeared to fall on deaf ears, other measures somewhat more forcible [e.g. trampling turbans underfoot] have been adopted.[8]

By January, the police were refusing to issue travel passes to Iranian men unless they were wearing the *kulah-i pahlavi*.

It was clear that Reza Shah considered this move would enhance national morale. As General Arfa, his chief of staff, later wrote

> [the Shah] believed like Ataturk in the moral influence of discarding national dress in favour of European dress, considering... his people would identify themselves with those of other countries and realise that as there was no fundamental difference between them and Europeans and Americans, there was no reason why they should not achieve the same advance (1964: 201).[9]

And indeed the Shah was heard to comment 'You look like one of them and their equal and not like a subordinate' when seeing his Foreign Minister in a morning coat (Wilber 1975: 233). In order to promote new thinking and 'uniformity' throughout the country, he said he was determined to have all Iranians wearing the same clothes, since when the Shirazis, Tabrizis, and all others no longer wear different costumes there will be no reason for difference among them (ibid., 232–3).[10]

Rumours spread through the capital that the law would be quickly followed by another forbidding women to wear the *chador* and *pecheh*. Already in Central Asia, women in Samarkand had ceremoniously burnt their veils in front of the Registan in 1927, and Amanullah of Afghanistan had banned the *burqa* on economic and sanitary grounds (see Scarce on veils).[11] The Queen herself had already caused a sensation by visiting the Qum shrine in a light-coloured *chador* rather than the customary black, and exposing part of her face in public.[12]

However, Amanullah had failed to win popular support for his reform programmes and was forced to abdicate in January 1929. Reza Shah too was meeting opposition to his Uniform Dress Law, with riots in Tabriz, Shiraz and Azerbaijan. Ambassador Clive was not alone in worrying the Shah might have misjudged the situation. In his eyes the issue of dress had provided a focus for discontent over conscription and heavy local taxes,[13] and he was aware that Shi'i theologians viewed 'the kolah and the short coat ... not merely unbecoming but ... actually ... tainted with heresy', pointing out that the peaked brim meant correct prostration in prayer could not be achieved (this was overcome by turning the peak to the back).[14] The *'ulama* also angrily criticised the consequent abolition of visual dress differences between Muslim and non-Muslim; the new codification had already abolished legal discrimination on religious grounds. British embassy staff waited anxiously to see if the Shah would insist on strict adherence to the new ruling in the Shi'i theological centres of Qum and Meshhed. They breathed more easily once they realised the exemption clauses were being interpreted somewhat generously in these cities, 'therefore, cut[ting] the ground under the feet of those who might otherwise have organised resistance to the proposed reforms'.[15]

The economic implications did not escape their notice. The Consul in Meshhed noted that local manufacturers, dyers and traders in silks, turban cloths, sashes etc. would lose custom, and that the poorer classes would find it difficult on their stretched budget to purchase the new clothing.[16] Indeed, in an attempt to minimize the impact on domestic textile-workshops, the Shah later re-issued the 1923 directives requiring all government and army personnel to wear garments of Iranian-made cloth.[17]

Indications of the importance of the clothing regulations to the minorities are indirectly revealed by certain Foreign Office documents. These reported that when agreeing to negotiate with the central regime to end hostilities in the summer of 1929, both the Qashqai and Kurdish tribal representatives demanded the return of their chiefs held in Tehran, exemption from military conscription, permission to possess arms and exemption from the Dress Reform Law.[18]

Reza Shah was to wait another five years before bringing in the next series of dress regulations. During his visit to Turkey in the spring of 1934 he ordered the brimmed hat (e.g. trilby or fedora) to be worn by all Iranian working men, despite stating before departing, that 'We have settled on the Pahlavi Iranian hat [as the 'national' head-gear]', and that western lounge suits were now the required dress for court officials.[19]

This was followed by the formal announcement in the Iranian Parliament on 6 June 1935 that the *kolah-i pahlavi* was abolished. Its passing was not greatly mourned, according to the ambassador:

the Pahlavi hat has rested uneasily on its wearers' heads. Neither becoming nor practical, it has never been popular. To devout Mahometans its protruding peak is a positive menace at prayer times, while on less solemn occasions its impeccable uniformity must have been the cause of acute distraction in gentlemen's cloak-rooms. I have once or twice made nervous enquiries as to its permanence, and have usually been informed that it is a 'hat of transition'. This definition has now been justified.[20]

The resulting demand for European hats allowed at least one official to profit greatly from his inside knowledge, buying up and reselling a stock of hats.

Rumours that these dress stipulations would be extended to the general public and include the banning of the *chador* resulted in huge demonstrations in Meshhed in early July, and unrest in Khurasan. The regime acted quickly and forcefully; by July 14 four to five hundred lay dead and eight hundred had been arrested in Meshhed, according to official figures. Four days later, with leading theologians either under arrest or banished, the law was passed. Officials in Meshhed were careful to carry both brimmed and Pahlavi hats, donning whichever seemed appropriate in the circumstances (Wilber 1975: 167).[21] The press pro-claimed that the origins of the brimmed hat lay in Sasanian times (thereby 'proving' it was a truly Iranian headgear), while the semi-official paper *Iran* described the Shah as tearing away the veil of obscurantism, of misery; at last, it rejoiced, Iranian men in their Western styled attire were emerging like butterflies from the chrysalis (Mass 1935: 415–6).

Aware that the *'ulama* opposed the law on the grounds that the *salat* (performance of prayer) would be rendered impossible, Reza Shah publicly rejected any idea that the decision was motivated by anti-Islamic sentiment:

The new hat has nothing to do with religion but it does have something to do with nationality. Previously those [? Westerners] who had worn it thought that this headgear conferred on them superiority over those who were not wearing it. We do not want others to think they are superior to us because of a minor difference in head covering (Wilber 1975: 166).

He confided in the British ambassador that the Iranian parliament worked better and more constructively now that all the deputies were dressed identically: before when 'all were attired in various garbs, there was no cohesion, no corporate feeling'.[22]

In this there was some implicit agreement in the Whitehall circles, the minutes recording that

> Eastern nationalism always seems to seek expression in headgear, and Persia is only following in the footsteps of Turkey and Iraq. But there is a method in this madness, since head-gear has in the past been one of the accepted methods of distinguishing between the various 'personal nationalities' among the subjects of oriental empires. To break down all such differences and amalgamate the various elements of the population into a 'nation' has been the object of all modern nationalist dictators.'[23]

Meanwhile provincial governors and officials were puzzling over what hat to wear where, when to raise it and when to remove it. The answers supplied by the Ministry of the Interior caused great amusement among Whitehall officials, who toyed with the idea of circulating them:[24]

1  The colonial helmet which will be exclusively in white and grey colour is used only during the summer days and until sunset.
2  The variety of straw hats (Panama) are also used during the summer.
3  The variety of felt hats, kepies, etcetera can be used day and night during the whole season, except at official occasions...
4  At the time of entering the room the hat must be taken off. For observing full honour, the hat must, of course, be placed outside the room, and at other occasions it can be held in [the] hand.
5  At times of meetings in the streets and public thoroughfares, as a mark of honour the smaller person (both as to position and age) must first take off his hat and then put it on after the same manner has been observed by the other party (i.e. after the other party has taken off his hat).
6  At instances when several persons are gathered together at a point or are passing by, in case another person meets them having acquaintance with one of the party, all the others must as a mark of honour take off their hats when an exchange of greetings is taking place between the two.[25]

A further official circular was issued in November detailing the proper use of black top hat (for all official occasions), the collapsible opera hat (not for day use), and the grey morning hat (for racing, garden-parties, manoeuvres).[26] To ease the financial burden, minor civil servants were granted one month's extra salary to cover the expense, but outside Tehran such items of dress were not readily available. Some resorted to ingenious invention, such as cutting up five gallon gasoline cans, beating the metal into a hat shape and painting it black. At one open air presentation, the sound of raindrops on such hats caused Reza Shah to think an assassination attempt was being made (Wilber 1975: 178–9).[27]

The clamp-down after the July 1934 Mashhad demonstrations gave Reza Shah the opportunity to extend the Dress Reform programme, to include the issue of veiling. Both women teachers and students of Tehran's School of Medicine and the Law School, and later of the University (1936) were first allowed and then ordered to attend unveiled (Savory 1978: 97). Women school teachers were told that salaries would be withheld and dismissal might follow if they wore the *chador* and *pecheh* at work (Savory 1978: 97; Reza Arasteh 1969: 185). The palace then announced in the spring of 1935 that no diplomas would be awarded to veiled students. Official pressure continued with the support of women's activist groups; in the summer of 1935, women wishing to renew their identify documents had to report unveiled to the police,[28] and military officers were warned against walking with veiled women in Tehran. Meanwhile a press campaign gathered momentum, reporting and photographing meetings of Girl Guides, women's groups and female athletes, and criticising hostility towards abolition as anti-social.[29] The Prime Minister held a party for members of his cabinet, high officials and their unveiled wives, not a great success, the British ambassador dryly noticed. Tehran buzzed with rumours that the *chador* would be banned for all females under the age of 40.[30] In the opinion of the ambassador:

> It is probable that the abolition of the veils will be accepted with the same resignation as other recent innovations...[but] if they start employing forcible methods... even the obedient Iranian may begin to show resentment.
>
> The Shah has probably judged his moment carefully, and one must assume that he is confident that religious influence is so completely eclipsed that the time has come to follow the Turkish example.[31]

The power of the *'ulama* had indeed been severely curtailed since Reza Shah took the throne in 1925. The number of active mosques was declining dramatically; in 1926 there were over 400 in Tehran but by 1941, only 24 remained. As mentioned above, Shari'a law had been largely replaced by new legal codes, so depriving the jurist/theologian of work and authority in the community. In 1934 religious endowment administration and monies were placed under government management. Public religious ceremonies were greatly curtailed and finally banned. There was no official recognition of Ramadan, and the rituals associated with the months of Muharram and Safar were limited to three days of observance (cf. Wilber 1975: 263; Arasteh 1964: 104). Education too was rapidly passing out of theological hands into government control, particularly in the case of girls' schooling.[32]

However, there was some doubt in Whitehall with one official wondering whether the Shah would 'succeed like the Ghazi [Kemal Atatürk] or follow Amanullah [of Afghanistan]' into exile.[33]

On January 8, 1936 the Shah, accompanied by the Queen and the two princesses, travelled to the Normal School in Tehran for the prize-giving.

For the first time the Royal ladies appeared in public unveiled (as were the school-girls and women teachers). This was no spontaneous gesture, for security forces had been ordered to remove any veiled women on the processional route before the royal party passed. However, the British ambassador reported that 'The Shah seems to realise that any general order to unveil would be a serious mistake.'[34]

Less than a fortnight later, official advice dealing with 'social etiquette of women and hints on conduct at both public and private assemblies' was published:

Women on entering public meetings must on no account remove their hats. They are not compelled to take off their coats and gloves. Umbrellas of course are an exception and should not be brought into the room... Those who have the habit of putting their handkerchiefs, cigarette cases or other articles in their breasts or up their sleeves must quit and use their bags for such things...Conversation about the dress and age of other ladies present is displeasing. To take fruit or sweets with gloves on is forbidden.'[35]

By the end of the month, the British Consul-general in Tabriz reported that government employees faced suspension if their wives appeared veiled at functions.[36] Lack of money to buy the new wardrobe of hat, coat, dress, gloves, bag etc. was no excuse; the central administration made a further advance of one month's salary, repayable over six months, to purchase clothing.[37]

The official announcement banning the *chador* and *pecheh* was made on 1st February.[38] Police and the security forces had orders to remove forcibly any worn in public, and they even entered homes to search for the offending items of dress.[39] Doctors were forbidden to admit veiled women into hospital, who were not allowed into cinemas and public baths; taxi and bus drivers were fined if they accepted veiled women as passengers.[40]

The *'ulama* declared the ban revealed the depth of Bahaist, Christian and Jewish influence at court as it was so anti-Qur'anic (Bagley 1971: 47). The pro-government press retorted that the Qur'anic and Prophet's injunctions regarding the veil applied only to Muhammad's wives, and to specific religious observance (e.g. performance of prayer); that widespread veiling had been introduced only in Abbasid times, and then as a result of external influence (Masse 1935: 416). The Embassy reported the great bitterness among the population, generated, it felt, by the cost involved in purchasing the new clothing; the *chador* had covered so much poverty.[41] To avoid the shortages experienced with male dress, government trade commissioners were sent to Germany and France to purchase 500,000 rials' worth of women's clothing (Wilber 1975: 174). Bazaar tailoring charges too were officially fixed, based on three types of establishment: a coat from 60 to 120 rials (US$ 5–10), evening gown 40 to 100, day dress 30 to 80, and hat 5 to 20 rials (Woodsmall 1936: 44). A total of £ 25,000 was also made available to assist hardship cases in purchasing the necessary clothing (Avery 1965: 292).

With the Allied occupation and consequent abdication and exile of Reza Shah in 1941, the young Muhammad Reza Shah desperate to win support rescinded the ban in regard to female university teachers and students. The Allied command made no objection. For its loyalty, the *'ulama* demanded in the following order, the re-instating of the veil, the return of *vaqf* endowments, foodstuffs at guaranteed low prices for the poor, and the restoration of Islamic teaching in schools. Declining to accept such rigorous terms but agreeing to non-enforcement of the ban, the young shah in return asked the *'ulama* to exert influence to curb the increasing number of attacks on unveiled women in the capital.[42] The religious grouping continued to make its position known; in 1949 Ayatollah Borujerdi issued a *fatwa* forbidding women to shop in bazaars without the *chador* (Savory 1978: 206)·

It is interesting to note briefly the role of clothing in the early days of the Iranian Islamic Revolution movement, as it reveals dress was still closely associated with political and religious allegiance. By the summer of 1977 Sattareh Farman Farmaian observed how Tehran students were displaying their interest in Islamic Marxism:

> More young men than I had ever seen were wearing the facial stubble or beards that renounced 'Westernism' and demonstrated Islamic zeal. At my own school [for Social Welfare & Health training] many male undergraduates were wearing buttoned shirts without ties to emphasize that they were not 'Westernizers'...many women students had defiantly put on the black chador or black clothes to show their support for both Islamic and Marxist economic theory (Farmaian 1992: 288).

After Black Friday (8 September 1978), when anti-Shah demonstrators were killed, 'Not shaving, or wearing a shirt without a tie, or a black dress and an 'Islamic' scarf, had become badges that showed one was on the right side [i.e. pro-Islamic revolution]' (*ibid.*, 297). For over a year the word *kravati* (tie-wearer) had come to be the fashionable term of disparagment for any intellectual[43] and smart, clean clothing was seen as *estekbar* (ostentation) and thus unfitting for devout Muslim men, in revolutionary circles.[44]

The *chador* was rapidly becoming an acknowledged symbol of rebellion against the established political order, although it did not necessarily imply support for the establishment of an Islamic state. Thus, after veiled women had been refused entry into university in 1977, it was symbolically donned as a sign of protest (against the Pahlavi regime) by most female demonstrators the following year.

In the eyes of the Iranian *'ulama* the *chador* manifested the overthrow of Western values. In his order banning co-educational schools (established in 1935) in the first week of March 1979 after the Shah's departure in January, Ayatollah Khomeini also directed all females in government employ not to work 'naked'. There was some confusion over the exact meaning of the term. When questioned, Ayatollah Taleghani gave a lengthy response, noting that women in other eastern countries had an historical (sic) tradition of wearing some form of *hijab* ('not specifically *chador*'),[45] and summarised Reza Shah's dress reforms as follows:

> He thought if he shortened dresses, if people wore coats and trousers and put on hats, if our women went without veils, then we would become progressive [i.e. advanced in science, industry, power, economy and politics] ... And what happened? We saw many of our women drawn into 'Westoxication' ... And what corruption ensued! (Tabari & Yeganeh 1982: 104–5).

Arguing that the *'ulama* wished to protect women's personalities, remove the social pressure of fashion, prevent family quarrels, Taleghani stated that Khomeini had not imposed rules regarding the wearing of a headscarf (and by implication, using less make-up);

> But we want to show that there has been a Revolution, a profound change, in our offices and ministries...So we ask of women to attend to their jobs in simple and dignified clothes and wear a scarf on their head (ibid. 107).

On March 8, 10,000 women marched in Tehran and another 3000 travelled to Qum protesting against Khomeini's decision; further demonstrations were held over the next few days. On March 13, the Ayatollah announced the *chador* was not compulsory but added it was 'the personal duty for Muslim women' to don it and that the garment was 'to be honoured as the flag of revolution'. The words recall those of Ibn Khaldun (d. 1406) quoted at the beginning of this study. All women in government and public employment were then directed to wear the *chador* on 5 July 1980, and then within the legal reform programme of 30 May 1981 (restoring Shari'a law), the wearing of *hijab* (either a *chador* or a full-length coat with long sleeves and *maqna'eh* or large head-scarf) was declared compulsory for all women over the age of 12, whether Muslim or not, non-compliance being punishable by one year's imprisonment (Paidar 1995: 232).

The New Order had once again meant New Dress.

# Notes

1  FO 371/18992 E4041/608/34 paper 28, dated 5 July 1935 signed A.E. Lambert. See note 29.
2  See also Sykes (1971: 198); Feuvrier (1906: 143); Bird Bishop (1891, 1: 216); Savage Landor (1903, I: 211–2).
3  FO 371/13071 E.4672/ 4672/34, Parr to Lord Cushendan 7 Sept 1928.
4  Sattareh Farman Farmaian (1992: 54) states that in fact the peakless version was designed by her father 'probably when he was war minister, and which had been known as 'the Farman-Farma cap'.'
5  FO 371/13781 E 353/95/34 dated December 31, 1928, 1929, from Clive to Chamberlain.

6  Translation of the edict is given in FO 371/13781 E 353/95/34 enclosure to document 1.

7  On Foran's figures (1993: 237) a fine of one tuman would have represented approximately 5 days' wages for a construction worker.

8  FO 371/13781 E 353/95/34 dated Jan 22, 1929.

9  It is interesting to note that firstly, the long robes and turbans were seen as marks of national identity, and as with Atatürk the retention of such dress was seen as an underlying cause of economic and technical stagnation, the donning of Western attire would inevitably lead, it was felt, to fresh thinking and motivation (see Baker 1986). A British diplomatic report from Istanbul concerning the 1925 Turkish dress laws requiring men to wear brimmed hats stated 'Or course, changing the headgear [from the fez] does not change the people's character and mentality. *But it is a step in the right direction.*' (emphasis added) E7672/4706/44 (FO 371/10870 dated 10 December 1925).

10  The official policy to 'purify' the language by removing foreign loan words, and banning teaching and public speaking in the languages of the ethnic minorities (e.g. Azari, Kurdish, Armenian) may be linked to this idea; as Reza Ghods suggests, 'The shah attempted to give the ethnically diverse nation a new, national identity connected to his own person' (1989: 107).

11  FO 371/13281 N 5412/ 10/97 dated 22 Oct 1928).

12  Learning that a member of the *'ulama* at the shrine had remonstrated with her, Reza Shah (or his aide; Avery 1965: 288) entered the complex in boots – itself a calculated insult – and personally set about the theologian; Paidar describes the queen and her daughter as wearing European dress. Akhavi (1980: 42) questions this episode. Around this time, six leading women activists were physically attacked in Shiraz for wearing dark, rather than black *chadors* in public; a similar incident happened in Tehran (Bamdad 1977: 85).

13  FO 371/13781 E 353/95/34 dated 31 December 1928 and E 1658/95/34 dated 12 March 1929. Taxes on sugar and tea were introduced in 1925 to finance the industrialisation programme.

14  FO 371/13781 E 1406/95/34 enclosure in no 1, Meshhed 14 February , 1929, Consul Biscoe to Clive, Tehran.

15  *Ibid.*

16  *Ibid.*

17  *Enc. Iranica*, 'Clothing; xi'.

18  FO 371/13781 E 2670/95/34 Tehran, dated 24 May 1929 (Qashqai); E 3351/ 95/34 dated 6 June 1929 (Kurds).

19  For an anecdote on the difficulties, faced by the royal entourage, regarding correct dress, see Arfa (1964: 244).

20  FO 371/18992 E 4041/608/34 Knatchbull-Hugessen to Hoare, dated 14 June 1935. The Shah attended the Majlis that day with his head uncovered (Avery 1965: 290); for the significance of this action, see Baker (1986:80).

21  Unofficial figures were much higher. FO 371/18997 E 4803 Meshhed, dated 14 July 35; full report in E 4871/4338/34 Tehran dated 25 July 1935. For Khurasan, E 4385 telegram dated 16 July 1935. In Tabriz, police delayed enforcement of the law presumably to lessen tension; E 4871/4338/34 Tehran, dated 25 July 1935.

22  FO 371/ 18992 E 4041/608/34 Knatchbull-Hugessen to Hoare, dated 14 June 1935 preceding minutes.

23  *Ibid.*

24  'It would be very tempting to print the enclosure … It is an entertaining situation, and the Persians are making themselves even more ridiculous than the

Turks did before them', signed Rendel FO 371/18992 minutes to E 4628/608/34.

25　Enclosure dated 7 July p. 51–2 in E 4628/608/34 which continues to advise in favour of dark, sombre clothing, clean and ironed and against wearing of white shoes and *givehs* (cotton slip-ons); and on the use of ties.

26　See references, note 22, 55.

27　Hat makers had resorted to similar action with tin in 1929 when faced with shortages in cardboard stiffening for the *kulah-i pahlavi*; FO 371/13781 E 1406/95/34, dated 23 February 1929. In Kirman, tailors hiked up their price 40% for making frock coats, required for the official celebrations of the Shah's birthday, FO 371/20048 E 2325/405/34 Kirman dated 19 March 1936.

28　FO 371/18992 E 4628/608/34 Tehran dated 12 July 1935.

29　Woodsmall (1936: 43–4); see also Massé (1935: 411–3) and FO371/20048 E 476/405/34.

30　FO 371/18992 E4628/608/34. It has been estimated that by the end of 1935 out of Tehran's total population of 300,000 (male and female), some 4000 women had discarded the *chador* and *pecheh*; Avery (1965: 291); Woodsmall (1936: 47).

31　FO 371 18992 E 4628/608/34 Tehran 12 July 1935. In fact the veil was never totally banned in Kemalist Turkey; see Woodsmall (1936: 366–7); Yalman (1956: 175).

32　In 1925 some 10,000 boys attended non-religious schools; by 1929, almost 138,900 boys and girls were registered, with a further 9661 in secondary schools, Savory (1978: 90). Kamrava (1992: 56) states that in 1910 there were 41 girls' schools teaching 2167 pupils; in 1929, 190 with 11,489 students, which rose in four years to 870 schools with 50,000 girls attending.

33　Minutes to FO 371/18992 E 4628/608/34, signed by Baggallay.

34　FO 371/20048 E 476/405/34 Tehran dated 11 Jan 1936.

35　*Ibid.*

36　*Ibid* E 994/405/34 Tehran 7 February 1936; see also E 1155/405/ 34 Tehran 20 February 1936 regarding January invitation to Tabriz reception; FO 371/20048 E 3515/405/34 Ahwaz.

37　*Ibid.*

38　Tual (1971: 96) gives the date as 8 January; Bagley (1971: 47) as 7 January.

39　*Enc. Iranica*, 'Clothing: xi.'.

40　FO 371/20048 E 1565/405/34 Tabriz 20 February 1936; Lenczowski (1978: 98).

41　FO 371/20048 E 1565/405/34 Tabriz 20 Feb 1936.

42　Akhavi (1980: 61); Wilber (1975: 174); Arfa (1965: 255–6); Lenczowski (1973: 97–8); Arasteh (1964: 183–5); Akhavi (1980: 61).

43　Foran (1993: 376). In some contemporary Muslim circles in Great Britain the wearing of a tie is seen as a proclamation of Christian faith, representing the cruxified Christ. In late 19th Istanbul some elderly men felt unable to sport ties, feeling that it conflicted with their religious beliefs (see Yalman 1956: 13).

44　*Enc. Iranica*, 'Clothing. xi.'.

45　He referred specifically to Indira Gandhi covering her hair with her sari (see Tabari & Yeganeh 1982).

# Bibliography

Akhavi, S. 1980. *Religion & Politics in Contemporary Iran.* Albany: SUNY Press.

Algar, H. 1969. *Religion & State in Iran.* Berkeley/LA: University of California Press.

Arasteh, A. Reza. 1964. *Man & Society in Iran.* Leiden: Brill.

—— 1969. *Education & Social Awakening.* Leiden: Brill.

Arfa. H. 1964. *Under Five Shahs.* London: John Murray.

Avery, P. 1965. *Modern Iran.* London: Benn.

Bagley, F. R. C. 1971. 'The Iranian Protection Law ...' *Iran & Islam,* (ed.) C. E. Bosworth. Edinburgh: Edinburgh University Press.

Baker, P.L. 1986. 'The Fez in Turkey: a Symbol of Modernization'. *Costume* (London) no. 20.

Bakhash, S. 1978. *Iran: Monarchy, Bureaucracy & Reform under the Qajars: 1858–1896.* MEC/Ithaca.

Bamdad, Badr ol-Moluk. 1977. *From Darkness into Light...* New York: Exposition.

Bird Bishop, I. 1891. *Journeys in Persia & Kurdistan,* Vol. 1. London: John Murray.

Diba, L. S. 1987. 'Visual & Written Sources: dating Eighteenth-century Silks' *Woven from the Soul, Spun from the Heart,* (ed.) Carol Bier, Washington DC: Textile Museum.

*Encyclopedia Iranica,* Ehsan Yarshaten, (ed.). 1992. 'Clothing', V: 719–871.

Farmaian, S.F. 1992. *Daughter of Persia.* London: Bantam.

Feuvrier, Dr. J. 1906. *Trois Ans la Cour de Perse.* Paris: Maloine.

Foran, J. 1993. *Fragile Resistance: Social Transformation in Iran from 1500 to the Revolution.* Boulder: Westview.

Ghods, M. Reza. 1989. *Iran in the Twentieth century.* London: Adamantine, Boulder: Rienner.

Ibn Khaldun, 1967. *The Muqaddimah: an Introduction to History* (ed.) F Rosenthal. Princeton: Princeton University Press.

Kamrava, M. 1992. *The Political History of Modern Iran.* Westport: Praeger.

Lorey, E. & Sladen, D. 1907. *Queer Things about Persia.* London: Nash.

Massé, H. 1935. 'Le devoilement des Iraniennes.' *Revue des Études Islamiques,* 9.

Naeshat, G. 1982. *The Origins of Modern Reform in Iran, 1970–80.* Urbana: University of Illinois Press.

Otter, J. 1248. *Voyage en Turquie et en Perse,* Vol. 1. Paris: Guerin.

Paidar, P. 1995. *Women & the Political Process in Twentieth-Century Iran.* Cambridge: Cambridge University Press.

Pittman. C. R. 1943. 'In defense of the Veil', *Muslim World,* 33, ??

Salem, E. A. 1977. *Hilāl ibn al-Muḥassin al-Ṣābiī 'Rustam dār al-Khīlāfah'.* Beirut: American University of Beirut.

Savage Landor, A. H. 1903. *Across Coveted Lands,* Vol. 1. New York: Scribners.

Savory, R. M. 1978. 'Social development in Iran during the Pahlavi Era'. In *Iran under the Pahlavis,* (ed.) George Lenczowski. Stanford: Hoover Institution.

—— 1980. 'Religion and Government in an Ithna Ashari Shi'i State', *Israel Oriental Studies,* 10.

Sparroy, W. 1902. *Persian Children of the Royal Family.* London: Lane.

Sykes, E. C. 1971. *Persia and its People.* London: Methuen.

Tabari, A. & Yeganeh, N. 1982. *In the Shadow of Islam.* London: Zed Books.

Tual, A. 1971. 'Variations et Usages du Voile dans Deux Villes d'Iran,' *Objets et Mondes,* 11.

Wilber, D. N. 1975. *Riza Shah Pahlavi: the Resurrection & Reconstruction of Iran.* New York: Exposition Press.

Wills, C. J. 1891. *In the Land of the Lion & Sun.* London: Ward Lock.

Woodsmall, R. F. 1936. *Muslim Women Enter a New World.* London: Allen & Unwin.

Yalman, A .E. 1956. *Turkey in My Time.* Norman: University of Oklahoma.

FO 371/10870 E 767214706/44;

FO 371/13071 E.4672/4672/341;

FO 371/13281 N 5412/10/97;

FO 371/13781 E 353/95/34; E 1658/95/32; E 1406/95/34; E 2670/95/34;

FO 371/18992 E 4041/608/34; E 4628/608/34; minutes to E 4628/608/34;

FO 371/18997 E 4803; E 4871/4338/34;

FO 371/20048 E 2325/405/34; E 1155/405/34.

# Index